To Mom.

About the Author

Barbara Czegel is president of SIRIUS3, a Toronto-based company that provides training for Help Desk professionals and facilitation of improvement initiatives for technology support areas. She has over 22 years of experience in both the technical and human facets of the computer industry. Ms. Czegel has been involved in planning, development, analysis, and support of retail business systems, planning systems, and manufacturing systems. She has justified, established, and managed Help Desk operations in corporate environments and is an experienced communicator and facilitator.

Ms. Czegel received her bachelor of science degree in Computer Science and Mathematics from the University of Toronto in 1975. She is a member of the Help Desk Institute and the Toronto local chapter of the Help Desk Institute.

Barbara Czegel can be reached at bczegel@sirius3.com. The SIRIUS3 Web site is at www.sirius3.com.

Barbara Czegel

Running
an
Effective
Help Desk

Second Edition

John Wiley & Sons, Inc.

New York • Chichester • Weinheim • Brisbane • Singapore • Toronto

Publisher: Robert Ipsen
Editor: Theresa Hudson
Managing Editor: Brian Snapp
Electronic Products, Associate Editor: Mike Sosa
Text Design & Composition: NK Graphics

Designations used by companies to distinguish their products are often claimed as trademarks. In all instances where John Wiley & Sons, Inc., is aware of a claim, the product names appear in initial capital or ALL CAPITAL LETTERS. Readers, however, should contact the appropriate companies for more complete information regarding trademarks and registration.

This book is printed on acid-free paper. ⊚

Published by John Wiley & Sons, Inc.

Published simultaneously in Canada.

This publication is designed to provide accurate and authoritative information in regard to the subject matter covered. It is sold with the understanding that the publisher is not engaged in professional services. If professional advice or other expert assistance is required, the services of a competent professional person should be sought.

Library of Congress Cataloging-in-Publication Data
Czegel, Barbara, 1953-
    Running an effective help desk / Barbara Czegel. —2nd. ed.
      p. cm.
    Includes index.
    ISBN 0-471-24816-9 (pbk.)
      1. Computer industry—Customer services—Management.
  2. Electronic office machine industry—Customer services—Management.   I. Title.
HD9696.C62C96   1998
004'.068'8—dc21
                                                               97-46069
                                                                CIP

Printed in the United States of America.

10 9 8 7 6 5 4 3 2 1

Contents

PART TWO   Basic Structure   39

CHAPTER TWO   Structure   41

CHAPTER THREE   Staffing   69

PART THREE   Internal Help Desk Processes   95

CHAPTER FOUR   Problem and Work Management   97

CHAPTER FIVE   Tracking   135

PART FOUR   Using Technology   **155**

CHAPTER SIX   **Help Desk Tools**   157

CHAPTER SEVEN   The Internet: Challenge and Opportunity   185

CHAPTER TEN   Marketing   281

CHAPTER ELEVEN   Cost-Benefit Analysis   315

CHAPTER TWELVE   Outsourcing   355

Preface

The world of Help Desks has changed since the first edition of this book. Help Desk tools have exploded. There are now literally hundreds of vendors offering some flavor of Help Desk tool. For Help Desks this means a wider selection, covering all budgets and all sizes of organization and a better chance to get exactly what you need. The Internet has woven its way into our daily lives and has become an integral part of the Help Desk function. The Help Desk itself has enjoyed a steadily increasing profile in the business world, and providing Help Desk services has become big business for third parties. *Running an Effective Help Desk*, second edition, incorporates these changes into the basic business of Help Desks spelled out in edition one.

The book is divided into six parts that discuss the foundation of Help Desks, their basic structure, internal Help Desk processes, using technology, and optimizing performance. Part 6 provides case studies and an example.

Chapter 1, which comprises all of Part 1, deals with getting focused on the business. This means defining mission, services, and objectives. To make sure you stay focused on the business while you are defining these, you need to understand what senior management expects from the Help Desk and where it is taking the business, what your customer profile looks like, and what the responsibility splits are between your Help Desk and other Information Technology (IT) groups.

Part 2, which encompasses Chapters 2 and 3, looks at how to go about setting up your Help Desk in terms of process structure, number of staff, number of Help Desks, and profile of staff. It addresses the consolidation of existing multiple Help Desks and suggests a design for managing staff turnover.

A critical success factor for running an effective Help Desk is to keep your problems under control. Part 3, on internal Help Desk processes (Chapters 4 and 5), discusses the tools and processes you need to use to achieve control. It looks at priorities, procedures, evaluation, and improvement and shows the benefits that the process of tracking calls brings to the Help Desk.

Part 4, on using technology (Chapters 6, 7, and 8), gives an overview of the types of tools available for Help Desk use, discusses the challenges and opportunities of the Internet, and shows how to set up a Help Desk Internet or intranet site.

Chapter 9, "Measuring Performance," is the first chapter of Part 5, on optimizing performance. It looks at the three critical aspects of performance and reviews the measures and perspectives that you need to take into account to get a true measure of performance. It suggests a method for calculating Help Desk return and Help Desk investment and gives a sample of a total performance report. The next chapter, "Marketing," looks at marketing the Help Desk in terms of image, selling value, education, and communication. The third chapter in the optimizing performance section is Chapter 11, "Cost-Benefit Analysis." As part of managing a Help Desk, you need to be in an ongoing measurement and improvement cycle. In order to cost justify some of these improvements you need to be able to put together a solid cost-benefit analysis. Chapter 11 gives you a template and three examples to help you. The final chapter in Part 5 deals with outsourcing. When outsourcing is used as a tool it can bring tangible benefits to the Help Desk, including reduced costs, increased flexibility, and improved performance. Chapter 12, "Outsourcing," discusses when to outsource, outsourcing options, and the outsourcing process.

The final section in the book, Part 6, contains case studies and an example. This section includes two case studies (Chapters 13 and 14) from the first edition: a Help Desk that is just starting up and a Help Desk that is performing well. The section also includes an example of a Help Desk intranet site (Chapter 15). The example shows you how to implement some of the suggestions made throughout the book and gives you a good starting point for developing your own intranet site.

The basic premises of Help Desk management have not changed from the first edition, but the environment in which they must be applied certainly has. This book shows you how you take advantage of the new tools and processes available to you to help you set up and/or manage your Help Desk more effectively.

What's New (In A Nutshell)

If you've already read the first edition, here is a guide to show you what has changed in edition two:

Part One: Foundation

Chapter One: Getting Focused   More emphasis has been placed on the mission statement. Examples and how to" information have been included.

Part Two: Basic Structure

Chapter Two: Structure   Information on levels of support, the front line, and multiple Help Desks has been carried over from the first edition and revised. New information includes a consolidation blueprint for multiple Help Desks and suggestions for calculating number of staff.

Chapter Three: Staffing   This is a new chapter. Some information has been carried over from the chapter on structure in the first edition. New material includes information on Help Desk roles, developing a grid to help you test for the skills you need, and planning for the turnover cycle.

Part Three: Internal Help Desk Processes

Chapter Four: Problem and Work Management

This chapter contains basically the same information as the first edition but includes a new priority example and expanded ideas on the tools necessary for control.

Chapter Five: Tracking

This chapter is now focused solely on tracking. Discussion of tracking tools has been moved to Chapter 6.

Part Four: Using Technology

Chapter Six: Help Desk Tools

This chapter has been updated to reflect the changes in the tools now available.

Chapter Seven: The Internet: Challenge and Opportunity

This chapter contains all new material and examples.

Chapter Eight: Setting Up a Help Desk Internet/Intranet Site

This chapter contains all new material and examples.

Part Five: Optimizing Performance

Chapter Nine: Measuring Performance

This chapter has been significantly revised to include a discussion of ROI (return on investment), and more specifics on how statistics can be used to measure and improve Help Desk performance. The service-level agreement and customer survey examples have been updated, as has the performance report example. A section on tips for Help Desks that are just starting up has been added.

Chapter Ten: Marketing

This chapter contains much new material. It offers a different perspective on marketing, which is viewed as having

	four components: image, selling, education, and communication. All the examples are new and reflect the importance of the Internet in marketing.
Chapter Eleven: Cost-Benefit Analysis	This chapter remains largely unchanged. Dollar values have been added and discussion of "the cost of doing nothing" has been added.
Chapter Twelve: Outsourcing	This chapter remains largely unchanged. An example of a request for proposal has been added.
Part Six: Case Studies and Example	
Chapter Thirteen: Help Desk Case No. 1: Setup	Unchanged from the first edition.
Chapter Fourteen: Help Desk Case No. 2: Working Well	Unchanged from the first edition (in the first edition this was labeled Case No. 3).
Chapter Fifteen: Example: A Help Desk Intranet Web Site	This chapter is new. It contains an example of a Help Desk intranet site.
A Further Resource	John Wiley & Sons, Inc. has made a Web site available to the author to provide readers and Internet surfers with ideas, guides, and information to complement this book. The companion Web site can be found at www.wiley.com/compbooks/czegel.
References and Further Reading	A list of miscellaneous resources is provided here.

Some material has been dropped from the first edition, specifically the chapter titled "Toward Automation" and the "Starting Automation" case study. Almost all the illustrations have been changed.

Acknowledgments

Thank you Les, for once again lending me your brain at regular intervals. I hope I haven't worn it out.

Thank you to the folks at Interlog Internet Services, particularly Scott Allan, for allowing me to include some of Interlog's Internet pages in this book.

Thank you to all of the people I have had the privilege to teach, for your endless questions, challenges, and ideas. All of you are in this book.

Thank you to everyone who puts out useful, free information on the Internet. You made writing this book a pleasure. You reflect the true spirit of the information highway.

Thank you to Chris and Care for giving me something to worry about besides this book.

Thank you to Megan, Shelley, Risk, Bari, and Jonno for giving me a reprieve from all things technical.

Thank you to Di and Phoenix for being true friends and never asking me "How's the book coming?"

Thank you again to Terri Hudson for the opportunity.

PART ONE

Foundation

Getting Focused

"If you don't know where you're going, most any road will take you there."

—Cheshire Cat, *Alice in Wonderland*

As a Help Desk, you have a limited budget, a limited head count, and only twenty-four hours in each day. You can try to do everything and end up doing many things poorly, or you can focus on providing a specific set of services that add value to the business and doing a quality job in each. Those services that you can't provide yourself can be dropped (if they are not important to the business), provided by another department, or outsourced.

Consider the Help Desk that is not focused. It might be new, unsure of exactly what it is supposed to do. Someone calls that Help Desk with a request to borrow a laptop computer. You answer the call. No one has made that request before. As a Help Desk employee wanting to please, you say "yes" and dig up one of the laptops that the team isn't using at the moment. The customer comes to get the laptop and is annoyed to find that it isn't loaded with the software required. You spend an hour loading the correct software (because the customer needs it that evening), while other more important problems sit waiting and calls accumulate. When the customer leaves, you scramble to get to the other calls, but a lot of customers are annoyed at having had to wait. The next morning the laptop isn't returned ("Oh, I thought I'd keep it for a couple of days—it's really coming in handy."). Your manager asks "Where's my laptop? I need it for a presentation to the logistics department." Oops. Your manager is very unhappy, as are the people in the logistics department who were promised a presentation but didn't get one. You start checking out the career classifieds during your break.

Later on in the day another customer calls and says, "I hear you loan out laptops—I need one for tonight." By this time, you've learned your lesson. "We don't lend laptops out" is what you tell the customer, rather curtly. The customer argues that someone else got a laptop just yesterday, which wasn't fair. You persist with a "no" and end up with an irate and unhappy customer.

You made a significant number of customers and your manager unhappy in order to satisfy one customer. By trying to do something that you couldn't handle, that you hadn't planned for, you not only alienated several customers, but you created unrealistic expectations and wasted a lot of time. There wasn't much business value in what you did.

Now let's turn that scenario around. The customer calls asking to borrow a laptop. You know what your services are, and lending out computer equipment is not one of them. "No," you reply, "we don't have any equipment for loan, but I can give you the name of a company that does rent out hardware." In thirty seconds you've handled a request that took you hours previously. You've satisfied your customer and have not kept any others waiting. If you didn't know the names of companies that provided the rental service, you could look the information up and get back to the customer and then save that information in a Help Desk reference library for quick access the next time you receive that same request. You could even work with the rental company to set up some kind of service-level agreement to make sure that any of your customers who called got the quick service they needed.

If your Help Desk is focused on the business, it is set up for success. It is providing the services that are most important to the business within a budget the business can afford. Your Help Desk probably looks something like this:

Help Desk staff and manager share a common understanding of how each call is to be handled and of the Help Desk mission.

You have a clear picture of your objectives, which is a good start toward attaining them.

Both you and your customers understand what your responsibilities are, which makes it easier for you to keep them satisfied.

You have the support of senior management and customers because you are adding value to the business.

You have the support of other Information Technology (IT) groups and have defined lines of responsibility.

In This Chapter

This chapter will discuss how to get your Help Desk focused on the business, whether it is just starting up or whether it requires some refocusing. Topics to be covered are as follows:

- Help Desk focus, defined
- Senior management input
- Working with other IT groups and creating a profile of your customers
- Customer profile
- Developing a mission
- Developing services
- Developing objectives
- A plan

Help Desk Focus, Defined

In a Help Desk, focus is defined by the following:

Mission

Objectives

Services

In defining focus, you need to make sure that you're focusing on the business. You need to get input from the following groups:

Senior management

Other IT groups

Customers

Figure 1.1 illustrates the definition of focus and what must go into it.

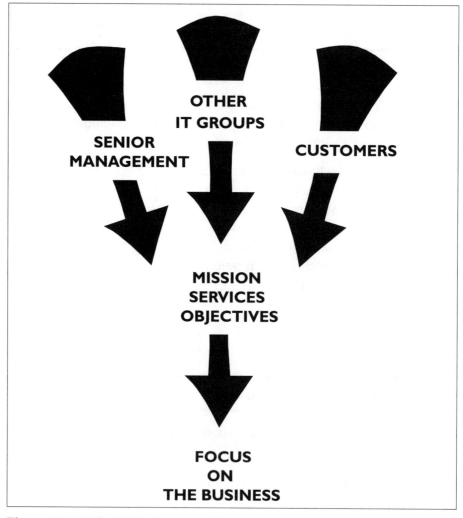

Figure 1.1   Help Desk focus.

Senior Management Input

The Help Desk is not usually a revenue-generating function and will be showing up on the ledgers as a cost. This makes it more important than ever to ensure that you know what senior management expects of you. You don't want to be caught in a situation where you are providing what management regards as an unnecessary service, especially when costs are being cut.

Senior management knows where the business is going, what its critical needs are. Information from senior management will help you choose, from all the things you could be doing, what your Help Desk should focus on doing for the business.

If senior management dictates a reduction in costs and head count, then your Help Desk might want to be highly automated, with several self-service options for customers. Alternatively, if you are supporting external customers and senior management is concerned about providing personal service to customers, then your Help Desk may have more human intervention and less obligatory automation.

Sometimes the direction the business is taking is not one you particularly want to follow. Consider the following scenario. Your Help Desk is focused on providing support for packaged desktop applications. Senior management knows that changes in the business will necessitate the purchase of several specialized applications. These applications are critical to the business and require twenty-four hour support. "This shouldn't be our job," you say, fearful of the new responsibilities and increased support hours. Senior management responds with "This is our critical support requirement. Standard desktop software is not. This is what the business needs. If you can't provide it perhaps somebody else can."

If you do not have the rapport you need with senior management to gain information about where the business is headed, you need to search for it. Talk to your own management, look at quarterly performance reports and objectives, invite yourself to business meetings whenever possible. Keep looking for information. It is, unfortunately, unlikely that someone will just hand it to you.

Some management expectations you might encounter are as follows:

1. Respond to business change quickly. Outsource whatever extra help you need.

2. Fix problems quickly—no computer or user downtime is acceptable. Don't let technology failure negatively impact any critical business functions.

3. Automate wherever possible—cut costs to the absolute minimum.

4. Monitor and report on technology use and performance (justify the capital expenditure).

5. Show a good return on investment (ROI).

A Help Desk that is unaware of what senior management expects is setting itself up for failure. Failure in the eyes of senior management could result in a shortened life for the Help Desk.

Working with Other IT Groups

Your IT partners can be your best friends and your worst enemies. You share the same customers and some common goals, you're both interested in ensuring that the technology is kept up and running, and you're both responsible for keeping that technology up and running. But just where that responsibility begins and ends for each of you is a potential source of conflict and the cause of many turf wars. In fact, there is potential there for two kinds of turf wars: the taking wars ("this is our responsibility, so butt out") and the giving-away wars ("this is not our responsibility—you should be taking care of it"). Each of these lead to the scenario, illustrated in Figure 1.2, of a ball being dropped—of a problem or request going unresolved because no one would take ownership. If you can eliminate or at least minimize these unproductive situations, you've a much better chance at coming to an agreement on division of responsibilities. Working together toward a common goal—meeting the needs of the business—will make everyone more lenient about where the divisions of responsibility are drawn.

Figure 1.2   Undefined responsibilities result in requests left unresolved.

Dividing responsibilities will take some time, but you don't have to wait until you're finished to continue setting your Help Desk focus. If all the groups involved agree not to let anything fall through the cracks while you are in the negotiation phase, regardless of whether it is their responsibility, you can keep your customers happy while you take the time to find a good solution. In fact, adopting the attitude of not letting anything fall through the cracks regardless of responsibility is one you want to encourage and promote, even after you've decided who does what. Fighting wastes time and energy that could be better spent providing improved service to your customers.

In learning IT expectations, and in negotiating what your responsibilities will be, don't try for perfect delineation. It just isn't possible. As technology keeps changing and new technology becomes available, lines of responsibility that were clear will become fuzzy. The whole process of delineating responsibilities will have to be ongoing to make sure that all aspects of supporting new technology are covered.

Before going to the rest of IT, take the time to think about what it makes sense for your responsibilities to be. Use this list as a starting point for discussion. It's easier to work with something that you can mark up and cross out than to start from scratch. Be careful to make it clear to your IT partners that this starting point is just that—it is not the world as you say it should be. People will get upset if they think you've made those kinds of decisions on your own.

In areas such as standards, client/server, PC software support, software maintenance, technology selection, and so on, support responsibilities will be foggy and will require some effort to define. Specialty software—software outside the standard PC or mainframe suite—might be a contentious issue. You probably cannot accept first-line support for something that is fairly specialized and time consuming to learn. You typically have a large customer base to keep happy and can't afford much specialization. But there are solutions that are a good compromise for everyone. In the case of specialty software, you might agree to get the first call but then pass it on directly to the group that knows the software. If you both work toward reaching this decision, it has a better chance of working, because you've both bought in. The Help Desk focus is on receiving and channeling the call; the focus of the other group is on resolving it.

You may also have other Help Desks within your IT organization. Getting together with them to clarify roles is a valuable exercise because you are probably going to be getting each other's calls—people will call the first number that looks like a help line when they run into trouble. It would be helpful to know who has the responsibility for and ability to do what, so you can get the customer's problem resolved even if the wrong Help Desk was contacted. One of the worst things that could happen to a customer is to be bounced between Help Desks: Help Desk A says, "This is a problem for Help Desk B; I'll transfer your call," while Help Desk B says, "Oh, this is handled by Help Desk A. I'll transfer you." If responsibilities are clear, and if each Help Desk has a "nothing falls through the cracks" attitude, this will never happen.

Some examples of IT responsibility splits include the following:

Standards. Help Desk participates in setting standards; IT is responsible for setting and enforcing those standards.

Problems with applications developed in house. IT is responsible for developing applications and for second-line support; Help Desk will take the first call and pass it on.

Help Desk is consulted in software selection, but another part of IT actually makes the selection. Help Desk is responsible for notifying everyone of the software installation, for doing the installation, and for getting a pilot out for testing to make sure that it works with all other technology components.

Help Desk monitors LAN performance and notifies application programmers of any problem applications. Application programmers address the problem applications.

Customer Profile

You want to know your customers because, very simply, you want to know what you have to support. One of your reasons for existence is to keep your customers productive (or to make them more productive). You need to know what they do. Knowing your customers means knowing:

Who they are, how many of them there are, and where they are

What technology they use

What they use it for

How often and when they use it

How technology-literate they are

How technology-friendly they are

What their priorities are

How controlled their environment is

What they want

Components of Customer Profile

Each of the categories of customer information listed in the previous section is examined in more detail in the following sections.

Who They Are, How Many of Them There Are, and Where They Are

You might be surprised by who your customers include. PCs, stand-alone or on their own small LANs, have a tendency to pop up everywhere. You might uncover small departments with outdated (or even ultramodern) equipment that have existed on their own, however efficiently or inefficiently, for years. One company Help Desk uncovered an Ethernet LAN in an area using CADD during a routine Help Desk call. It was a total surprise to them. It was also a total surprise to the customers who had made the call—they hadn't realized they were on a LAN. Before the Help Desk came into existence, they were being supported by an external company that came every once in a while or when there was a problem, did things, and then left. The Help Desk only found out about the LAN when the customers called with some problems that required the PCs to be opened up. The area was eventually converted to a standard configuration, but supporting them in the interim was painful.

You need to flush all these customers out in order to be able to reach them through your marketing and to help make sure that they at least know what technology is available, what the standards are, what you offer, and where to get support if you can't provide it. If they're on their own and suddenly have a catastrophe and call for your help, it could mean a lot of expense for you—especially if major things must be fixed very quickly. You'll have to call in outside help or ignore a lot of other inside customers. It makes more sense to spend time up front finding out who and where your customers are and then slowly bringing them on board and up to standards—not that this will be easy. If they refuse your advice and you aren't able to support them, perhaps contracting for external support could be a solution. They would pay, and senior management would either approve it or not, in which case you could make a case for a standard configuration.

If all the PCs in your company are networked together, asset management software will be able to find them all. You'll know where everyone is. If you still have standalone PCs you might need some kind of a "calling all PCs" campaign.

Knowing the number of customers you have gives you an idea of how many potential callers to the Help Desk there are—this will help you determine call traffic and staffing requirements.

If your customers are spread out over several remote locations, some aspects of support, such as servicing their hardware, will be more complex than with local customers. You will need to make provisions to ensure that the service is provided and that you are kept abreast of everything that's done, so your hardware/software inventory is kept current and your call-tracking information is complete. You might outsource the servicing and have the outsourcing company update your hardware/software inventory and your call-tracking system directly.

What Technology They Use

Customers are generally not impressed by technology, especially when it isn't working. They're not interested in the differences between expanded memory and extended memory or why they don't have enough of one or the other. They don't care that the bridge from the mainframe to the LAN is down; they don't care about control unit failures or whether hubs are intelligent. They just want the damned computers to work so they can get their jobs done. You may find it infuriating at times that they don't want to hear your explanations of why the LAN is down (and that they don't accept it with a "well, I understand"), but you have to remember: They're trying desperately to get their jobs done, probably under a tight deadline, and *you* (in the guise of an uncooperative PC or terminal or other technology) are preventing them from doing just that. If the technology is not working, then the business is not working, and someone is losing money and perhaps jobs. No downtime is acceptable.

Your users might not care about technology, but you must. You need to know what you will be supporting. An environment of completely standard Pentiums and laser printers with a stable LAN linked to a mainframe is a much different support picture than an environment consisting of everything from a low-end 286 to a Pentium Pro, with every model of clone imaginable, and a tenuous (read, "always going down") mainframe link. In the same way, an environment of completely standard software is very different from an environment in which you have customers using several different brands of products such as word processors and spreadsheets. Knowing what technology is used will give you a better idea of how big the support requirement is. This will help you determine what aspects of support you need to focus on, what problems to expect, what things you need to clean up, how many people you need, and what services you might outsource.

If you have an inventory of all your hardware and software assets, then you already know what hardware/software you have; if you don't, now is the time to get one.

What They Use It For

Help Desk customers call the Help Desk when they can't use the technology to do what they need to do. Unfortunately for you, "using the technology" can mean just about anything from keying in letters to running mission-critical applications such as order processors, and can mean the difference between two support staff and forty support staff. To determine how much support is needed, you need to know what your customers are doing, not just what software they're using. PC users might use Word for Windows for letters or documents, or they might have developed several macros for production applications using Word. Supporting the former is quite different from supporting the latter.

Knowing what they use the technology for also helps to better prepare you for when the technology has to change. For example, you might have an accounting department that is using Lotus 1-2-3 macros written by a keen summer student. Meanwhile, you are trying to standardize on Excel, another spreadsheet package. Unfortunately for you, the accounting employees don't know how the macros work; they just use them. You want to convert those macros to Excel, but Excel doesn't translate those very complicated macros nicely, and you don't have the time or resources to rewrite them. It's much better to know up front, when you're planning for the Excel conversion, that such macros exist. It would be painful to be hit by them as you go about installing Excel. It would certainly slow down your conversion.

Getting this kind of information is not a trivial matter, but the effort will be worth it. You'll have to talk to your customers, perhaps attend departmental meetings, and watch them at work whenever you get the chance. Do this continuously. You might start up customer focus groups in which the group members do that work for you. They can bring back information on what their areas are doing, and let you know what kind of support they do or will require. If you do decide to go with focus groups, you'll have to make it worthwhile for customers to join. You might consider offering early software releases for testing, free education, or other perks.

How Often and When They Use It

Do your customers use the technology you support twenty-four hours a day or only 9 A.M. to 5 P.M.? Do they work extra hours on regular occasions (e.g., at the end of the month)? You need to know this so you can balance your staff against the support load traffic. Figure 1.3 shows a typical distribution of technology use over a day. You might have staggered working hours in your group one or more staff members starting as early as 7 A.M. to check out the networks and provide support for any early customers. and one or more staff members finishing as late as 7 P.M. to provide support for the late workers and perhaps to do some maintenance work on the LAN when the traffic is lighter. The peak hours will have the heaviest support coverage, while the fringe hours will have the lightest coverage. Your peak hours might actually be early in the morning or late in the evening, in which case you would stagger your hours differently to accommodate the peaks. You might also be able to offer prearranged support for those times that your customers work extra hours—such as the end of the month or the end of the year.

The key to being able to provide all this support is to know the requirements beforehand so you can offer suggestions and alternatives. The reality might be that you just don't have enough staff or budget to provide extra occasional support. If that is the case, then one option might be to negotiate with the department in question to have them pay for extra support. You might outsource some standard support so your staff members who know the systems involved could provide the extra support. Being proactive and finding out which of your customers need

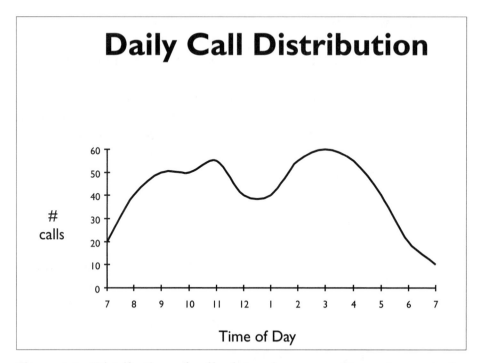

Figure 1.3 Distribution of calls determines support requirements for different time periods.

extra support and when, and setting up alternatives before the support is actually required, will prevent the panic and potential customer disappointment that result when unexpected support is requested at the last minute.

If you have network monitoring tools, you will be able to get the information you need to determine customer workload patterns just by looking at the network usage statistics over a given period. Looking at the pattern of calls into the Help Desk will also give you some information about when the customer load is the heaviest—if you have call distribution technology, then you will be getting this information automatically. If you don't have any way of getting this information from your system, you'll have to talk to your customers. You can use E-mail to explain what information you need and why. Your customers will probably respond willingly with the information required because it is in their best interests to do so. If you have customer focus groups, you can get some of the information you need from them.

How Technology-Literate They Are

How well do your customers understand their technology? Do they just perform the same tasks continuously, panicking if they have to do something new or if they run into problems, or are they reasonably knowledgeable about the systems they use and comfortable with trying new things? More of the former kind of customer will mean a heavier support load for you and perhaps a need to provide more in-depth training for your customers. They will expect and need a lot more help just doing the basics than the more self-sufficient customer. If training is not one of the services you provide, you will want to at least arrange for external training for these customers. If you are using external training, you will need to make sure that it is appropriate for your environment. It is very frustrating and unproductive for a customer to attend training and then return to the work environment to find that things are set up very differently than they were in the training environment.

On the other side of the coin are power users. Power users can be both a blessing and a big problem. If you can work with them to harness their energy, enthusiasm, and curiosity into pilot projects, software trials focus groups, or help groups, they can be a valuable resource. If, however, you can't or don't work with them, they may cause you grief by doing things on their own: Changing configuration files, installing illegal software, and so on, all of which will cost you significant support time.

Knowing what kind of customers you have will give you a better idea of how much of a load they will be, what you will need to do to improve their level of literacy, where potential problem areas lie, and where some potential resources are. Learning what kind of users you have will take time and will be a matter of monitoring the kinds of calls you get and where they come from. You could ask for volunteers for software piloting—this could flush out some power users. You might not have this information if you're just starting up a Help Desk. In this case, you might want to go to various areas and find out how they were getting support, and this might point you to both the power users and those customers needing extra help.

How Technology-Friendly They Are

How technology-friendly your customers are, or are willing to become, will determine how automated you can be, at least initially. It will also determine what tools you will be able to use to greatest advantage with your customers. Will your customers talk to voice mail? Will they use an automated system? In some companies, voice mail is still considered the ultimate evil invention and people will not use it. Installing a voice mail system to record support calls that come in while no one is there, or while all the phones are busy, may not be a good idea in an environment that doesn't use voice mail. You'll end up with customers who are irritated, or who may come to where the support desk is physically to find a human being, or who complain to senior management. And senior management is not always enamored with voice mail or other automation either. If you can't automate, if you can't use tools such as voice mail, you will be looking at a more expensive support load—more staff—until you can convince your customers that automation works when used properly (and naturally you will use it properly), and that it is absolutely necessary for the health of the business. Needless to say, this is not an overnight endeavor, but knowing that you need to address this issue will allow you to plan for it and work toward it.

To find out how technology-friendly your customers are, check to see what technology they're currently using. Find out whether other technology has been tried, and try some pilots of your own. Don't be deterred if at first your customers tell you they won't like being talked to by a machine or dealing with other forms of automation. Let them try it. They may just love it, especially if it gets them a quick solution to their problem. They can help you market it to the rest of your customers.

What Their Priorities Are

What are your customers' priorities? You can't handle all the problems that come up at once, so you have to have some mechanism for determining which are the most important. The problems that are most important are those that will have the greatest impact on the business. If a company is dependent on a network for gathering all of its data for nightly processing—be it payments, orders, or whatever—that network had better be high on your list of things that are most important. The same goes for specific applications. If your ordering application is a high priority and there's a problem with it, you'd better ensure that your staff understand the priority. Otherwise, they might end up spending time on a less important problem while that one is still outstanding.

Aside from talking directly to your customers, there are various other sources of priorities: job scheduling information, IT application analysts (they will most likely know where specific applications fit into the priority hierarchy), company mission statements, and company business plans. These will all give you valuable information about what applications or technologies are most important to a company.

Beware of priorities that reflect what customers want rather than what the business needs. Figure 1.4 shows how these can differ. You will want to double-check the priorities you get directly from customers against other sources. Once you establish and communicate priorities (see Chapter 4), you might encounter some disagreement from customers. Be careful of trying to adjust priorities yourself. If your customers belong to the same company and can't agree on a resolution for conflicting priorities, either you or they will have to go to a higher au-

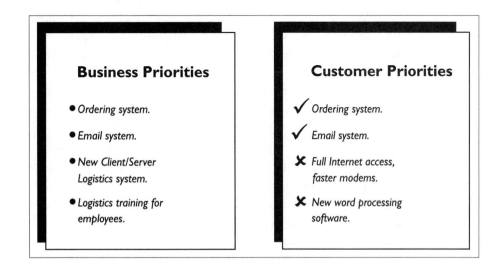

Figure 1.4   Beware of customer priorities that are not business priorities.

thority to get the priority resolved. If your customers belong to different companies, they may pay a premium for higher priorities or may have some kind of agreement stating exact priorities. You need to know what these are. If two problems happen at the same time and the priority is not resolved, you will lose valuable time if you try to resolve the priority rather than solve the problems, or you may work on the wrong problem first. If you are in such a support situation, you might actually have extra staff just to ensure that each company you support gets the agreed-upon priority.

You need to work by priorities that are determined by the business and understood by your customers. If you choose not to do this, working by your own priorities instead—perhaps ignoring a critical customer's problem to install some terrific new technology—you could find yourself out of business.

How Controlled Their Environment Is

The reality is that you may work in an environment in which everything the user wants the user gets. Setting any kind of standards or limitations in this kind of environment is next to impossible. Unless you can change the whole environment, you're stuck with it and have to accept the limitations under which you will work. Your customers have more clout than you, so in any kind of confrontation you would lose. Accept that you can't change this overnight. Any kind of legislation would mean revolution. You have to convince your customers that what you are offering is better.

This kind of environment would certainly have a strong effect on your services. You would, at least initially, have to support just about anything that came up. You would need to allocate time to selling standards, and you would most likely have to have a base of external contacts to help you out with your hardware and software support.

Alternatively, if the environment you support is highly standardized, life on the Help Desk is going to be a lot easier. You will be able to automate more easily, and you won't need as much breadth of expertise because you will be supporting a limited number of products. You won't have as many technology incompatibility problems as in an nonstandardized environment, so getting things working and keeping them working will be easier.

What They Want

Asking your customers what services they want that they don't currently have could be very dangerous—you could be setting very unrealistic expectations. Don't ask unless you're willing to listen to the responses and address each one. If people ask for things and those things are not delivered, they're going to want to know why they didn't get them.

Honesty is the best approach when trying to get an idea of what customers need without giving them the impression that you're going to deliver everything. Let them know up front that you would like to know what services they need but that you are constrained by a budget so you will only be able to provide those that deliver the most value to the business. Your customers should be able to recognize the legitimacy of what you are trying to do.

Getting to Know Your Customers

How do you find out all these things about your customers without moving in with them? Aside from the suggestions already made, you can attend customer departmental meetings, drop in to talk to your customers informally, call selected customers, constantly check what is happening whenever you happen to be in a customer's area, hold focus groups, send out surveys, and invite customers to participate in the planning or changing of the Help Desk. But remember, when you ask their opinion be prepared to listen and be prepared to hear things that you may not agree with. If you ask and then ignore, you're starting off on the wrong foot and have lessened your chance of success significantly.

You may not be able to get all of the information we talked about here. Time is sometimes an enemy. You'll just have to build or change using the information that you do have and then adjust your processes as the feedback comes in. Gathering information is really an ongoing process—get information, change; get feedback, change; get more feed-

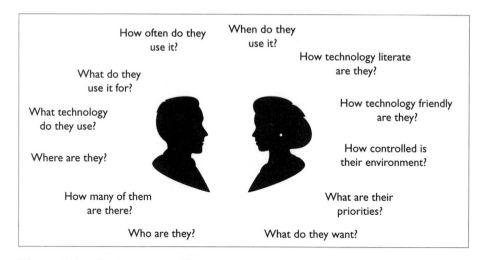

Figure 1.5   Customer profile.

back, change; and so on. The more information you do have, the better chance you'll have at success. (See Figure 1.5.)

Sample Customer Profile

Your customers are everyone in the corporation; not everyone has a PC or a terminal, but everyone has access to one. There are about 2,000 of these customers, and they are in four different locations, all within one state.

They use PCs for both LAN and mainframe access. There are a profusion of IBM clones—about six makes and, within those, both 486s and Pentiums of various speeds. Memories range from 16 megabytes to 32 megabytes, and hard drives from 250 megabytes to 7 gigabytes. Other technology includes a variety of printers, mostly laser printers of one type, a few CD-ROMs, and the mainframe. There is also a super server linking information from several smaller networks and the mainframe together. Software is divided between Windows 3.1 and Windows 95, and the network operating system is Novell. There is a standard for software, but it is loose and can be bypassed fairly easily. You have three word processors, two spreadsheets, four database packages, and two graphics packages. There is also a small department of text editors using Macs. They are hooked together by an AppleTalk network, which is standing on its own.

The greatest use of PCs is for word processing and spreadsheets. Client/server applications are just starting and will reach production in the next six months or so. Word processors are used mostly for correspondence and text editing; spreadsheets make heavy use of macros and are used for calculating input into larger (mainframe) systems. You suspect that some of these macros are not quite correct and that there is not a great understanding of what they do. Several mission-critical applications run on the mainframe. About one-third of your customers use the Internet.

Customer use of technology takes place from 7:30 A.M. until 6 P.M., with the heaviest use between 10 A.M. and 4 P.M. There is some use after 6 P.M., but this is infrequent and the load is very light—just one or two users trying to get some extra work done. When big projects are coming due, about three times a year, some extra support time is required. After 6 P.M., production batch processing starts on the mainframe and finishes early the next morning.

Most people are not willing to take the time to go to external courses and have not been properly trained in the use of the packages and hardware that they are using. The Help Desk gets a lot of calls with very elementary questions and problems. On the other hand, you have a pocket of Mac users who think they know it all. You wish they did.

The company implemented voice mail a few years ago, and it has been very well received. There is a fair amount of travel going on in the company, so many people conduct a large proportion of their business via voice mail.

The priorities are the network (including the mainframe), database access, ordering applications, distribution applications, credit card applications, and links to retail systems.

The customers want to be able to solve all things instantly with a single phone call. You know you won't be able to give them that for a while yet, and you're kind of sorry you asked.

What This Suggests

Your customer profile is only one of four inputs into developing your list of services and objectives, but taken on its own it can suggest several things that your Help Desk should consider doing to improve service and prevent problems. These, of course, must be tempered by budget, management, and the rest of IT. Using the profile described previously, some suggestions might be as follows:

> Have staggered hours for your staff to cover the Help Desk from 7 A.M. to 7 P.M. Discuss the need for occasional extra support with your customers to ensure that it is there when required.

> Outsource hardware maintenance. You cannot do this as cost effectively or with as quick a response as the maintenance company can because it has easy access to all the parts required and the technical expertise necessary to keep the hardware maintained.

> Work with the IT group that sets standards to encourage them to make the standards official rather than loose and to make compliance mandatory. This means you will have to do a fair bit of marketing of the advantages of having standards and selling of the chosen standards.

> Use (or purchase) a network monitor and automated asset management software to check network traffic and the configuration of network components to ensure that your network can handle the client/server systems being designed. The asset management software will tell you which machines, if any, need to be upgraded to handle the new system.

> Encourage and promote training in standard software packages. You don't have a training group, so you will outsource the training, but you will work closely with the trainers to ensure that your customers are getting the training they need. You will also keep track of call statistics for questions and problems, so you can show customers the number of calls their lack of training is causing and demonstrate that they are tying Help Desk resources up for other customers.

> Identify power users and get them on your side before they cause too much trouble. Get them involved in testing new software and upgrades and making recommendations.

> Check out customer priorities with other sources, including management, to make sure they are valid; communicate these to the Help Desk staff. Incorporate these priorities into your Help Desk software if possible.

Thank your customers for their input regarding what they would like to see on the Help Desk and get back to them with your list of services, explaining your budget constraints. Ask for their feedback.

Your Mission

A mission is a declaration of purpose, values, direction. It is a strategy for handling customers, for doing business. It governs every interaction your Help Desk has with your customers. It determines how each Help Desk team member will deal with a call, problem, request, and so on. It is your "modus operandi."

Characteristics of a Mission

Your mission will typically be one to five paragraphs long. Sometimes it will be a statement only, sometimes it will be a statement followed by values—or how you plan to achieve your mission. There is no hard-and-fast rule about what a mission should look like, but it should be:

> **Believable.** Your staff need to believe in the mission. Something like "Exceed customer expectations" will receive very little buy-in if you're just trying to keep your head above water, trying not to let your problems take over.
>
> **Achievable.** Your mission needs to be achievable. "Strive to thrill the customer at every opportunity" is not achievable. In most cases it would take more than a call to the Help Desk to thrill your customers (unless you choose to provide a very different set of services.)
>
> **Recognizable.** After each call you need to know whether you fulfilled your mission. Did you give "best value first time?" In other words, did you solve as much of the problem before you passed it on? Did you "focus on the needs of the business first" by resolving the customer's immediate problems before worrying about the technological problem? If you can't recognize when you are fulfilling the mission then it's not much use having one.

Example No. 1

Mission:

"To help the customer make the best use of technology in support of the business."

Values:

We resolve problems, not symptoms.

We are proactive, actively seeking to prevent problems and eliminate reasons for calls.

We treat customers courteously and professionally.

Our top priority is to minimize the downtime of our customers.

Example No. 2

Mission:

"Focus on the needs of the business first."

Putting a Mission Together

There is only one rule for putting a mission together, but it's a very big one: Let the people who will be living it do it.

If you have a tendency to try to get people to do things your way, butt out. Help Desk managers often resort to "legalese" when trying to create mission statements. They come up with missions like "We need to maximize the value of the corporation's investment in technology." What does this mean to the person answering the phones? Nothing! Something like "We resolve as much as possible at the first call" is simpler but probably more meaningful.

Some suggestions:

Have the Help Desk team discuss a strategy for running the Help Desk, how they should be handling each call. This should give them a mission statement.

Another way of approaching the creation of a mission is to think of comments about the Help Desk that you would like to hear about from customers. Build your mission around these comments.

You will find that the act of putting a mission together will go a long way toward clarifying responsibilities, objectives, and services.

Keeping a Mission Alive

As the business changes, so will your mission. The mission you have while your Help Desk is in start-up mode will probably be different from the mission you have two years later when your environment is more mature and your support structure is in place and working well.

Your Services

The services that your Help Desk provides are determined by your customer profile, senior management, other IT groups, and, of course, your budget. The more services you offer and the more things you support, the more thinly spread your staff and resources will be. You need to focus on providing those services that give best value to the business. You also need to keep the cost of offering these services within the budget that you have (or negotiate a larger one!).

Caution: Too Many Services

If you try to provide too many services or support too broad a range of products, you are setting yourself up for failure. You could end up in a situation in which customers with important needs are forced to wait while you provide a service that is not as important.

Stretching the Budget

Customers may be happy to pay for services that you cannot provide. For example, an option popular with customers is to have someone come into their department on a daily basis to give just-in-time help to people while they work—to show them better ways of doing things, to help them do new things, to answer their questions. They are typically more than willing to pay for this themselves.

Characteristics of Services

Services must be:

> **Manageable.** Make sure your Help Desk doesn't take on more than it can handle.
>
> **Supportive of the business.** You have limited resources. Make best use of them by focusing on the services that deliver the best value to the business. Use input from customers, senior management, and other IT areas.
>
> **Well understood and well defined.** If they aren't, customers may have expectations far beyond what your Help Desk can possibly provide. The closer your customer's expectations are to reality, the more satisfied they will be. They won't get unpleasant surprises. Services also need to be well defined to ensure that staff are clear on what they should be focusing on and are not distracted from the important calls by requests or problems of lesser importance. Remember to talk to other IT areas to make sure that all responsibilities are covered and nothing of importance is dropped.

When Things Change

You will want to adjust your services regularly, as the business changes, as your customers change, as your budget changes. Your goal always is to provide the best value to the business within the budget you have.

A Sample List of Services

> Provide support between 7 A.M. and 7 P.M.
>
> Allow customers to use E-mail, the phone, or voice mail to request support.
>
> Provide support for all standard (or preaccepted) software and all standard (or preaccepted) hardware. Software or hardware falling outside of this will be a lower priority.

Provide a central point of contact for any problems with technology. The Help Desk is responsible for problem recording, tracking, ownership, and resolution. Problems that cannot be resolved immediately are passed on to the appropriate areas but monitored to make sure they get resolved.

Maintain a Help Desk intranet web site.

Monitor LAN performance and notify appropriate groups of any potential problems.

Monitor problem trends and notify appropriate groups of recurring problems so that a permanent solution can be found.

Maintain hardware/software inventory.

Provide hardware maintenance (outsourced to an external vendor).

Offer training/education—either recommend or, if need dictates, administer a special information seminar.

Offer software testing (only for operability in the technology environment) for upgrades and new software.

Offer software sourcing, purchase, licensing, and installation.

Offer hardware sourcing, purchase, and installation.

Provide consulting: hardware/software recommendations based on user requirements.

Participate in groups determining standards for hardware and software.

Provide performance reporting—system and Help Desk.

Broadcast information about system availability.

Your Objectives

If you think of services as your products, you can think of objectives as your sales quotas or targets. Things will not improve or change on your Help Desk without some kind of momentum, and your objectives define that momentum. If you aren't setting objectives, you aren't improving, changing, measuring yourself. You can't possibly keep up with the business you're supporting.

Objectives must do the following:

Support the business and fulfill the Help Desk mission.

Be clear.

Be measurable.

Be owned.

Objectives must also be attainable. If you are setting objectives that you don't really think you can achieve, you are setting yourself up for failure. It's like agreeing to a project deadline that you know you cannot meet. You won't meet it—at least, you won't meet it with the quality of product that is expected. Management will be disappointed, your project will be a failure, and you will be history, or at least not in line for a promotion. If objectives are to be what you are measured by, then they are worth fighting for.

Clear

There should be no ambiguity in your objectives. People should understand what you're trying to achieve. For example, "Bring in training for customers" is not very clear. What training? Which customers? Does training need to be enforced? Alternatively, "arrange for basic Excel training for the forty customers in finance, starting in September. Ensure each person in the department is trained within four months" is clearer. Responsibility is clearer.

Measurable

Objectives are not much use if you can't measure whether or not you've attained them. If you don't know how you will measure an objective, don't set it. "Increase first-line resolution rate" is not measurable. Have you succeeded even if you increase it by .04 percent? "Increase first-line resolution rate from 60 percent to 80 percent" is better but not good enough. What is the time frame? Best of all is "Increase first-line resolution rate from 60 percent to 80 percent in four months (by April of this year)." That objective will be very easy to measure. Consider these examples:

1. "Increase positive response on weekly customer sampling surveys from 30 percent to 50 percent in four months' time." Very easy to measure (as long as you've defined what a positive response is).

2. "Improve team morale." Not measurable. You need to take a baseline measure. Draft up a survey to give your team. Then you have a base from which to measure. "Increase positive monthly survey responses from Help Desk team from 10 percent to 60 percent."

3. "Put marketing plan in place." Not clear—what does "in place" mean? And by when? Better would be "Create a marketing plan by March 5, to start March 10."

4. "Increase self-sufficiency of customers." Not clear. And not at all measurable. Better would be "Reduce number of calls per day from 300 to 200 within four months (by making customers self-sufficient)." Your objective is call reduction. Your plan for doing this includes various initiatives to promote self-sufficiency.

Owned

Once you set an objective, make sure someone is working toward achieving it. It is common on a Help Desk for staff to not know what the objectives for their team are. If they don't know they should be working on call reduction, the calls are not going to be reduced; if they don't know about the goal to increase first-line resolution, then the resolution rate will not get better. If the whole team should be working on an objective, let them know.

Measuring Success

Measure performance against objectives. Achieving objectives is a cause for celebration. Missing objectives is an opportunity to learn what could be done differently next time. Objectives will move you ahead. If you have no goals, you don't really know where you're going and you cannot be focused.

A Plan

Getting a plan together to implement your services and objectives, as your mission mandates, may seem an obvious step, but many Help Desks do not have any kind of a plan. And if it's not written down somewhere, it's not a plan. If you don't have a plan, the process of getting from where you are now to where your objectives say you want to be falls into the same category as an act of God.

You do need a plan, whether you're starting a Help Desk or running (and improving) an existing one. Your plan is a map that shows the path for attaining your objectives and providing your services. Your plan will help keep you on track and will help ensure that you meet your objectives in the time you need to. A plan will even help you determine whether your objectives are attainable, so you will want to do some preliminary planning before you set your objectives.

Your plan must take reality into account, and, unfortunately, reality may mean that you have to support an unstable environment while you get things up and running or improve things. Reality is the business screaming, "My PC is broken, fix it" and senior management nagging, "Will you please just stop this fooling around and fix the network? We've got a business to run here!" In this kind of environment, it is easy to get pulled into the whirlpool of endless support—you never have time to improve things, so they keep breaking and people keep calling you. More and more PCs get installed, and the problem is compounded daily.

A plan is more important than ever in this kind of environment. A plan will allow you to make compromises and to show management and customers why they are necessary. A plan will give you ammunition for setting attainable objectives. Perhaps you might have to move a little more slowly with your changes, so you can still maintain the current environment, or perhaps you can arrange for some temporary extra help.

Write your plan down and review it often. Use it to check on your own progress. Give it to management so they may check on yours.

Time and Reality

You have it all. Services, objectives, a mission to operate by, and a plan to make it all happen. You are focused on the business. How long did all of this take you? It didn't happen overnight. It may have taken a year; probably it took about four months. It may have happened completely apart from the support environment and may have been the real beginning of the Help Desk, or it may have taken place in the midst of chaos and confusion as you struggled to support the mess that already existed and that you inherited (or created). Also, some of it may not have happened just as it is laid out in this chapter. Perhaps you couldn't get all the parameters. Perhaps you couldn't get input from management or you couldn't get some of your customer information. But you took whatever information you had and used it to develop your services, objectives, strategy, and plan, recognizing that you would probably have to adjust as you got more information and more feedback.

Are You Finished?

You have your focus, your formula for success. But are you finished? No! You need to revisit all the components of your focus regularly—every quarter, say—to make sure they are still valid in your environment, which will probably have changed significantly since you set your focus. If your customers are asking constantly for a service that you don't provide, maybe you should provide that service. If cost cuts have been stepped up, you may have to change your objectives and your strategy. Automating wherever possible might be your new strategy, and your objectives would reflect this—you would be looking at each area of your Help Desk operations and seeing where you could automate. As new technology becomes available, you might have to adjust your services and objectives to be able to support it or use it. A focus that changes as your environment changes, as the business changes, will ensure that you keep following success even when success changes direction. Your formula for success won't ever be out of date.

Example: The ABC Help Desk

Senior Management Input

Fix problems quickly—no computer or user downtime is acceptable. Don't let technology failure negatively impact any critical business functions.

Automate wherever possible—keep costs to the absolute minimum.

Respond to business change quickly.

Responsibility Splits with Other IT Groups

For problems with internally developed applications, the Help Desk will get the initial call but will pass it on to the applications group for resolution. The Help Desk will maintain its intranet web page, but network technical support will maintain the intranet platform, informing the Help Desk when it changes.

The Help Desk is consulted in software selection, but another part of IT actually makes the selection. The Help Desk is responsible for notifying everyone of the installation, for doing the installation, and for getting a pilot out for testing to make sure that it works with all other technology components.

Customer Profile

There are 1,500 users in two adjacent buildings (almost everyone in the company).

Each user has either an IBM-compatible PC (ranging from a 486 to a Pentium Pro) or an Apple and is hooked to a small mainframe via a LAN. There are about twenty-five standalone PCs. Laser printers are one of three makes; impact printers are any of a variety of makes. Software has been standardized to a few Windows applications.

All users have full access to the Internet.

Applications are being migrated to the LAN from the mainframe. Most customers will be accessing client/server applications from their PCs within the next six months. Currently, most customers use their PCs only for word processing, spreadsheet applications, host access, and Internet access (heavy research requirements).

Customers work mostly from 8 A.M. to 6 P.M., but a few come in early and a few stay late. At year's end, some extra support is required to provide help for customers doing year-end calculations, should they need it.

Ten percent of customers work from home.

Most customers are familiar with how to use the standard software but are complaining that they cannot use the Internet effectively for research; they don't know where to find things.

E-mail is used heavily; voice mail is used only by certain departments. Generally, customers have no problem accepting new technology.

Priorities are the network and the applications being migrated to client/server.

Mission

To help customers get the most out of their technology. Values:

Get customers up and running as soon as possible.

Solve problems, don't just apply fixes.

Offer customers hints and tips, answers to frequently asked questions, training suggestions. Take every opportunity to educate customers.

Services

Offer support 7 A.M. to 7 P.M.; extra support available by request, arranged for in advance.

Allow customers to use E-mail, phone mail, or the phone to request support.

Offer single point of contact for all technology problems: Calls that cannot be resolved within ten minutes will be passed to second-level analysts. All calls are tracked from open to close.

Offer management of hardware and software assets.

Provide hardware maintenance—Help Desk has actually outsourced this; a person from the outsourcing company works as part of the Help Desk, maintaining hardware and investigating hardware failures.

Maintain Help Desk intranet web site.

Create and maintain service-level agreements with each major customer group.

Source and purchase hardware and software.

Participate in setting standards and changemanagement.

Monitor LAN performance and notify appropriate groups of any potential problems.

Monitor problem trends and notify appropriate groups of recurring problems so that a solution can be found.

Participate in setting standards.

Arrange for training for products being supported.

Objectives for Next Six Months

1. Increase number of problems resolved at first call to 80 percent from 70 percent.
2. Upgrade PCs to a level that can handle client/server application (using asset management tool to find PCs that need upgrading).
3. Source and offer training on using the Internet.

Key Points Covered in This Chapter

On a Help Desk, setting yourself up for success means getting focused on the business, concentrating on doing the things that add most value to the business. Focus on a Help Desk is defined by:

Mission

Services

Objectives

To make sure your mission, services, and objectives are focused on the business, you must get input from three areas:

Senior management. You need to know where the business is going and what it needs from the Help Desk.

Other IT groups. You want to make sure that responsibility splits are clearly defined, that no balls are dropped.

Customers. You need to create a profile of your customers so that you really understand what you need to provide for them.

Getting focused won't just happen on its own, you need a plan. If you're drowning in support, a plan will help you ensure that you actually spend time on getting focused and not just on fire fighting. You can outsource extra help while you get yourself focused.

As the business changes so will your focus. Review your mission, objectives, and services every quarter and update them as necessary.

PART TWO

Basic Structure

Structure

The structure of a Help Desk is a reflection of its focus. Just as the focus of each Help Desk is unique and depends on the business it supports, its mission, services, and objectives, so too is its structure. There is a tendency in the Help Desk world to try to find the perfect Help Desk and use it as a model. Unfortunately, there is no such thing as a Help Desk that is perfect for every organization. What works perfectly for one organization may fail miserably in yours. Use input from other Help Desks, take a close look at them, but then find the structure that's right for your Help Desk and don't worry about how it differs from the others.

In This Chapter

This chapter will discuss how to structure your Help Desk, from levels of support through staffing requirements to consolidation of multiple Help Desks. Specific topics to be discussed are the following:

41

- Typical Help Desk structure
- The front line
- Second and third levels of support
- Staffing level factors
- Estimating required staffing: formulas, rules of thumb, and software
- Multiple Help Desks
- Consolidating Help Desks

Typical Help Desk Structure

Figure 2.1 shows the call-handling structure of a typical Help Desk. Calls come into the front line. If the front line can't handle a call, it is passed on to the second line of support or to a specialized area such as hardware maintenance. If the second line can't resolve the call or if the call requires specialized skills, the call is passed to the third line of support, which is typically another information technology (IT) area or an area external to the organization, such as a vendor.

Help Desks usually reside in an IT area such as enterprise operations, but depending on the business, they might also be found in business areas.

The Front Line

The structure of the front line can make or break the Help Desk. It is the point of first contact with the customer, the first chance to help the customer. Front lines are usually structured as either *Dispatch*, in which the call is answered and then dispatched to a second level, or *Resolve*, in which the front line analyst tries to resolve the call, only passing it on if it cannot be resolved within a certain amount of time. A Resolve front line may dispatch calls that require specialized support, such as hardware maintenance.

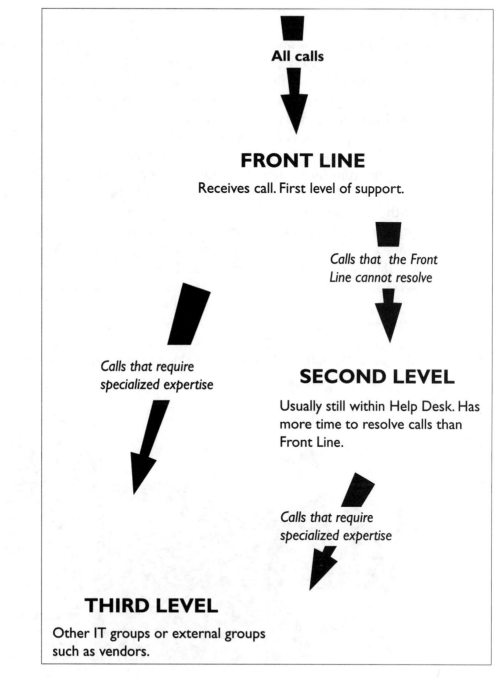

All calls

FRONT LINE

Receives call. First level of support.

Calls that the Front Line cannot resolve

Calls that require specialized expertise

SECOND LEVEL

Usually still within Help Desk. Has more time to resolve calls than Front Line.

Calls that require specialized expertise

THIRD LEVEL

Other IT groups or external groups such as vendors.

Figure 2.1   Typical Help Desk structure.

Dispatch

In a Dispatch front line structure, the people on the Help Desk who get the first call typically do not have the knowledge to resolve the problem or question. Instead, they act as operators who take the call and route it to the appropriate area for resolution. They may transfer the call without logging it, or they may log it and then pass it on. They take no further responsibility for the call. Calls are answered quickly but they are not necessarily resolved quickly. The people who receive the dispatched calls in this structure form the second line of support. These people could be analysts within the Help Desk, or they could be experts in other parts of the organization. They would be responsible for picking up logged problems, getting the appropriate people involved to get the problems solved, getting back to the customer, and closing the problems.

If the second line is not within the Help Desk, or does not have a firm service-level agreement with the Help Desk, resolution times may start to creep up. The Dispatch structure falls apart completely if there is absolutely no formalized commitment by the second line of support to resolve calls. Figure 2.2 illustrates the backlog that is created in this situation. The calls will be dispatched to people who either cannot or do not want to resolve them.

Figure 2.2   Potential pitfall of a Dispatch front line structure.

Resolve

In a Resolve structure, the front line tries to resolve each call that comes in. It is staffed with people who are technically and analytically skilled and who are devoted to resolving the calls that come into the Help Desk. Calls are passed on only if resolving them will take longer than is practical on the Help Desk—calls might be coming in and waiting while the first call is being worked on. Customers typically only have to describe their problem once—to the person who will be handling it. Tools such as knowledge bases, expert systems, and remote diagnostic software are often used on a Resolve front line to increase the percentage of calls resolved at point of call.

A Comparison

With a Dispatch structure, the customers get their Help Desk calls answered quickly, but this says nothing about when the calls actually get resolved. As mentioned previously, Help Desk operators can answer and pass on a lot of calls—a lot more than front line staff who try to resolve the calls—but in doing so they may be creating a continuously increasing backlog. All those passed-on calls queue up for handling by analysts. If that queue is too long—a problem that may be caused by not enough analysts, too heavy a workload, or unbalanced priorities—then customers have to wait a long time before their problems get resolved. When calls are resolved by analysts outside the Help Desk, this problem becomes more pronounced (see Figure 2.2). It is difficult to control the priorities of people outside of your own department. A formalized service-level agreement with all second levels of support is absolutely critical if a Dispatch front line is to be in any way successful.

Another potential problem with Dispatch front lines is that customers soon learn who actually resolves the problems and start calling these people directly, rather than going through the front line. They don't want to have to describe their problem to more than one person, and they want to talk to the person who will actually be able to help them. Unfortunately, this kind of activity interferes with the workloads of the analysts and disrupts the balance of priorities.

The cost of acquiring the skills to get a job on a Dispatch front line is less than for a Resolve front line job, but the job of logging calls and passing them on can quickly become monotonous. Career prospects for people in a Dispatch front line are limited. There is not much opportunity for learning or skill expansion.

With a Resolve front line structure, your front line staff members are actually trying to resolve the problems, answer the questions, and service the requests. Each person is spending more time on the phone. Other calls are constantly coming in, so you need to put some kind of controls in to make sure that the queues don't become unreasonable in length. You may need to set a time limit. If a call cannot be resolved within a specific amount of time—say, five or ten minutes, then it should be passed on.

To get the most out of a Resolve front line structure—to increase the number of calls that can be resolved at point of call—you will most likely need to use tools such as knowledge bases, expert systems, and remote control software (see Chapter 6). Tools such as Interactive Voice Response (IVR) can be used to automate routine tasks so that customers can resolve some of their own problems, freeing up front line staff for more critical issues.

The higher skill levels required on a Resolve front line, although more expensive than skills on a Dispatch front line, mean that you could more easily rotate staff responsibilities with other levels in the Help Desk, for purposes of cross training and enhancing skills and experience. Staff could work on the front line for a few months, then move into other Help Desk areas such as software testing and installation. Your analysts could keep their technology skills sharp by working with new and upgraded products on the back lines of the Help Desk, yet stay close to the customers—know what their problems are, what they use, and what they need—by spending time on the front line. Working on the front line also would give staff an appreciation of the Help Desk workload and a better understanding of the urgency of the problems that might be passed on to them while they are in other roles. Analysts from areas other than the Help Desk might also benefit by spending some time on the front line. Developers would learn a lot about what kind of problems customers tend to have with systems and what customers want. This could only improve the design of the products they create. The rotation process also creates backups—if someone on the front line is absent, you can rotate another analyst who has spent time on the front line into the position temporarily.

The Resolve front line structure, especially when it is combined with automation that eliminates routine, mundane tasks, makes for an interesting and challenging place to work. Working on the front line offers staff a wonderful opportunity to get an overview of all the systems in the corporation, talk to customers from all areas of the business, and learn what is most important to the business. Staff also get exposure to all the technology being used, often before anyone else in the corporation, and their technology knowledge base expands greatly. All of this is valuable training that makes staff more marketable when they are transferred to other areas.

A summary of the comparison between the Dispatch and Resolve structures is presented in Table 2.1.

Table 2.1   Dispatch versus Resolve Front Lines

	Dispatch	*Resolve*
Initial Response Time	**Low**	**Higher.** A limit may have to be placed on how long an analyst spends on each call so that other customers are not kept waiting. Tools such as automatic call distributors can be used to handle incoming calls as effectively as possible.
Time per Call	**Low**	**Higher.** The analyst will actually try to resolve the problem. After a specified time limit, the analyst will pass any still unresolved calls on to the next level of support.
Resolution Time	**Can get out of control**	**Lower** for most problems. Most problems will be resolved immediately by the person answering the phone.
Investment in Skills	**Low**	**High.** Expensive technical and analytical skills are required.
Investment in Tools	**Low**	**High.** If calls are to be resolved at point of call, analysts will need access to tools such as knowledge bases, expert systems, and remote control software.

(continues)

Table 2.1   Dispatch versus Resolve Front Lines (*continued*)

	Dispatch	*Resolve*
Job Interest	**Low**	**High,** especially if automation such as an IVR is used to eliminate the repetitive, mundane calls.
Career Prospects	**Not good**	**Excellent**
Customer Satisfaction	**May be low.** Frustrated customers may starting calling the analysts directly, resulting in lost statistics and interrupted workloads.	**Higher.** Customers need to explain their problems only once—to the people who actually resolve the problem. Most of the time the customers have their problem resolved while they're still on the phone.
Critical Success Factors	Service-level agreements with all areas receiving passed-on calls.	**High skills** and **good tools**

Second and Third Levels of Support

The second level of support in a Help Desk usually consists of Help Desk analysts who are doing other things besides resolving problems passed on by the front line. Analysts in the second level of support may actually take turns rotating through the front line, so they get a chance to experience both the problem-resolving and the project side of the Help Desk. Functions performed by second-level analysts depend on the services provided by the Help Desk but may include software testing and installation, call elimination initiatives, marketing initiatives, surveying customers, and maintaining Help Desk Web site information such as hints and tips, frequently asked questions (FAQs), standards and policy information, and system information. Ideally, second-level support analysts work on Help Desk improvement initiatives. Not only is this good for the health of the Help Desk but it's good for the health of the Help Desk analyst in terms of job satisfaction and growth.

Third levels of support typically involve areas outside of the Help Desk such as technical support, database administration, program development, and network administration. Depending on Help Desk services, some of these areas may actually reside within the Help Desk. Third levels of support might also include third parties who are providing services such as hardware maintenance to Help Desks and vendors of Help Desk tools and products that Help Desk customers use.

Terms of support outside of the Help Desk need to be formalized so there is a clear understanding on both sides of the responsibilities involved in passing on and receiving Help Desk problems. A problem that may seem important to a Help Desk analyst who has actually spoken to the desperate customer may not seem as important to the network administrator on whose desk it may eventually fall (see Figure 2.2). A weakly defined third level of support can completely undermine strong first and second levels.

Staffing Level Factors

The million-dollar question is "What number of staff is ideal for my Help Desk?" Why isn't this an easy question to answer? Why can't you just copy the solution of someone else who has already figured it out? The answer to the latter is, because no two Help Desks are exactly alike. Say someone tells you they run their Help Desk with ten people. Does this mean you should be able to run your Help Desk with ten people? Consider the following:

Who do they include in those ten people? Just front line staff? Do they include all levels of support?

What does their customer profile look like?

What are their call volumes and call distribution like?

What hours do they support?

What services do they provide?

How complex is their environment?

How skilled are the people on the Help Desk?

What does their budget look like?

What does the organization they support expect of them?

Do they feel they are performing well?

Does their senior management feel they are performing well?

Consider the examples in Table 2.2. This is sample data taken from an informal survey of Help Desk analysts. In each case, the analysts state the calls they receive per month, the number of customers they support, and the number of staff on their Help Desk or in their support area. The data in the table, although it has no statistical significance, serves to illustrate how dangerous comparisons to other Help Desks can be without an understanding of the details of the other environment. Compare examples 2 and 5. In example 2, each customer support person handles 200 calls per month, approximately four times the number handled by each support person in example 5. Does this mean that the Help Desk in example 2 is doing a better job? Absolutely not. Help Desk 5 might be handling much more complex problems than Help Desk 2. Each problem might take hours or days to resolve. Help Desk 5 might well be the Help Desk that is doing the better job.

Table 2.2   Examples of Help Desk Staffing Levels

Example 1	Calls per month:	1,700
	Customers supported:	1,500
	Help Desk staff:	5 first level, 11 second level.
	Customers per support person:	94
	Calls per month per support person:	106
	Calls per month per customer:	1.1

Table 2.2 (*continued*)

Example 2	Calls per month:	2,800
	Customers supported:	1,500. Of these, 1,200 are internal, 300 external.
	Help Desk staff:	4 first level, 10 second level.
	Customers per support person:	107
	Calls per month per support person:	200
	Calls per month per customer:	1.9
Example 3	Calls per month:	1,650
	Customers supported:	4,000
	Help Desk staff:	5
	Customers per support person:	800
	Calls per month per support person:	330
	Calls per month per customer:	.4
Example 4	Calls per month:	775
	Customers supported:	300
	Help Desk staff:	3, but can escalate to approximately 12 IT staff.
	Customers per support person:	100 (ignoring the staff that can be escalated to).
	Calls per month per support person:	258
	Calls per month per customer:	2.6
Example 5	Calls per month:	10,000
	Customers supported:	8,000
	Help Desk staff:	170 technical support staff, 8 dispatchers.
	Customers per support person:	45 (including the dispatchers).
	Calls per month per support person:	56
	Calls per month per customer:	1.25

We've discussed why calculating staff required is not necessarily easy; now let's look at what needs to be taken into account when deciding on this number. There are several factors that will affect your Help Desk staffing levels. These include the following:

- Services you need to provide
- Objectives you need to meet
- The profile of your customers
- Call volume and distribution
- Complexity of environment
- Skill level of staff
- Your budget

Services

Very simply, if you offer a service you need to include someone on the Help Desk to provide that service, unless it is automated or outsourced. The more services you provide, the more such people you will need. The number of staff will also depend on the number of hours of support you need to provide. A Help Desk that operates twenty-four hours a day, seven days a week, will have 118 hours more to cover each week than one that operates ten hours a day, five days a week.

Objectives

If you need to do more than just answer phones, if you need to be proactive, reacting quickly to the business and in a state of ongoing improvement, then you need to set objectives for these activities and you need to assign people to them. You will need to take this into account when calculating number of staff.

Customer Profile

All the factors that go into a customer profile—complexity of functions performed, skill levels, and so on (see Chapter 1)—will affect the number of staff your Help Desk requires.

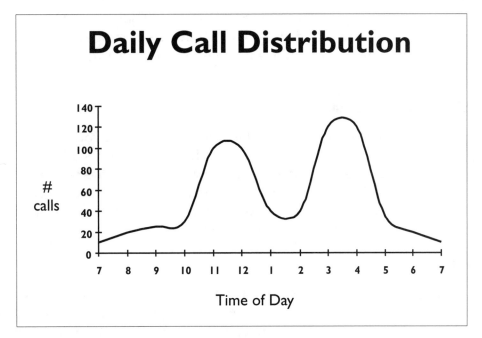

Figure 2.3 You need to take call volume and distribution into account when determining number of staff required for your Help Desk.

Call Volume and Distribution

Say your Help Desk daily call volume and distribution looks like the example in Figure 2.3. You can look at number of calls in a month and calculate staff using that number as input, but consider the peaks you're dealing with. You have two peaks during the day. If you calculate staffing for the whole day based on the levels in those peaks, you'll be overstaffing. If you ignore the peaks, you'll be understaffed during the peaks. Your solution in this case might be to staff for fairly stable times and outsource daily extra help during peak hours.

Complexity of Environment

The more complex your technological environment, the more support it will require. For example, an organization with a wide area network (WAN) that spans the globe, linking 20,000 users and doing all of their business electronically, will have very different support requirements from an organization that has a much smaller WAN that spans only one state and does very little business electronically. Standardized environments require much less support than environments in which anything goes.

Skill Levels of Staff

How much are you willing to pay for staff? If you aren't willing to pay top dollar you will have to settle for less skilled staff and possibly more staff. The more highly skilled your staff are, the more productive they will be. If you do decide to skimp on staff skill level you may find yourself paying more for extra training or extra help (to say nothing of what it might be costing your customers).

Budget

Ultimately, if you can't get money to get what you want, you'll have to settle for what you can get (see Chapter 11, "Cost-Benefit Analysis," to make sure you're asking in the right way). If there is not much money for head count you might still be able to outsource extra help because outsourcing usually comes out of the expense bucket.

Estimating Required Staffing: Formulas, Rules of Thumb, and Software

Having discussed all the factors that will go into determining the actual number of people you have on your Help Desk (see Figure 2.4), we'll now discuss formulas and rules of thumb you can use to get an initial estimate of the people you will need or to validate the number you do have.

Measuring Performance in an Up-and-Running Help Desk

If your Help Desk is already up and running and you are measuring performance (see Chapter 9) your performance will give you a good indication of whether or not you have the right number of people and which way to adjust. For example, you should probably look at your staffing levels and your call levels if objectives are not achieved and agreed-

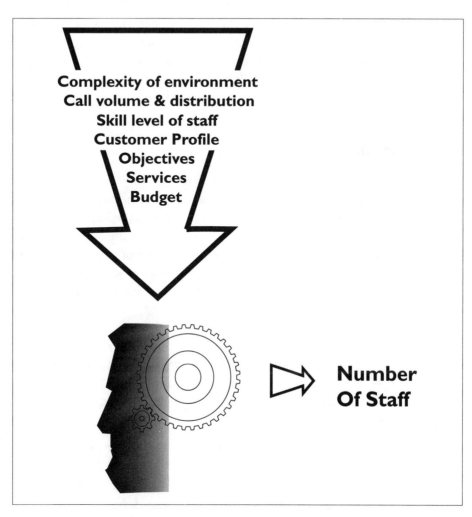

Figure 2.4   Many factors need to be taken into account when calculating staffing levels.

upon service levels such as resolution times and percentage of calls re-solved at point of call are not met. The former might be too low, the lat-ter too high for the environment being supported, or both.

Forecasting Packages

Forecasting demand is a complex science. If your Help Desk is large, a forecasting package might be the way to go for you. There are many forecasting packages available that can help you forecast customer demand and calculate staffing projections. Staffing projections will help you stay ahead of the game, giving you an idea of what your staffing requirements will look like in the future. Scheduling packages are available (often paired with the forecasting) to help you schedule staff based on call levels.

Quick Staff Requirement Formula

If you just want a quick indication, there is a very simple, commonly used formula that will give you a good idea of the staff required to answer calls. The formula is simply *total expected call time for a specific time period* divided by *time one person will actually be available for that period*. In more detail and selecting a time frame of one month, the formula is as follows: (Expected number of calls per month × Expected average duration of call) ÷ (Working hours per month × Estimated utilization × Percentage availability).

> **Expected number of calls per month, expected average duration of call.** If you have no call history you'll have to estimate these. Call duration must be expressed in hours.
>
> **Working hours per month.** This is the hours per working day, totaled for a month, that an analyst will be working at this job. If we say that the working day is eight hours and subtract 1.5 hours for lunch and breaks, we're left with 6.5 hours on the job per day. Over one month, or twenty-one working days, this becomes 136.5 hours.
>
> **Estimated utilization.** The person doing this job will not be on the phone 100 percent of the time. There will be time between calls. Since your numerator in the formula deals with actual call time, your denominator must also. The estimated utilization figure is your estimate of what percentage of time the analyst actually spends on the phone (or answering E-mail, if you get requests or problems that way). This figure is typically somewhere between 75 percent and 85 percent (for phone calls).
>
> **Percentage availability.** Your analyst will be taking vacation time, attending training, taking occasional sick leave, and so on. In reality, only a portion of analysts' time is usable time. Your human resources

department can tell you what figure your organization uses. It is typically 85 percent. Let's take an example. Say you estimate 2,500 calls per month, averaging twelve minutes (or .2 hours) per call. Each analyst will be on the phones 136.5 hours each month (6.5 hours per day for twenty-one days); you want to see a utilization of 75 percent, and 85 percent of the analyst's time is usable. Your formula becomes $(2,500 \times .2) \div (136.5 \times .75 \times .85)$ which gives you 5.7 people required.

A good exercise is to vary your number of calls per month and your call duration to see what happens to your staffing requirements. If you're just starting, it will give you a better understanding of how the numbers work and what kind of a range you might be working in. As your true call volume and profile changes, you will have a better understanding of how your staffing requirements will change. The *Microsoft Sourcebook for the Help Desk* (Microsoft Press, 1995) gives an excellent detailed explanation of this formula and its use.

Remember, this formula is very simple and does not take into account factors such as call distribution (e.g., peaks in call traffic) and any wide variances in call duration (could depend on type of call). The formula may tell you that you need six people on the Help Desk, but in reality you may need only four in the morning and eight during your peak afternoon hours. Similarly, on some days, your call durations may be much higher than usual because you are getting a lot of complex calls, and in order to handle those calls you'll need more people than your simple formula forecasted.

Calculating Required Staff for Project Work

What if you have people who do project work? How would you go about calculating the number of staff required? If you want to calculate staff required for project work you can use a formula similar to the quick staff requirement formula given in the preceding section: (Estimated hours of project work for the month) ÷ (Working hours per month × Percentage availability). The utilization would be 100 percent, since project work would be a continuous activity with no wait time.

For example, say we estimate that we will do 500 hours of project work in one month. We will leave work hours at 136.5 and availability at 85 percent. This gives us (500) ÷ (136.5 × .85) = 4.3 people required.

Calculating Required Staff for Combined Phone and Help Desk

What if we want a combined Help Desk where the analysts are spending some time on the phone and some time on the Help Desk? If you have analysts with combined responsibilities, then you would simply use each formula as presented in the previous sections, making sure that your working hours represent full working days, and then add the results. If we combined the previous examples, our Help Desk would have to handle 2,500 twelve-minute calls per month plus 500 hours of project work. We would need a total of 5.7 + 4.3 = 10 people. (We could add the decimals since responsibilities are being shared.) We would have to divide up hours between the Help Desk and project work in such a way as to make sure that our call time and project time requirements were satisfied.

If you want a starting point for estimating call volume, a rule of thumb commonly used in the industry is that you can expect 1.2 to 1.5 calls per month from each customer you support. The higher end of the range would imply a less skilled customer base or a more aggressive technological environment. Remember, this is just a rule of thumb, not a magic number.

Whatever method you choose, you will most likely go through a process of calculation and adjustment. Outsourcing extra help during this time is a good way of getting the extra help when you're not sure whether you'll need it or not in the future.

Multiple Help Desks

There are a lot of historical reasons for having more than one Help Desk. Most of them are just that—historical. When PCs first started coming in, if support structures were set up they were usually set up to be completely separate from any existing mainframe support structures. This may have worked for standalone PCs, but when PCs started accessing mainframes via LANs, difficulties became apparent. When problems occurred, it was often difficult to tell whether they originated from the LAN or the mainframe. If there were problems with the mainframe, the mainframe support group didn't always bother to tell the PC support group, and vice versa. Both groups could be trying to solve the same problem, which was a waste of time for at least one of them. Customers didn't always know who they should call for support: Was the problem a PC issue or a mainframe issue? Even more basic than that, was the box on their desk a PC or a terminal? In some companies, as specialized applications were created special groups (with separate phone numbers or E-mail IDs) were set up to provide support for them. In that kind of environment, a customer could get really confused—when something went wrong, was it a PC problem, a mainframe problem, or an application problem? And if it was an application problem, which application was causing the problem?

In one extreme case, a bank found itself with more than ninety Help Desks, which had sprung up as various applications were developed. When a new application was developed, a hotline support number was established for it. Things got a bit out of control, and support became a real headache for both the IT staff and the 50,000 end users. Communication between Help Desks was a nightmare: When one Help Desk implemented a new technology, other Help Desks might not learn about it until they started getting calls about it. There was much duplication of effort. Fortunately, the bank realized the severity of the situation and the ninety Help Desks were consolidated to three, one for each geographical region the bank serviced. This resulted in a dramatic improvement in service levels, and thus a much happier customer base.

These kinds of multiple support structures are the legacy that many of us are left with today; in fact, many of us are still creating this kind of legacy for the future. We have to make sure that our Help Desk structures are not confusing our customers, that they are not causing duplication of effort, and that they are as efficient as possible, with no superfluous layers or divisions.

If your customers are confused about who to call, chances are you have too many Help Desks. If your Help Desks share the same customer base, you probably have too many Help Desks. A PC Help Desk that services the same customers as a mainframe Help Desk, and vice versa, is one too many Help Desks. Such Help Desks should be consolidated. To leave them separate is to invite confusion, duplication of effort, and general inefficiency.

Consolidation Advantages

Some advantages to having consolidated Help Desks are as follows:

1. **One source for information.** If something is wrong with a server, with any network component, or with the mainframe, the Help Desk will know about it. In a multiple Help Desk environment, there is always the danger that one Help Desk does not know when another has detected a problem in its particular piece of the environment. This could result in the wasted effort of trying to resolve a problem that has already been recognized and addressed and in the dispersal of false information to customers.

2. **Better use of staff.** Generally, a consolidated Help Desk requires fewer staff than the sum of the component Help Desks. The higher call load will be easier to balance between staff members and will be less susceptible to dramatic fluctuations. Staff on the consolidated Help Desk will have the opportunity to develop a broader knowledge base. They will have a more complete picture of what is happening, which will make it easier for them to resolve problems. They will gain experience in a broader base of technologies. The Help Desk will become a more interesting place to work.

3. **Better use of technology.** On a consolidated Help Desk, duplication of Help Desk tools will be eliminated, and tools can be more easily integrated so that their functionality and accuracy increases. Tools for one Help Desk generally cost less than the sum of tools for several individual Help Desks.

4. **More consistent service.** A consolidated Help Desk makes it easier to provide consistent service to customers. Putting procedures in place to ensure consistent service is easier with a single Help Desk than across multiple Help Desks. Similarly, monitoring and managing these procedures is easier in a single Help Desk environment.

5. **Less expensive.** A consolidated Help Desk will most likely be less expensive to run than several smaller Help Desks. Savings can be realized on tools, on staff, and on office space.

This is not to say that it's always wrong to have more than one Help Desk. If you have separate customer bases with separate requirements and support needs, more than one Help Desk might well be the way to go. In the case of the bank that consolidated ninety Help Desks into three, each of the three Help Desks supports a different client base in a different part of the country. A pharmaceutical company with 5,500 PC customers spread among several buildings decided to create several satellite Help Desks to bring support closer to the customers. The Help Desks are administered centrally and draw on the same resources.

Another organization found it advantageous to have a separate Help Desk to service the support requirements for its stores. The stores have their own computer systems and are hooked into the corporate network. The store Help Desk provides help seventeen hours a day, across the country, in two languages. The support staff must have detailed knowledge of the store systems—including the cash register systems—and are, in fact, required to have actual store experience.

Living with Multiple Help Desks

If, for whatever reason, you find yourself with more than one Help Desk, there are things you can do to help ensure that communication between Help Desks does take place and customer service does not suffer.

Have regular meetings between Help Desks. Talk about problem trends, new technology or techniques being employed, and anything unusual that has occurred. Also, review the effectiveness of communication between Help Desks.

Use the same Help Desk software if possible, including a common problem database, so that problems can be passed back and forth easily and workloads can be viewed.

Ensure that each Help Desk understands what its responsibilities are and what the responsibilities of the other Help Desks are. Knowing who does what will help ensure that customers aren't bounced between Help Desks and that there are no cracks for problems to fall through.

Set up procedures to keep each Help Desk informed of problems and new developments. Don't leave this up to the discretion of the staff. Set up clear procedures, ensure that staff understand them and their importance, and ensure they are being followed. If there is a problem on the mainframe, it is important that the PC Help Desk knows this because they will be getting calls about it.

Set up Help Desk procedures together. Wherever possible, try to make sure that procedures on each Help Desk are the same, to help ensure consistency of service to the customers.

Share training—try to use the same courses so that training received and skills gained are consistent.

The more consistent Help Desks are in the service they deliver to their customers, the more successful they will be.

Consolidating Help Desks

Consolidating existing Help Desks is not an easy task. There are several processes that you should go through before you try to put the new Help Desk into place. These include the following:

1. Validate your consolidation, making sure it is something you should be doing.
2. Gather information from all the Help Desks being consolidated.
3. Gather information from the business.
4. Design the new Help Desk.

Suggestions for each of these processes are given in the following sections, along with a few notes about the consolidation project itself.

Validate Your Consolidation

Before you make any moves toward consolidation, you should determine if consolidation is something you should be doing. This may sound contrary to what you've just been reading, but, as with other IT trends, the consolidation trend sometimes swings too far. Organizations have started consolidating Help Desks for everything from PCs to overflowed toilets to credit card inquiries. Sometimes consolidation simply does not make sense. When you're about to embark on a Help Desk consolidation project, you need to ask yourself the following questions, and if you don't have good answers go no further.

> What are you looking to accomplish through consolidation? What's in it for the business (such as positive financial impact)?

> What are your current biggest support issues or concerns? How will consolidation help resolve them?

Gather Information: The Help Desks

Make sure you understand the magnitude of what you are trying to consolidate. Gather information from all Help Desks being considered for the consolidation. Take an inventory of the following:

- Functions performed
- Technology supported
- Help Desk technology used
- People and skills

Talk to *and listen to* people on each Help Desk (sometimes they see and hear things that you cannot). What are their concerns about consolidation? Do they feel consolidation is or is not a good idea and why?

Gather Information: The Business

Talk to the business customers who will be supported by the consolidated Help Desk. What are their concerns about consolidation? Which Help Desk functions are most important to them? You need to make sure these won't get lost. Try to determine what impact consolidation will have on them.

Design the New Help Desk

There are several things you need to consider when you design your new Help Desk. These include the following:

1. **First-level call resolution.** In a consolidated support area, people might be required to support a wider range of products. This could significantly decrease first-level resolution rates (the percentage of calls resolved at point of call).

   Could telephone equipment be set up to channel calls to the appropriate people to keep first level resolution rates up?

   Would everyone be able to access any available reference information or knowledge base tools to get at problem resolution information?

   What else could be done to keep first level resolution rates from being negatively impacted?

2. **Call handling.** In a consolidated environment, call handling might be more complex, for example, passing calls on to other levels of support. You may need to set up clear procedures and service-level agreements with all secondary levels of support.

   What procedures are currently in place for call handling? How do these have to be changed?

   What call priorities are currently in place? Will these still hold?

3. **Impact on customers.** Customers hate surprises. Anything that will change their current levels of service—the services the Help Desk provides for them now—needs to be marketed so that they are aware of it ahead of time.

   Will customers know who to call for help?

   Will customer service levels remain the same, get better, or be degraded?

   Will the consolidated Help Desk offer new services such as self-help? How would these impact customers?

4. **Tools.** A Help Desk that is supporting a wider base of technology may need new tools, which may be different from all current tools.

   Could one call management tool handle the requirements of all the support areas being consolidated? What data conversion or building is required?

   What training would be required?

   What other tools would be required?

5. **People.** You need to consider the skills and staffing levels required on the consolidated Help Desk.

   What training is required (at consolidation and on an ongoing basis)?

   What will consolidation do to morale, job interest, job opportunities?

   How can you keep people involved in the consolidation while still keeping the support areas staffed?

6. **Focus.** You need to make sure that your new Help Desk is focused on the business. You need to look at your new customer profile, what management expects from the consolidated Help Desk, and what the responsibility splits are with other IT areas. You can then develop a mission, list of services, and objectives to get your Help Desk focused. (See Chapter 1 for help.)

Notes on the Consolidation Project

Your Project team should include the following:

Help Desk staff

Staff representing secondary areas of support

Staff representing all IT areas affected by the consolidation

Customers

Some other suggestions:

This project will be a lot easier if you have cooperation from all Help Desk staff. Keep them informed of your intent and progress. If you intend to lay staff off or relocate them, let people know that this possibility exists and what you will do to help people find new jobs within the corporation or outside of it.

Market the new Help Desk (see Chapter 10 for ideas).

You should be able to build a solid cost justification for consolidation. If you can't, you probably shouldn't be consolidating. A good justification together with your project plan will help ensure that the consolidation project maintains the priority it deserves when other important projects come up.

Key Points Covered in This Chapter

In a Help Desk structure there are usually three levels of support: the front line, which actually takes the calls; the second level, which usually resides within the Help Desk and handles calls the front line cannot; and the third level, which consists of people (typically outside of the Help Desk), with specialized skills.

The front line can be structured as Dispatch, which simply takes calls and passes them on to another level of support, or Resolve, which actually tries to resolve each call that comes in. See Table 2.1 for a comparison of Dispatch and Resolve.

Determining staffing levels for a Help Desk is a complex process and needs to include consideration of the following factors:

Services you need to provide

Objectives you need to meet

The profile of your customers

Call volume and distribution

The complexity of the environment

The skill level of staff

Your budget

An environment with multiple Help Desks is often fraught with confusion and duplication of effort. Consolidating multiple Help Desks can resolve these issues by offering the following:

One source of information

Better use of staff

Better use of tools

More consistent service

Lower cost

When you have to live with multiple Help Desks, there are several things you can do to improve communication and help ensure that service does not suffer:

Hold regular meetings between Help Desks.

Use common Help Desk software.

Ensure mutual understanding of responsibilities.

Set up procedures for keeping each other informed of problems and new developments

Set up Help Desk procedures together.

Share training.

When embarking on a consolidation of Help Desks there are several processes that you need to go through before you start the merge:

Make sure consolidation is something you should be doing.

Gather information from all Help Desks being consolidated to ensure all services are covered and all issues and concerns are addressed.

Gather information from the business. You want to make sure that customers will not be losing anything from the consolidation and that their concerns are heard and addressed.

Before you begin your Help Desk design, consider factors such as first-level call resolution, complexity of call handling, ease of use for customers, the Help Desk tools that will be required, and the staff training and skills that will be required.

Focus your Help Desk on the business.

CHAPTER THREE

Staffing

Gone are the days when all the Help Desk analyst did was answer the phone. The roles a Help Desk analyst must play have expanded and are more demanding than ever.

In This Chapter

This chapter will discuss the factors involved in staffing a Help Desk. The following topics will be discussed in detail:

- Roles Help Desk analysts play
- Skills required
- Hiring the skills you need
- Planning for turnover
- Training for staff
- Help Desk environment

We will also look at examples of

a Help Desk analyst job description

a Help Desk manager job description

Roles Help Desk Analysts Play

There are seven major roles that Help Desk analysts must take on on a day-to-day basis (see Figure 3.1):

Partner/shareholder in the mission, services, and objectives of the Help Desk

Problem eliminator to solve, prevent, and eliminate problems

Communicator

Marketer

Data gatherer

Expert

Customer service representative

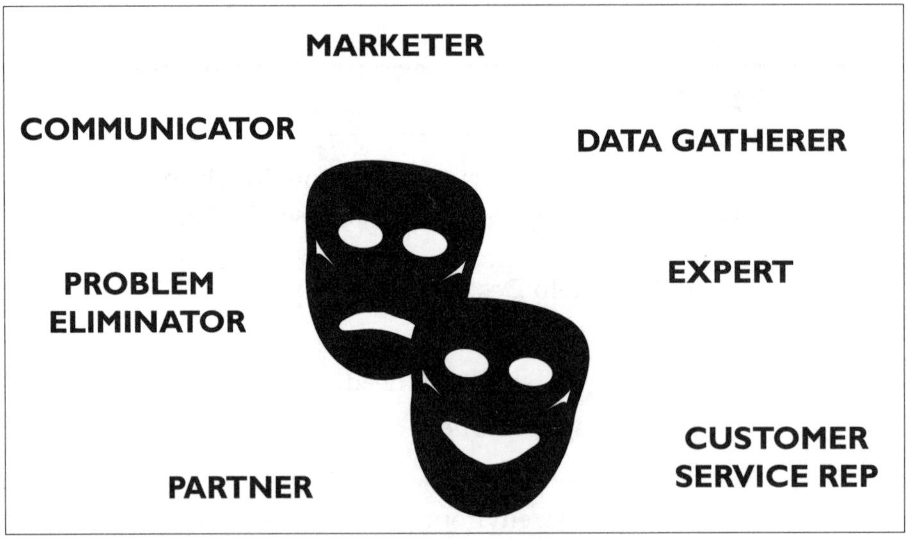

Figure 3.1   Roles that Help Desk analysts must play.

Partner/Shareholder

Help Desk analysts who don't buy into the Help Desk mission—into the role the Help Desk is trying to play—can jeopardize the success of the Help Desk. They will unintentionally sabotage initiatives by not really trying. For example, a Help Desk might be trying to install an IVR system that allows customers to perform certain tasks on their own, such as checking on the status of their problems or requests. Say a customer calls the Help Desk and bypasses the IVR to talk to a real person. "I don't really like to talk to machines," the customer confides, "I prefer talking to a live person." The Help Desk analyst who is not a partner in the mission of the Help Desk, who has not bought into the IVR project, will think "I knew customers wouldn't like this" and will answer, "That's okay. I'll do it for you." That analyst is undermining the success of the IVR project. An analyst who was playing the role of a partner in the Help Desk mission would have answered that customer by saying "Let me walk you through it. You'll find it's very quick and easy. Next time, try it on your own and let us know what you think." The second analyst is ensuring the success of the project by encouraging—teaching—the customer to use the IVR system.

Taking on the role of partner/shareholder means the following:

Living the Help Desk mission, being part of the team

Providing agreed-upon Help Desk services, staying within these services and not doing extras that may appease customers but take away from time that can be spent on activities that are more critical to the business

Understanding Help Desk priorities and objectives and taking an active role in accomplishing these objectives

Problem Eliminator

Help Desk analysts need to eliminate problems, not just solve them. They need to focus on eliminating reasons for calls, on increasing the uptime of their customers. This means assuming such problem-solving responsibilities as

Logging and updating problem profiles

Investigating causes, testing solutions, and putting solutions in place

Escalating when necessary

Help Desk analysts must also do the following:

Work to eliminate recurring problems.

Watch for trends that indicate potential problems and then eliminate the problems before they happen.

Communicator

The Help Desk analyst is the customer's first point of contact. The analyst has a big job to do just in listening for the problem, getting a resolution across to the customer, and getting feedback from the customer. But his or her role as a communicator is even more important (see Figure 3.2). The Help Desk analyst must not only interact with the customer but must

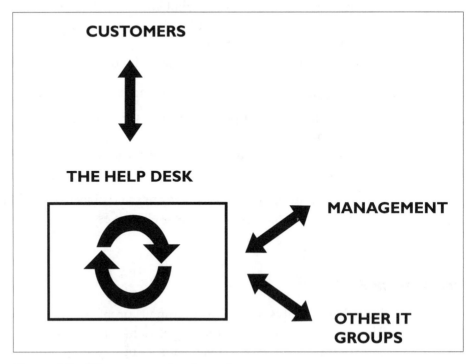

Figure 3.2   The communication role.

Pass feedback from customers on to other IT areas or to management.

Participate in groups such as standards, change management, and disaster recovery to provide input on customer impact and to collect information about upcoming changes.

Constantly communicate with peers, exchanging information about problems and about anything new in the environment.

Marketer

Every customer interaction is a marketing opportunity that a Help Desk analyst must take advantage of. The Help Desk analyst must do the following:

Promote a professional Help Desk image.

Sell the value of the Help Desk, it successes and accomplishments.

Promote effective use of technology.

Communicate anything that affects the technological environment.

See Chapter 10 for more information on marketing.

Data Gatherer

Running a Help Desk means gathering a lot of data for the purpose of resolving problems and evaluating and improving the Help Desk. Help Desk analysts take a role in these processes by

Tracking and gathering data from calls to update knowledge bases and to identify any significant trends.

Gathering feedback from customers via surveys.

Expert

Help Desk analysts are expected to be experts in the products they support. Because of the continuing importance of customer service skills, we seek Help Desk staff who are good communicators and can handle even very negative behavior well and we sometimes underestimate the importance of technical ability. No matter how skilled a person is in terms of soft skills, if he or she has a problem learning technical things then that person probably does not belong on a Help Desk.

Playing the role of expert means that a Help Desk analyst must:

Keep current on all the technology used in the environment supported.

Get the right training at the right time (hopefully before the technology is rolled out to the customers!).

Take seminars, join user groups, read trade magazines, and visit trade Internet Web sites to keep up to date with technology and the Help Desk industry.

Customer Service Representative

Being a customer service representative on a Help Desk is not an easy role to play. It involves dealing with, and responding positively to, complaints, problems, and sometimes negative and emotional behavior. In order to play this role the Help Desk analyst must learn to think of the customer as the most important part of the job. Without customers, there would be no job. The analyst must think of each customer interaction as an opportunity to help that customer, not as an interruption. This is not easy to do when the customer is being emotional, negative, or challenging in some way. To fulfill the customer service representative role, the Help Desk analyst is going to need some training.

The importance of each of these seven roles in an organization will depend on factors such as the focus of the Help Desk (mission, services, objectives), the customer profile, individual job descriptions, the technological Help Desk environment (tools used), and the Help Desk structure.

Skills Required

In order for Help Desk analysts to be able to take on the roles discussed in the preceding section, they must possess certain skills. The most important of these are the following:

Focus. The ability to remain focused on the mission, on what's important to the business despite the distractions of day-to-day Help Desk life.

Problem solving. The ability to identify and resolve problems quickly and effectively.

Proaction. The ability to take initiative to make improvements.

Communication. The ability to listen to customers and staff and convey ideas effectively.

Technical skills. The ability to learn technical product information quickly and accurately.

Customer skills. The ability to interact with customers in a polite and professional manner.

Help Desk staff may also need skills that are company-specific, such as a specific level of experience, maturity, and/or professionalism. The Help Desk staff's working habits and character also need to fit into the organization and into the Help Desk.

Hiring the Skills You Need

It is instructive to encounter Help Desks that just can't seem to get the right staff. They keep hiring and letting go because staff just don't measure up. The problem may not be the people they're hiring. It may actually be their hiring practices. If you don't change your hiring practices, you will keep hiring the same kind of people over and over. In order to ensure that you get out of that negative cycle and actually change how you hire, you need to put together a skills requirement grid that details the skills you require; how important they are to you; and what kinds of questions, scenarios, or observations you can use to test for them. Table 3.1 illustrates a sample grid that shows these possible questions, scenarios, and observations.

Table 3.1 Example of a Skills Requirement Grid

Skill / Description / Questions, Scenarios, Observations	*Required/ Preferred*

Focus   **Required**

Commitment to team/department/company; understanding of Help Desk role in the company.

Questions:

"Tell me about your Help Desk/department mission and how you helped fulfill it."

"Tell me about your Help Desk/department goals and how you helped achieve them."

"What were the main services/products of your Help Desk/department?"

"How did your Help Desk/department contribute to the performance of the company?"

"What do you consider the most important aspects of your job? Why?" (Take note: Are these related to the business, to Help Desk goals? How important are these really?)

Problem Solving   **Required**

Understands entire process from logging to informing customer solution is in place; knows when to escalate; implements solutions not fixes.

Questions:

"Describe to me the steps involved in solving a typical problem in your job." (Take note: Does the candidate mention testing, communication with the customer?)

"If you were working on a difficult problem, how would you decide if and when you needed to go for help?"

"Give me examples of some major problems that you felt you resolved well and describe how you went about solving them from start to finish."

"Give me an example of a problem you felt you did not handle well. What would you do differently next time?"

Table 3.1 (*continued*)

Skill / Description / Questions, Scenarios, Observations	*Required/ Preferred*

Scenarios:

> Select a problem that you would expect the candidate to be able to handle almost from day one. Describe the symptoms. Ask the candidate to describe the first step(s) he/she would take toward solving the problem. (Take note: Look for responses such as "I would ask the customer questions to make sure I really understood the problem" or whatever makes sense for the problem in question.)

Proaction   **Preferred**

> Anticipates customer needs; looks for ways to make things better for the customer, to eliminate recurring problems, calls and prevent problems, calls; is constantly learning.

Questions:

> "Describe what you feel has been your greatest accomplishment in your job." (Take note: Does it indicate taking initiative?)
>
> "Describe what you feel has been your biggest failure and why it happened. What are you doing to prevent it from happening again?"
>
> "What area or skills do you need to improve on, in the next year, say?" (Take note: Is the candidate thinking about how to improve?)
>
> "Describe ways in which you took initiative to make improvements on your Help Desk."
> Or:
> "Describe some actions you took to eliminate calls on your Help Desk."
>
> "Describe ways in which you took initiative to make things better for your customers in some way."
>
> "Describe any instances in which you actually prevented specific problems."

Scenarios:

> "You've been getting a lot of calls recently about how to use a specific application. What do you do?"
>
> "One of your customers keeps having to reboot his/her PC. You get another call from the same customer and you think his/her PC has to be rebooted. What do you do?" (Take note: Does the candidate suggest fixing the underlying problem?)

(*continues*)

Table 3.1   Example of a Skills Requirement Grid (*continued*)

Skill / Description / Questions, Scenarios, Observations	*Required/ Preferred*

Communication   **Required**

Good listener; good at getting message across; communicates well with peers, management, and customers.

Questions:

"What are your strengths as a communicator? Your weaknesses?"

"Describe the toughest communication challenge you had on your Help Desk and how you handled it."

"Were any of your peers poor communicators? How did you handle the situation?" (Take note: Who, really, was the poor communicator? Candidate or peer?)

"Describe how often you communicate with your manager and what you talk about."

"Are you involved in any committees or focus groups outside of the Help Desk (but still within the company)? Describe your involvement."

Observations:

Does the candidate listen actively?

How good is the candidate at getting his/her ideas across?

How does the candidate use body language?

Scenarios:

Everyone on the Help Desk is busy on the phones. You get a call from a customer and after a few questions you realize the customer's PC has a virus. What do you do? (Take note: Does the candidate suggest informing other Help Desk staff?)

Technical Skills   **Required**

Working knowledge of Windows 95 and standard Microsoft desktop products; working knowledge of Novell.

Scenarios:

Put together a verbal/oral test for the candidate. Include questions/problems that you would expect the candidate to be able to handle from day one on the job. Be realistic. Gear the level of question/problem to the level you are looking for. Test the questions/problems out on Help Desk staff. Get feedback from them.

Table 3.1   (*continued*)

Skill / Description / Questions, Scenarios, Observations	Required/ Preferred

Customer Skills   Required

Regards customer as most important part of job; respectful of customers; empathetic; able to handle challenging behavior.

Questions:

"What do you do in instances in which customers call you for services or information that your Help Desk does not provide?" (Take note: Did the candidate offer the customers any alternatives?)

"When you miss a promised deadline or make a mistake doing something for a customer, what do you do?"

"Have you ever had an interaction with an angry customer? Describe it." Or: "If a customer shouted at you, how would you react?" Or: "Describe encounters you have had with difficult customers." (Take note: Look for signs that the candidate realizes there might be stresses and pressures behind that anger. Look for empathy. Listen for what the candidate considers a difficult customer to be.)

"Do you get unreasonable requests from customers? Describe some of these requests and how you handled them."

"What do you like most about your customers?"
"What do you like least about your customers?"

Scenarios:

You get a call from a customer who is extremely upset. The customer is working on an important assignment for the president. It's due this morning. Yesterday, the customer's PC was working; this morning it isn't. You suspect that the PC is simply unplugged—all the carpeting in the building was cleaned last night. How would you handle this?

You are working the early morning shift on your Help Desk. Things are chugging along nicely until you get a frantic call from a customer who is desperate to get onto the Internet to send off an E-mail but can't because the system denies log in. The customer is angry and shouts at you saying your service is very poor. You check the log and see that the customer changed the login password on the security system yesterday but did not change it in the login script. You have to tell the

(*continues*)

Table 3.1   Example of a Skills Requirement Grid (*continued*)

Skill / Description / Questions, Scenarios, Observations	*Required/ Preferred*

customer this carefully so as not to imply that the customer is stupid. How would you handle this?

Professionalism	**Preferred**

Confident; honest; tactful; image-aware.

Questions:

"What do you feel are the most important qualities to have when you are dealing with customers in a technology support environment?"

"What are some of the traits that you feel define professional behavior?"

Observations:

How confident is the candidate?

How comfortable is the candidate?

Does the candidate feel comfortable admitting his/her mistakes?

Does the candidate refer to customers and peers respectfully?

Do you feel the candidate is honest?

Do you feel the candidate has good control over his/her temper?

Scenarios:

A customer calls claiming he ordered a laptop on a specific date. You check and see that it was actually ordered a week later than that date. You tell the customer. This means he will get the PC a week later than he thought. He disagrees with your date and gets angry. You check again. He may have asked for the purchase requisition to be signed on the date he gave you but you did not get the order until a week later. What do you do? How do you handle this situation?

Experience	**Required**

Minimum two years in a support environment as a front line Help Desk analyst.

Questions:

"What are/were the main responsibilities of your job?"

"Did you have any supervisory responsibilities? Describe them. Were you responsible for giving performance appraisals?"

"Did you have any planning responsibilities? Describe them."

Table 3.1 (*continued*)

Skill / Description / Questions, Scenarios, Observations	*Required/ Preferred*

"Were you responsible for interviewing and hiring? Describe some of the candidates you hired (in terms of position) and your role in the hiring."

"Who does your performance appraisal?"

Observations:

Check the candidate's resume for years worked in each position, career progression, etc. Ask questions to clarify or if you suspect that information is "inflated in importance." Check references.

Team/Company Fit	**Required**

Absolutely always on time; enjoys working in a very casual environment (in terms of dress, relationships, communications); willing to work one Saturday each month; doesn't need any hand-holding.

Questions:

"How many hours do you have to work each week to get your job done?"

"How stressful is your environment? Give examples."

"How do you best learn?"

"Describe the amount of structure, direction, feedback you would consider ideal in your job."

"What is your approach to balancing your career with your personal life?"

"What do you want to be doing in five years' time?"

Observations:

General behavior. Would your other staff be comfortable with this person and vice versa?

Do this person's work ethics match the company's?

Where Do You Find Them?

Where can you look for potential Help Desk employees? You need not limit yourself to looking in technical areas. If potential employees have the ability to learn technical skills (and it is very important to check that this ability is there) they need not have a technical background if you are willing and able to take on the training investment required. The following kinds of people often make good Help Desk employees:

1. **People who work with people.** A big bonus here is that these people probably have most of the nontechnical skills you're looking for: communication, problem solving, proaction, customer service.

   Administrators

   Teachers

   Human resource workers

   Marketing people

   Tellers

2. **People who work with technology.** These people are most likely to have the technical expertise you require, especially if you want them to be fully productive from day one.

   People already working in support

   Technology salespeople

   People from other IT areas

3. **Students.** A student's incredible enthusiasm and eagerness to learn often more than make up for lack of experience and expertise. Students are good for part-time or summer help or for fixed-duration placement as part of cooperative learning programs. You wouldn't put a student on the front line right away, but every Help Desk has noncritical work that a student could do well.

Planning for Turnover

Turnover is traditionally high in a Help Desk environment. Planning for turnover means that you are less likely to be caught unprepared when someone does leave. Learn to think of employees in terms of limited stay. Change your interviewing and hiring practices to reflect the limited stay philosophy so that you are not trying to hire for "forever."

Figure out approximately how long people stay on your Help Desk, on average. When you hire, think of the employee as coming on to your Help Desk for only that specific period. For example, say employees stay with your Help Desk for an average of two years. If you were hiring a person, you would assume that the person was only going to stay two years. This will affect the type of employee you hire. Do you spend more and get a more highly skilled employee who can be fully productive almost from day one (see Figure 3.3), or do you spend less and get a less skilled employee who will not be fully productive until a certain amount of experience is gained or training is taken (see Figure 3.4)? You'd have to balance the cost of the more expensive employee against the costs associated with the less skilled employee, specifically, money and time for training; the time it would take another Help Desk employee to do the

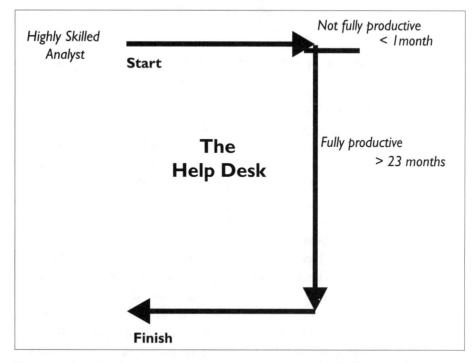

Figure 3.3   The turnover cycle: Taking on a highly skilled employee.

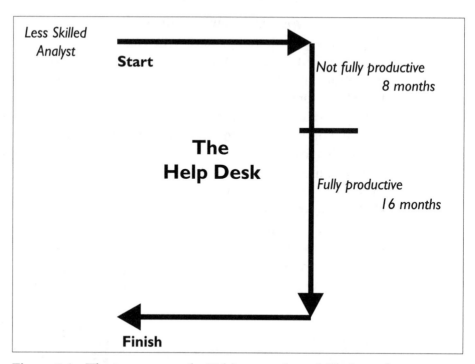

Figure 3.4 The turnover cycle: Taking on a less skilled employee.

work that the new employee cannot yet do; the work that will be waiting because of this; and possibly increased customer wait time and decreased customer satisfaction. Table 3.2 shows a comparison.

Create an ongoing training cycle and plan. Have your team research courses available and match these with skills required. Let everyone contribute to this training menu of technical, procedural, and personal skills. Be in a constant state of training and change. Plan for ongoing staff replenishment.

If you have an up-to-date menu of training available with an associated plan, people will just cycle in and out of training, updating skills as required. New employees coming into this process will simply go right into the cycle; the training will already have been researched and sourced. Keep your skills and requirements grid up to date, and get your whole team involved in doing this. Don't be scrambling in the few minutes before the interview trying to think of questions to ask.

Table 3.2   Costs Associated with Potential Employee's Skill Level

COSTS	*Highly skilled*	*Less skilled*
Salary	Higher	Lower
Time employee is not up to full productivity	Little or none	Could be significant
Time required by other employees to help this employee	Little or none	Could be significant
Negative impact on service to customers	Little or none	Could be significant
Cost of training required to get employee up to full productivity	Little or none	Could be significant

Always be on the lookout for potential employees. Help Desk employees come from many types of environments. If you keep your eyes open in your day-to-day interactions, you may spot someone who would be a good fit for your Help Desk. You could offer that person a rotational assignment through the Help Desk to see if it would be something he or she would be interested in. If you do this on an ongoing basis, even when you aren't hiring, you may find yourself with someone ready to step into a Help Desk position when an opening does occur. Encourage rotation assignments with other departments. This will help keep the Help Desk in a state of change and will expose more potential Help Desk employees to the Help Desk.

Always be on the lookout for potential career moves for employees. Talk about potential career moves at your Help Desk meetings, and have your employees make suggestions. Oddly enough, sometimes just knowing that there is somewhere for them to move to will make people stay! Don't act upset when people tell you they're thinking of leaving. Suggest places for them to go. This attitude will soon be reflected in the image the Help Desk has. People may start thinking of the Help Desk as a springboard to many other opportunities.

Don't let anyone, including yourself, get too comfortable. Make change the normal state of affairs on your Help Desk.

Training for Staff

One of the biggest mistakes Help Desk managers make in trying to stay within their budget is letting people learn on the job. Learning on the job encourages the bad practice of learning other people's mistakes and inefficiencies. It teaches how a certain person or application uses a tool, not what the tool is capable of and what it might be used for in the future. Training is an investment in the present and future of the Help Desk. If you don't spend enough on it, you'll get what you paid for.

The kind of training your Help Desk staff will need might include the following:

1. **Technical training**

   Help Desk tools

   Foundation products, such as LANs and LAN operating systems

   Products currently being supported by the Help Desk

2. **Procedural training**

   Help Desk procedures in use at your organization (this training should be offered by your Help Desk)

   General procedures and skills for setting up, running, or improving a Help Desk

3. **Personal training**

   Delivering quality service to customers (this training should include any organizational initiatives)

   Communication skills

   Problem solving

If you're planning for turnover, you'll have a training plan in place for each specific skill that you require of your Help Desk staff. You need to assess the skill level of each analyst and decide what training that analyst needs. You also need to make sure that the training is actually taken. People sometimes have to be convinced that the organization will not fall to pieces if they are away for a few days.

On-site training can be beneficial if all of the staff taking the training are at the same level of a specific skill, but it will fail if there is too much of a difference in skill levels. For example, if you bring an Effective Listening seminar on site and some of your staff have never attended any kind of communication training while others have taken every communication course ever given, the seminar will most likely fail for the latter group.

Have the procedures you use on your Help Desk documented or incorporated into your tools to ensure that each new person is getting the same training and that it is consistent. Passing on procedures by word of mouth will mean that they will change with each iteration, and important steps might be missed. Reviewing procedures frequently will help weed out processes that no longer make sense.

Help Desk staff should be trained on new products before anyone else—certainly before the products are tested or released to the customers. It is most embarrassing for a Help Desk employee to get a call about a product that was rolled out by the Help Desk but the Help Desk employee knows nothing about it.

Training is sometimes, strangely enough, used as a reward, a morale builder. Training is not a reward; it is a requirement. Very simply, if you don't hire the skills, you have to teach the skills, otherwise they won't be there. They won't magically appear. What you invest in training will be returned to you in improved Help Desk employee performance, a more professional Help Desk, improved use of Help Desk tools, a better overall understanding of technology in use and technology available, and an innovative Help Desk environment where people are always looking for ways to improve. Your customers will notice the difference.

Help Desk Environment

In the olden days, the Help Desk was closeted in the cold, airless, windowless computer room. It was like being in a refrigerator. The only real benefit was that your sandwiches stayed fresh. Unfortunately, many organizations still live in the old days when it comes to Help Desk location. We expect our Help Desk analysts to be pleasant, helpful, cheerful, and productive for the whole day while they are being bombarded with problems, negative behavior, and complaints. How do we help them do their jobs? We put them into a cold, airless, cramped space, away from everyone else, with no windows so they won't be tempted to look outside. It just doesn't make sense.

What do Help Desk analysts need in terms of environment?

Light, Space, Air, and Comfortable Office Equipment

People are like a lot of other mammals. They need light, air, exercise, and proximity to their own kind. You can't necessarily ensure that they get exercise, but you can give them the other things. Position your Help Desk in an area with windows, if possible. If not, make sure that the area is brightly lit. There are several alternatives to fluorescent lighting, which seems to bother a lot of people, and it might be worth your while to look into these. Ensure that ventilation is adequate. Too many office spaces are stuffy and dry. Plants, where possible, will also improve the environment. Large potted plants that sit on the floor are better than smaller shelf plants because they do not clutter shelf or desk space, they are larger and can be appreciated by more people, and they can be used as screens when necessary. Using a large plant as a screen often creates a more pleasant, open work space than installing a solid partition.

Actual physical comfort is one of the first things to consider. Your staff, especially those who sit answering the phone, need comfortable furniture, the best video display screens you can afford, and headsets that allow them to have their hands free. Let them be involved in selecting equipment wherever possible.

Easy Access to Each Other and to Other Support Groups

The roles of Help Desk analysts dictate that they need to be in touch with other people—their peers, technical support staff, application support staff, network support staff. When they are provided with easy access to each other, problems and potential solutions are discussed more readily and information is passed more easily and naturally. People are closer to each other's environments and have a better understanding of what they entail. It's easy for a person to call across to an adjoining desk, "Has anyone heard anything about a virus on the third floor?" Sometimes verbal communication just can't be beat.

An Interesting Job

Automation is probably the best way to achieve a more pleasant Help Desk environment. If you can automate the routine, repetitive work and give customers the ability to solve some of their own problems, then the actual work that Help Desk staff do will be more interesting and challenging. The number of uninteresting and repetitive problems coming in will drop, and Help Desk staff can focus on analyzing problem trends and eliminating the causes of more critical problems.

Time Away from the Phones

If you have enough staff, you can have them rotate through phone duty so they're answering the phones for a certain number of hours and doing project work for the remainder of the day. Time away from the phones will help keep your analysts from getting burned out and give them a chance to make improvements, do project work, and widen their skill base.

One option that you might consider is allowing Help Desk staff to work from home. This is not for everyone, and it is not possible in all environments. It might be worthwhile, however, if you have Help Desk staff who want to work from home and are disciplined enough to work on their own, if the technology necessary to set this up is readily available, and if communication links can be set up between all necessary contacts. You will have to balance the costs of the technology against any benefits you feel could be realized. Benefits might include happier and more productive staff and a decrease in office space requirements. Disadvantages might be less opportunity for informal communication and information exchange with peers, being excluded from team activities due to physical distance, being forgotten when information is being passed around to Help Desk staff, and perhaps missing out on information critical to effective Help Desk function.

Look at the environment that your Help Desk is in and ask yourself whether you would want to work there. If not, maybe you're not getting as much out of your Help Desk as you could be and you should consider changing a few things. The people to ask for advice about this are the Help Desk staff.

Job Descriptions

Job descriptions should not be cast in stone. As the business changes, the focus of the Help Desk will change and the responsibilities of the Help Desk manager and staff will change. Review and update job descriptions at least once a year.

Use job descriptions in your hiring process. Job descriptions should be given to potential employees so they have a clear idea of what the job entails. Then there will be less chance of a new employee complaining, "This is not the job I was offered!" Use job descriptions to help prepare for the interviewing process. Review roles and skills so you can look for them in potential candidates.

Performance reviews should be based on job descriptions as well as objectives (or specific assignments). Employees should be measured not only on performance versus objectives but also on how they fulfilled each of the responsibilities listed in their job descriptions.

Example No. 1: Job Description for a Help Desk Analyst

Goal

Analyze and resolve problems with the aim of eliminating recurrences and reducing calls to the Help Desk.

Responsibilities

1. **Problem analysis and resolution**

   Log all Help Desk calls.

   Analyze and resolve problems according to priorities and time frames laid out in the Help Desk service level agreements, escalating when necessary.

2. **Problem prevention**

Fix causes, not just symptoms, doing what is necessary to prevent problems from recurring.

Investigate and implement ways of reducing calls to the Help Desk.

3. **Participation in external groups**

Take an active role in monthly IT problem and change management meetings with the goal of ensuring that all new and updated systems going into production have as few problems as possible.

Participate in the corporate standards committee, providing other committee members with data on the impact of any changes or additions to standard technology.

Participate in customer focus groups, providing technical hints and tips to participants and bringing back feedback to improve the Help Desk.

4. **Communication**

Create/maintain an on-line Help Desk intranet site containing information on (at least) standards, security policies, technology ordering, and technical hints and tips.

Keep peers and manager informed of trends, significant problems, unexpected delays.

Keep customers informed of global problems or scheduled downtime. Also, keep them informed of progress on problems that cannot be resolved at point of call.

Call a sampling (approximately 10 percent) of customers back each day to ensure that the problems they had were fixed properly and to solicit feedback and ideas for the Help Desk.

5. **Training**

Take the training required, technical as well as interpersonal.

Keep up to date on technology and methods.

Example No. 2: Job Description for a Help Desk Manager

Goal

To support technology being used by the business with the realization that technology is critical to the business's ability to compete and survive.

Responsibilities

1. **Focus on the business**

   Create/maintain mission, services, and quarterly objectives for the Help Desk.

   Get input from customers, management, and other IT groups.

   Ensure participation and buy-in from Help Desk staff.

2. **Help Desk performance**

   Measure and report on Help Desk performance.

   Ensure all service-level agreements are met and objectives are achieved.

   Manage and allocate Help Desk budget.

   Generate quarterly performance report to senior management (both IT and the business).

3. **Help Desk function**

   Manage the day-to-day function of the Help Desk, ensuring that priorities are followed and procedures are working. Evaluate and improve on an ongoing basis.

4. **Planning**

   Create an annual plan for the Help Desk. Update quarterly.

   Keep up to date on technology and new support ideas and techniques.

5. **Staffing**

   Ensure that each person on the Help Desk is a good fit for the role.

   Ensure that all staff receive adequate technical and interpersonal training.

Key Points Covered in This Chapter

There are seven major roles that Help Desk analysts must take on on a day-to-day basis.

Partner/shareholder

Problem eliminator

Communicator

Marketer

Data gatherer

Expert

Customer service representative

In order for Help Desk analysts to be able to take on these roles, they must possess certain skills. The most important of these are the following:

Focus

Problem solving

Proaction

Communication

Technical skills

Customer skills

In order to ensure that you get the kind of people you want on your Help Desk, you need to put together a skills requirement grid like that shown in Table 3.1.

Turnover is traditionally high in a Help Desk environment. Planning for turnover means that you will be less likely to be caught unprepared when someone does leave.

Learn to think of employees in terms of limited stay.

Create an ongoing training cycle and plan.

Keep your skills and requirements grid up to date.

Always be on the lookout for potential employees.

Encourage rotation assignments with other departments.

Always be on the lookout for potential career moves for employees.

Help Desk staff need to be trained properly and should not be forced to learn on the job. Learning on the job might mean picking up other people's bad habits or learning only how a tool is used by the Help Desk, rather than what it is capable of and what it might be used for in the future.

If we want our Help Desk staff to be at their best the full working day we need to create good working environments for them. This means providing the following:

Light, space, air, and comfortable office equipment.

Easy access to each other and to other support groups.

Interesting work. We need to outsource or automate mundane, repetitive tasks.

Time away from the phones.

PART THREE

Internal Help
Desk Processes

CHAPTER FOUR

Problem and Work Management

"Be thankful for problems. If they were less difficult, someone with less ability might have your job."

—Bits & Pieces

Each call coming into the Help Desk means that a customer is working at less than optimal productivity. Your job, as a Help Desk staffer, is to get that customer up to full productivity as soon as possible. When the calls start coming fast and furious, this is not easy to do. You start working on one problem, and then you get a customer who is absolutely frantic and demands your immediate help. How do you decide who gets served first? "First come, first served" doesn't make allowances for the fact that some problems are more important than others. You decide, for example, that the second call must be more important because the customer sounds so frantic and you put the first request aside to work on the second. Before you get started, however, another call comes in that sounds even more frantic than the previous one, and the cycle starts over. You find yourself with several things put aside while you work frantically on several more. Calls start coming in from customers asking why their work hasn't been completed. You haven't logged anything because you haven't had time.

Your Help Desk is now totally out of control, as illustrated in Figure 4.1. The problems have taken control and are doing a good job managing you. You don't have a chance to resolve one before you have to drop it

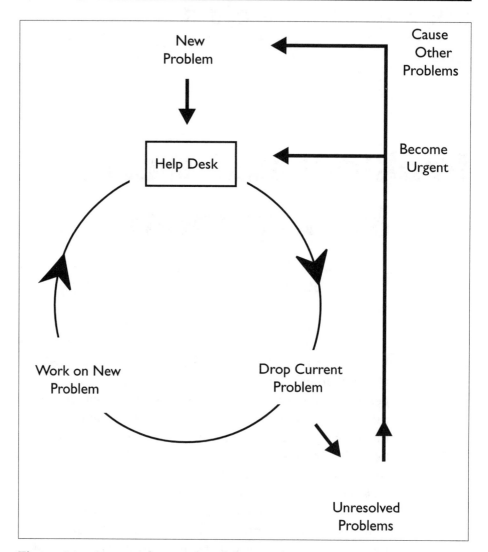

Figure 4.1   An out-of-control problem cycle.

and start on another one—a cycle that's difficult to get out of. The number of calls will keep increasing because you won't be able to finish everything properly, and you aren't doing anything to make things better. The calls that you have put aside onto the Help Desk pile of unresolved problems start taking on a life of their own. Some become urgent and come back into the Help Desk. Others cause more problems that come back into the Help Desk as new problems. You aren't logging many calls so you don't have statistics that can help you get a handle on what you're dealing with. How do you get out of this vicious cycle? By putting a program of problem and work management in place.

There are several things you need to do to prevent problems from taking over:

Get focused on the business (see Chapter 1).

Structure your levels of support to minimize resolution times. One of the best ways to do this is to have a Resolve front line, resolving as many problems as possible (80 percent and up) at point of call (see Chapter 2).

Get the Help Desk tools you need and make effective use of them (see Chapter 6).

Know what is most important to the business and work on those things first.

Set up and follow procedures to ensure correct and consistent service.

Constantly evaluate Help Desk function to make sure everything is working.

Eliminate the need for as many of the calls as possible.

These seven points describe the most important components of effective Help Desk problem and work management: *focus, structure, tools, priorities, procedures, evaluation,* and *improvement.*

If you aren't focused on the business, you might be spreading yourself too thinly, doing many things poorly, and maybe even doing things that aren't important to the business.

If your Help Desk is structured poorly you may be handling each call too many times or you may be passing the calls around for too long before actually trying to resolve them, increasing resolution time.

If you don't have the tools you need, you don't know what your call profile looks like and you won't know where to start to improve things—which types of calls to address first. You are probably also spending too much time on mundane repetitive tasks, time you could be spending getting yourself back in control.

If your priorities aren't well defined, Help Desk staff will work on the things they think are important, which may bear no resemblance to what's in your plan, what you have committed to, or what is important to the business.

If your procedures aren't well defined, your customers will get different service depending on who answers the phone. A customer trying to type a letter might call up extremely upset and frustrated, complaining that the word processing software is not working properly. The Help Desk operator, intimidated by the upset customer, promises, "We'll get to it right away." Meanwhile, a customer who needs to do some price updates is waiting to get a problem with the pricing software configuration fixed. The first problem gets priority over the second, even though the second is much more serious, and each of the customers gets a very different level of service.

Constantly evaluating how your Help Desk is working will ensure that any unbalanced priorities are quickly corrected and will address any issues involving procedures that are incorrect or improperly followed. Evaluation also involves monitoring the progress of planned work and making sure it gets done.

Planning improvements should be an ongoing function of your Help Desk. You have to be constantly looking for ways to reduce the number of calls and improve service to the customers. You want to be able to keep the number of calls under strict control. If the numbers start creeping up, you need to address the situation immediately and not wait until it is out of control.

In This Chapter

The first three components of effective Help Desk problem and work management are covered to some degree in other chapters (Chapters 1, 2, and 6). This chapter discusses the remaining four components, specifically:

- Priorities
- Procedures

- Evaluation
- Improvement

Priorities

Somehow you need to ensure that your Help Desk resolves the problems that are most critical to the business before all others. At the same time, you want to make sure that the work you have planned to improve service to your customers gets done. Setting priorities will help you address both of these requirements. Priorities will prevent the scenarios in which every call becomes an emergency based on how upset the caller is and work is started and then dropped midstream when something perceived as more important comes along. How angry a customer is should not play a part in the priority a problem is assigned, and there should be no "perceived" priorities—only clearly defined, well-understood ones.

What Needs Priorities?

Calls that are resolved by the Help Desk at point of call are commonly called *incidents*. They are resolved in the order in which they are received. Calls that need to be passed on, or are not resolved right away for whatever reason, need to have a priority assigned. These calls can typically be broken down into the following categories:

Problems

Problems are interruptions in service to customers. Something is wrong with hardware, software, or procedures, and as a result the technology is not working as it should. Customers are prevented from achieving optimal productivity at their jobs.

Requests

Customers making requests are asking for services that are part of the Help Desk's advertised list of services. These might include training, ordering PCs, and so on.

Questions

Questions are queries about how to perform specific tasks using technology. Application questions are of the type, "How do I pull my spreadsheet into my word processing package?" Procedural questions are of the type, "How do I download a file from the mainframe?" or "How can I send this document to someone who is not on the LAN?" Consulting questions might include "What software should I use to create a newsletter?" or "Is there anything that can help me do this on a PC?"

Calls coming into the Help Desk are not the only thing you need to set priorities for. You need to make sure that work that you have planned, and perhaps some that you have not planned but has become necessary, gets done. You have to be able to prioritize work, planned and unplanned, against everything else going on in your Help Desk.

Planned Work

Planned work is work that the Help Desk has committed to in its objectives. This might include upgrades to software or hardware and work to eliminate problems or automate solutions.

Unplanned Work

Unplanned work is work that has not been planned for but that has been made necessary by unforeseen circumstances. Often, unplanned work is necessary to prevent future problems. For example, an unexpected and significant increase in the number of users storing information in the public files on the LAN server means that something needs to be done quickly to prevent a service interruption caused by lack of storage. Adding to or reorganizing storage may not have been planned for, but in these circumstances it takes priority over planned work.

In order to ensure that all of your Help Desk resources are not pulled into resolving problems, leaving you with no resources to do anything else that needs to be done, you need to set your priority structure so that your work and services have a priority at least equal to nonemergency problems, and you need to stick to it. This won't work, however, if you simply have too few staff. The problems, requests, questions, and planned work will pile up, unfinished, while Help Desk staff struggle to get out from under it all.

Your priorities also need to be in line with your mission and objectives. They need to be working for you, not against you, in support of your efforts to carry out your mission and reach your objectives. For example, if your mission is to make customers self-sufficient, then you might want to place a lower priority on questions or problems of a learning type and a higher priority on requests for training or coaching. If one of your objectives is to implement integrated voice response (IVR), then that needs to have a priority at least as high as that of training and coaching requests. Figure 4.2 illustrates how a Help Desk might assign priorities.

Determining Impact on the Business

Priorities ultimately need to measure impact on the business. Impact on the business involves potential income lost. If a newspaper can't take

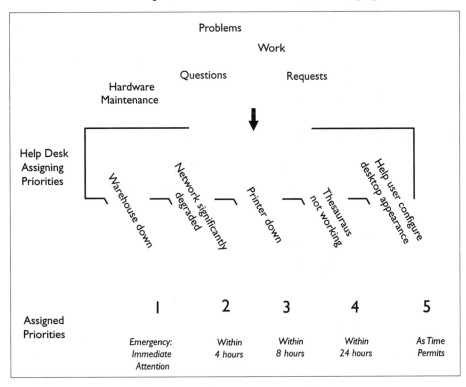

Figure 4.2   How a Help Desk might assign priorities.

Figure 4.3   Determining impact on the business.

ads or a stockbroker can't buy or sell stock, severe financial repercussions are involved. If a cash register can't function, sales can't be entered and customers who are waiting impatiently might be lost forever. If, however, the result of a problem is that performance reports will be a day late, the financial impact on the business will be negligible. Having an impact on the business is defined as having a negative financial effect on the business—whether it be directly and immediately, or further into the future, such as by losing customers now. Operational systems such as order taking tend to have the biggest impact on the business, while administrative systems such as accounts receivable, although important, have less.

   Impact on the business, as shown in Figure 4.3, can be determined by looking at two entities: the importance of the component involved and the severity of the event.

Important Components

When a call comes into the Help Desk, the first indication of how critical it is is the importance of the component involved. Important components can be the following:

- Technology (hardware and software systems)
- Projects
- People

Technology

Technology that is critical to an organization, specifically, computer hardware and software, is the technology it needs to run its daily business. For example, shipping and receiving systems are critical for warehouses, point-of-sale systems are critical for stores, and airline reservation systems are critical for airlines. Mainframes are critical. When any of these systems fail, there is no easy bypass. Large stores cannot function without their cash register systems—pulling out a calculator and tallying customer purchases by hand just wouldn't be practical, not to mention the fact that inventory and sales activity information would be lost. Similarly, warehouses cannot ship anything when the systems that put their loads together and pull stock are down, and airlines have no way of tracking reservations without their reservation systems. Each minute that these systems are nonfunctional means significant losses in revenue to the businesses involved. Problems must be fixed quickly.

Critical technology will vary from one organization to the next. A good place to find this kind of information is in a company's disaster recovery plan. All of the most critical systems and hardware will be listed there.

Projects

When organizations are in a highly competitive mode, as most are today, projects that have the potential to put them ahead of the competition become critical. Anything stopping these projects, such as technology problems, is really stopping the organization from getting ahead of the competition.

People

Organizations may have people critical to the business: people who need high-priority problem resolution wherever they are, whatever computer they happen to be using. An example of such a person might be the hands-on president of a small company, someone constantly making critical business decisions and making deals for new business.

Severity of Event

The severity of an event, such as a problem, can be measured by how much function the component in question has lost. Is the component completely shut down, unable to function at all, or is it still functioning but at a degraded rate? How widespread are the effects of the event? Is the impact localized, with only one person impacted, or is it widespread, with whole departments impacted?

A newspaper that sells ads considers its ad sales systems, which include workstations, network, and ad sales software, as critical to the business. If the network goes down and no one can sell ads, that newspaper all of a sudden is not making money. It's losing significant revenue with every minute the network is down. That problem gets the highest priority. If only one of the PCs on the network is down, or if network response is degraded, the newspaper is still getting some revenue but not as much as it should be getting. The paper is still losing money. The business is impacted, so the problem must get a high priority. If, however, one of the people on the ad sales network wants a custom screen saver installed, that person may just have to wait. Although ad sales is a critical system, the severity of the event—the custom screen saver not being installed—is nil. Our priorities should be helping us ensure that we never spend time on the latter type of problem or request while severe problems such as the ones described earlier are outstanding.

Priority Scales

You will need some kind of scale to measure priority. A commonly used scale is one with values ranging from 1 to 5, where 1 denotes the highest priority and 5 the lowest. Sometimes priorities are built from a combination of scales and based on values such as impact and impairment, where impact indicates the impact of the problem on the business and impairment describes the usability of the problem component (system, application, hardware). Regardless of the values used, what is most important in a scale is the clarity of the definition. The definition should make it clear to the person assigning priorities what the priority should be. Often, the priority will be obvious. "The warehouse is down," "no one can take any ads," or "the mainframe is down" are pretty good indications that you have a serious, top-priority problem on your hands. On the other hand, "The colors on my screen look kind of washed out" probably won't have you pushing the panic button. Other times, the priority will not be as easy to determine, and this is when a clear definition will help. If the definition refers to critical or noncritical components, then a list of critical components should accompany it. Response times are often tied into priority definitions to further clarify what each priority means. Service-level agreements use this kind of priority-response relationship to define and measure service levels.

Scales for Problems

Priority scales for problems are structured on business impact. Priority assignments try to measure the impact on the business using the formula described previously, specifically, importance of component plus severity of problem. This section contains four examples of priority scales for problems, each measuring business value in slightly different ways.

The first example, shown in Table 4.1, is a priority definition for all problems coming into the Help Desk. In reality, this definition would be accompanied by a list of critical components and users.

Table 4.1 Priority Scale for Problems, Example 1

Priority	Definition	Example
1	Critical component(s) down. Business is impacted.	Warehouse systems have crashed. No merchandise is going into or coming out of the warehouse. As a result, business is severely affected.
2	Critical component(s) degraded. Business is impacted.	Response time on the LAN supporting staff responsible for taking ads has doubled for some reason. Number of ads that can be taken has decreased. Revenue lost.
3	Multiple, noncritical components down or degraded; business not impacted.	One ring on the LAN has lost access to the company's E-mail system.
4	Single noncritical component down or degraded; business not impacted.	A programmer is unable to print consistently.
5	Little or no impact. Problem could be cosmetic.	A customer is missing some of the standard Windows background patterns ("wallpaper").

**Table 4.2   Priority Scale for Problems, Example 2:
A Narrow Application, Well Defined**

Priority	Definition
1 System Failure	Cannot use the registers to process customer transactions.
2 Off-line Registers	Registers are working but are off line to the controller. Price lookup is not available.
3 Controller Functions	Certain controller functions such as cash balancing are not working—can continue with other daily functions; or Credit authorization is not available; or Sales cannot be transmitted to the store back-end computer (if this lasts for more than two days it becomes a priority 1; or Controller printer is not working; or Backup did not end successfully.
4 Register Hardware	Register hardware such as the printer, cash drawer, or keyboard is not working.
5 General Questions	Have a question about system operations or require general information.

The second priority definition, shown in Table 4.2, is one with a much narrower application: a single system (a cash register system). The definition for each priority is much more specific than in the previous example.

The third example, shown in Table 4.3, is designed for wide use and deals with a different kind of scale, which is based on impact and impairment. Impact is a measure of the business impact of the problem, while impairment describes how serious the problem is in terms of the remaining functionality of the problem component. A list of components classified as "critical" and "very critical" would have to accompany the definitions of impact. Help Desk action and final problem priority would depend on the combination of impact and impairment. For ex-

Table 4.3   Priority Scale for Problems, Example 3:
Using Two Measures, Impact and Impairment

Impact	Definition
1 Severe	Component is very critical to the business and multiple users are negatively affected.
2 Major	Component is critical to the business and multiple users are negatively affected.
3 Limited	Component not critical to business; few users negatively affected.

Impairment	Definition
1	Component is shut down; no bypass or alternative available.
2	Component severely degraded. Limited function.
3	Component degraded but usable, or bypass or alternative available.

ample, an impact 1, impairment 3, would get a lower priority than either an impact 1, impairment 1, or an impact 2, impairment 1.

In the fourth example, all problems are given a severity code based on criteria as specified in Table 4.4, and are assigned an initial priority of 7. The Help Desk manager will change the priority (which can range from 7 to 1) within the severity category to bring calls to the top as re-

Table 4.4   Priority Scale for Problems, Example 4:
Priorities Are Assigned within Each Severity Category

Severity	Definitions
1	Major service interruption to majority of customers.
2	Significant. Affects fifty or more customers or a critical unit/process.
3	Important. Affects three or more customers but does not cripple a unit/process.
4	Affects fewer than three customers.
5	Moves/Installs.
6	Questions/Other.

quired. In this way, analysts taking problems/requests off of the queue know exactly which problems/requests are of most importance.

Scales for Questions

Questions are a bit of a dilemma for the Help Desk. You want to help your customers with their questions, but you want them to be as self-sufficient as possible, both for their own good and for the good of the Help Desk. The better they understand the tools they are using, the better use they can make of them. For example, customers using word processing software will not be getting the most out of the software or making the best use of their time if all they know how to do is to enter and spell-check text. They won't know about time-saving features such as linking and embedding data from other software packages and creating templates for entering data. Customers who do understand their tools will make fewer calls to the Help Desk, lessening the Help Desk call load and leaving resources free for more serious issues.

As a Help Desk, what you want to discourage is having customers try to learn how to use a tool through calls to the Help Desk. This is a waste of time for the Help Desk, which should be spending its time on more serious problems, and a waste of time for the customer, who is spending a lot of time trying to figure the tool out. What would make much more sense, from a cost and effectiveness point of view, is for the customer to take the appropriate training. Setting priorities should discourage these kinds of calls.

There are exceptions, however. If you are dealing with a critical user who needs a question answered in order to perform a business function, then that question needs a higher priority, regardless of whether it is the result of a lack of proper training. In this case, the question of training can be addressed later, using information gathered from call tracking. (This is one example of why it is important to log everything).

Using the same scale of priority definitions for problems as in Table 4.1, a sample priority definition for questions is shown in Table 4.5.

Scales for Requests

Your Help Desk should only be responding to requests that are included in your list of services. If you receive requests for services not on your

Table 4.5 Priority Scale for Questions

Priority	Definition	Example
2	Critical user, can't get business done.	User needs to know how to download critical financial data from the mainframe so that it can be transmitted via PC and modem.
5	Everything else.	"How do I put a border around my document?"

list, then you need to refuse them by suggesting where customers might go to get the service required. Tracking such requests will indicate whether you should think about changing or adding to your services. Requests that are on your list of services will require a priority, but they may be channeled off to specific areas—such as PC ordering—that will be setting the priority, possibly with the customer's input.

Regardless of who is assigning them, priorities for requests must be flexible enough to handle any exceptions and emergencies that come up. For example, someone might ask, "Please change my profile to allow me to access the figures I need to prepare a special performance report for the president. It's needed ASAP." A critical business decision might be waiting on that report.

You need to be flexible, but you also need some method for controlling "emergency" requests. If all the requests coming in are emergencies, then 99.9 percent of them probably aren't. You can try explaining to your customers that their emergency means that someone else loses priority— some other part of the business might have to wait for something. If this isn't enough to get them to downgrade the importance of their (non-emergency) requests, you will have to go to some other kind of control, such as management sign-offs or having the customers speak to the groups that will be affected by their "emergency" priorities. For example, if department A calls and asks for ten PCs "in a hurry; this is an emergency," you might tell them that you will service their request if they get approval from department B, who has also ordered some PCs but is ahead of them in the priority queue. Letting the customers sort out the priorities in this way usually means that the real priority emerges. (Telling a Help Desk that this is an emergency is one thing, but having to explain it to the manager of a department who will have to wait for PCs is quite a different thing.) It also means that the Help Desk is not trying to prioritize for the business. The business is performing this function itself.

If customers are having a hard time accepting priorities, you might want to take the issues off line and visit the specific customers or groups individually. You can take the time to explain how much lead time is needed for the Help Desk to service their requests. You can also show them how their "emergencies" affect the business and how additional or improved planning on their part would ensure that their requests get serviced without a negative impact on other parts of the business that might have problems or requests of higher priority.

A sample priority definition for requests is shown in Table 4.6.

Scales for Work

Planned work needs to get a high enough priority to ensure that it gets done, especially if the resources doing the work are the same as those taking care of the problems, questions, and requests. You have objectives and service-level agreements to meet and improvements to make, none of which will get done if you give work too low a priority. Problems, questions, and requests will drain away your resources. If the staff members you allocate for planned work are different from those handling the day-to-day calls, you most likely won't have the problem of staff being pulled away to work on calls. What you might have to face, however, is resource drain from unplanned work, work that the Help Desk has not

Table 4.6 Priority Scale for Requests

Priority	Definition	Example
2	Emergency requirement.	Install special software ASAP to allow the business to put on a special promotion to respond to the competition.
3	All other requests for services supported by the Help Desk.	Order a PC.

planned for in this time period (usually a quarter). Some unplanned work is inevitable. A technological environment rarely stands still, and things change at a pace that cannot always be planned. You may need to do some work to stop a recurring problem that is causing a lot of calls, or you may need to do some maintenance to prevent problems in the near future. Other unplanned work does not have as much business value— for example, Help Desk staff spending time investigating interesting software or upgrading Help Desk software to get the new features, regardless of the fact the work was not scheduled until next quarter. You may find that staff don't even tell you about unplanned work, preferring to do it on the side and not considering that it is ultimately interfering with the business. Unplanned work should take precedence over planned work only if it is in the interests of the business for it to do so.

Planned work and unplanned work that must be done in the interests of the business should get the same priority as problems that don't affect the business (a 3 in our previous examples). Other unplanned work should be put off until it can be included in a plan.

A sample priority definition for work is shown in Table 4.7.

Putting It All Together

If the same staff are handling problems, work, questions, and requests (or some combination of these), you'll need to ensure that the priorities make sense in relation to each other. Your resulting priority structure might look something like Table 4.8.

Getting Support for Priorities

In order to honor priorities, you will need the cooperation of your customers, the rest of IT—specifically, those areas within IT that work on resolving some of your calls—and your vendors. Customers must accept the fact that if an application more critical to the business than the one they are using goes down, it will get priority over any problem they might have. They must accept that they cannot call the Help Desk up and whine or shout their way to a higher priority. The needs of the business must come first. IT areas that support the Help Desk—for example, application support areas—must be willing to abide by established priorities and allocate the necessary time and resources to fixing high-

Table 4.7   **Priority Scale for Work**

Priority	Definition	Example
3	Planned work.	Upgrade the LAN operating system.
	Unplanned work that is necessary to prevent serious problems.	There has been an unexpected increase in the number of users putting data on a shared server, which has resulted in increased network traffic and a decrease in available space. In order to prevent potential problems that may bring individual users or the whole network down, a server upgrade is required. The server upgrade was not planned for in this quarter; it was put into a future quarter.
	Unplanned work that will resolve recurring problems that are putting a strain on Help Desk resources.	Customers using DOS applications often have problems printing. When this happens, Help Desk staff must reset the printer interface. In order to get rid of this problem, which is causing an increasing number of Help Desk calls, the upgrade of the DOS applications to the Windows versions has been moved forward and will replace some other planned work.

priority problems as quickly as possible. Vendors must understand your priorities when you call for help. They need to know how seriously you are affected by a problem and must be willing to respond to high priorities quickly to honor service agreements.

To get this kind of cooperation, you need to communicate priorities so that everyone understands what the priorities are, the reasoning behind them, and their importance to the business. In fact, in setting up a priority structure, you should be getting input from or working with your customers, the rest of IT, and your vendors.

Part of the communication about priorities to customers, the rest of IT, and vendors should be information about who decides what priority a problem should have. Choices include the Help Desk, the customer, or the Help Desk and customer together. One Help Desk that supports a live retail environment gives the responsibility for setting priorities completely to the customers. When customers call in to report a problem to

Table 4.8   A Priority Scale for All Events

Priority	Problems	Work	Questions	Requests
1	Critical component(s) down. Business is impacted.	N/A	N/A	N/A
2	Critical component(s) degraded. Business is impacted	N/A	Critical user, can't get business done. Business is impacted.	Emergency Requirement. Business is impacted.
3	Multiple, noncritical components down or degraded. Busniess not impacted.	Planned work or unplanned work is necessary to prevent serious problems or unplanned work that will resolve recurring problems that are putting a strain on Help Desk resources.	N/A	All other request for services supported by the Help Desk.
4	Single, noncritical component down or degraded. Business not impacted.	N/A	N/A	N/A
5	Little or no impact. Problem could be cosmetic.	N/A	Everything else.	N/A

the IVR system that front ends the Help Desk, they are asked to enter a priority from 1 (highest) to 5 (lowest). Priorities are clearly defined, well communicated, and understood by all customers. Another Help Desk within the same company has a clear understanding of the most important systems, applications, and users and has chosen to set priorities itself. This seems to be the most common choice for assigning priorities among Help Desks. According to the Help Desk Institute's 1997 *Help Desk and Customer Support Practices Report*, in approximately 40 percent of Help Desks, priorities are assigned by Help Desk staff or by persons that the call is passed on to. Another 33 percent of Help Desks assign priorities jointly with customers, and only 7 percent of Help Desks rely on customers to set priorities. The remaining Help Desks either do not prioritize calls or handle calls in the order in which they are received.

Changing Priorities Once They Are Set

Occasionally, you may want to change the priorities of problems, requests, or work. Priorities may have been entered in error, or they may be upgraded to a more severe level as time goes on. For example, something that is down for an hour may not affect the business, but if that same thing is down for half a day, it may. (An example of this is a function that has to be performed in the morning, but when in the morning does not matter.) You might want to change priorities when you put in a temporary fix that lessens the problem's severity but leaves the problem still outstanding. For example, if a critical printer is down you may borrow one from another department.

How long something has been in a queue is often used as a factor in deciding when to change priorities, but you want to be very careful about this. If something has been in a queue for too long, that might be an indication that it is of such a low priority that you shouldn't be doing it, that you don't have enough staff to handle your workload, or that your priorities are unbalanced for your environment. Rather than unthinkingly upgrading the priorities of older problems and requests, you should address the reason why they've been in the queue for so long.

Changes in priorities need to be controlled carefully to make sure they do not interfere with your priority structure and the distribution of work. If you are constantly changing priorities, then your priority structure is not working and should be revised. Changing priorities should be an exception, not a regular occurrence.

Flexibility is key to making your priorities work. You don't want your priority definition to add needless red tape or to become a bottleneck, but you do want to make sure that the important things get handled before all others. Be sensitive to the needs of your customers and the business you support.

Procedures

Procedures are necessary to ensure Help Desk success, especially in the following areas:

1. Consistency and correctness of service. Help Desk staff aren't making up the rules as they go along. If customers know that they're going to get the results they need when they call the Help Desk, they're going to keep calling the Help Desk. They won't be tempted to go elsewhere to get help.

2. Procedures also help customers make better use of the Help Desk. If the Help Desk asks for specific information each time a customer calls, customers will start having that information ready when they call. This will save the Help Desk time and get the customer's call processed faster.

3. Having documented procedures in place also makes automation easier and use of Help Desk tools more effective. A process that is documented is much easier to automate than one that exists only as hearsay or in several versions. A Help Desk tool that routes logged Help Desk calls into various queues depending on who will be resolving the calls is useful only if procedures are in place to ensure that the calls are picked off of the queue and resolved.

Someone once said to me "I don't want to have to define rigorous procedures. I want things to flow naturally." Rivers flow naturally. But they only flow naturally because the riverbed is solid, immovable, often cast in stone.

Figure 4.4 shows how quality and accuracy improve as the definition of procedures increases. Automation is considered the highest level of procedure definition.

Procedures are most effective when developed and documented by the people who currently perform them or who will be performing

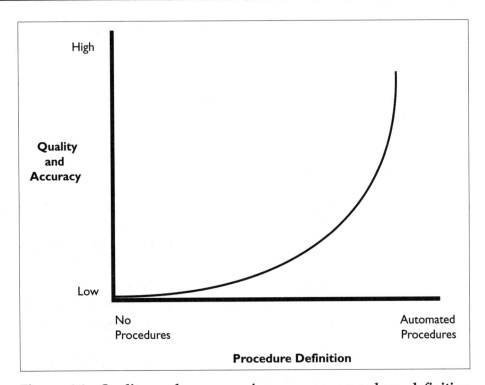

Figure 4.4   Quality and accuracy improve as procedure definition increases.

them. Internal procedures for tasks such as taking calls, resolving problems, and handling requests should be set up by the Help Desk staff who do these tasks on a day-to-day basis. Any procedures that involve other departments should be set up jointly with people from those departments. People who will be using procedures have a vested interest in making sure that they make sense, are easy to follow, and can be updated easily. Documenting procedures gives the people doing the documenting a greater understanding of the procedures and can lead to the identification of possible improvements, inconsistencies, and errors.

Customers need to be informed of any procedures that they need to follow when calling the Help Desk—for example, any sign-offs they need when purchasing a PC. You may want or need to involve them in developing these procedures as well.

Documenting procedures in a way that ensures they will be used and can be easily updated is often difficult. Creating them is the easy part. Getting people to use them is the challenge. The only way to guarantee that a procedure is followed consistently is to automate it. Assuming that you have not automated all of your procedures, there are some things you can do to help ensure that your procedures are referred to and used:

Keep procedures as short and simple as possible.

Keep procedures in a central location, such as an intranet site, accessible to all Help Desk staff. In the same place, keep information that your procedures might refer to, such as priority definitions and routing information.

Have regular reviews and revisions of your procedures—keep them current and alive. Assign someone responsibility for both reviewing and revising procedures. You can rotate this task.

Integrate your procedures into any Help Desk tools you use, wherever possible. Let the tool prompt staff through the procedure, or use the tool to automate the procedure.

Have Help Desk staff create procedures. Give them ownership.

Make sure Help Desk staff understand what role they play in each procedure.

There are also some things you should avoid doing when setting procedures:

Do not duplicate information that is stored and maintained elsewhere. Cross-reference it instead. The duplication of what already exists will create a maintenance nightmare. This means that a set of notes on how to use software, or any form of software documentation, has no place in procedures. It makes more sense to go to the original documentation for that information.

Don't attempt to train people in using tools in your procedures. This is ineffective as a training method and leads to ungainly procedures that are hard to maintain. The same applies to skills such as communication, dealing with customers, and so on. People should not be learning skills from procedures—they should be getting those skills from training programs. Training programs will teach people what tools are capable of, not just how tools are used in a specific procedure. Training in skills such as communication and dealing with customers will involve practice and feedback—a much more effective way of learning a skill than reading about it.

You need to have procedures in place to describe how to deliver each of the services you offer. These will vary from Help Desk to Help Desk, depending on the services offered, but some common ones may include the following:

Handling a call

Resolving a problem

Answering a question

Servicing a request

Handling an emergency

Informing customers of system problems

Reporting

Disaster recovery

Communicating with other Help Desks

Specific processes internal to your Help Desk

If your Help Desk makes use of some kind of Help Desk software, then you may not need procedures for many of these. They can be programmed to happen automatically.

You also need procedures for those internal processes specific to your Help Desk. These might include any activities that need to be performed at the beginning and ending of Help Desk shifts, work status reporting, getting fill-in help for staff that call in sick, and so on.

Handling a Call

Information necessary to describe call-handling procedures includes the following:

- Greeting to be used
- Call logging

    What to log (everything!)

    How to log

- Assigning a priority
- Routing a call

    When to route a call

    How to route a call

    Where to route the call

Your Help Desk software can probably be set up to prompt you through logging and routing a call so you won't need to document any details on these tasks. Information on whom to route calls to can exist in a central procedures library. Depending on the Help Desk system you have, you might be able to store and update this information in the system itself.

Resolving a Problem

Procedures for problem resolution include details on the following:

Picking up a problem

How to take ownership of a problem

Checking for trends

Getting help

Closing a problem

Picking up a problem could suggest how to take ownership of a problem. Checking for trends could be accomplished by your Help Desk system, depending on its sophistication. Getting help could suggest whom to go to or what systems or documents to reference to get further help in specific areas. Closing a problem could include any required interactions with the customer.

Answering a Question

Procedures for questions might include the following:

- **Checking for trends.** See whether this customer had called previously with questions and perhaps required some training.

- **Making recommendations.** Recommend training to customers. This includes referencing courses available and giving (or sending) the customer all of the required information. If your Help Desk is really cracking down on training questions, this procedure might involve something a little more formal, such as sending a memo off to the customer's manager.

- **Getting help.** Describe where to get further information on specific subjects.

- **Closing a question.** Determine whether a question should be added to an existing frequently asked questions (FAQ) list.

Servicing a Request

Procedures for servicing requests (that are on the Help Desk list of services) include information on what the Help Desk must do and provide and what is required from the customer. For example, in the case of PC purchases, the customer might be required to get senior management sign-off on a purchase requisition before submitting a request for a PC purchase to the Help Desk. In turn, the Help Desk would place the order and give the customer an estimated installation date.

Handling an Emergency

Emergencies are a priority of 1 or better. Procedures for handling emergencies need to include information on how to set escalation procedures into motion and on whom to keep informed at what stages of the emergency.

Informing Customers of System Problems

Procedures to inform customers of system problems typically include information on whose responsibility this communication is, what media to use to broadcast information, and to whom to broadcast it.

Reporting

Reporting procedures contain information on what to report on, how frequently, and to whom. Depending on the sophistication of your Help Desk software, you may be able to set your system up so that reports are generated at preset intervals and even sent to the appropriate people automatically and electronically.

Disaster Recovery

Disaster recovery procedures are usually part of larger, companywide procedures (and documents) and are best set up in conjunction with any dedicated disaster recovery groups.

Communicating with Other Help Desks

Communicating with the other Help Desks (if any) within your organization is necessary to ensure that all Help Desks are kept informed of what is going on in the technological environment so they can resolve customer problems more effectively. They can maximize the problem-solving information at their disposal and minimize the duplication of effort. Things that your Help Desk may want to communicate to other Help Desks include the following:

Major problems in your area of responsibility

Major problems in their areas that have come to your attention

Problems that were reported to you but that need to be resolved by other Help Desks

Changes in your Help Desk environment, including new or upgraded technology and services

Other Help Desks will have corresponding procedures to make sure they communicated the same information to you. Wherever possible you should make use of automation such as your Help Desk management software to program procedures to happen automatically.

Internal Processes

You also need procedures for those internal processes specific to your Help Desk. These might include any activities that need to be performed at the beginning and ending of Help Desk shifts, work status reporting, getting fill-in help for staff that call in sick, and so on.

Evaluation

Evaluating the activities of your Help Desk on an ongoing basis is necessary to ensure that your Help Desk is functioning effectively. As shown in Figure 4.5, evaluation checks that

Procedures are correct, understood, and being followed.

Priorities are balanced and are being followed.

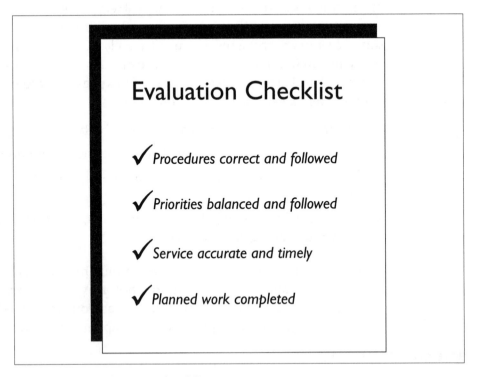

Figure 4.5   Evaluation checklist.

Service delivered is accurate and is accomplished within an acceptable time frame.

Planned work is completed.

Procedures

Written procedures are in constant danger of being ignored and forgotten. You have to make sure that your procedures are alive, that they are updated constantly, and that they change as your environment changes. You can assign someone the task of reviewing procedures with the Help Desk team every month or so at one of your team meetings. If you have procedures with other departments—they may be providing second-level support—you need to review those with the people in those departments to make sure that the procedures still make sense. You also have to make sure that procedures are being followed, both within your team and in other departments. There will be a better chance that this is happening if your procedures make sense, are understood, and change with the environment. Your Help Desk system will give you an indication of whether people are following procedures. It will report on logs not closed properly, problems not fixed properly, information missing, and so on. A daily or weekly review of the status of the Help Desk logs should bring these situations to light.

Priorities

When priorities are unbalanced, or are not being followed properly, you could find yourself with too many high-priority calls or calls that are waiting too long for service. Help Desk staff might be assigning too high a priority to calls that do not merit it. This could be the result of anxious users convincing the Help Desk staff that the problem is really severe or just a lack of understanding by Help Desk staff of what constitutes a high priority. You might also have a situation where the priorities assigned are too low. The logged call might sit in a queue forever, waiting to be serviced. You need to use your Help Desk system statistics to keep an eye out for these situations so that your customers get service based on what is most important for the business. If your priorities aren't working, change them—as your environment changes, they may need to be updated. Make sure that Help Desk staff, other support staff, vendors, and customers understand the priorities.

Service

When a problem is resolved and a log closed, you need to make sure that the customer was satisfied with the resolution—that it was performed correctly and within an acceptable amount of time. One way to do this is to send your customers notices when logs are closed, informing them that the problem was resolved and telling them to call the Help Desk if they were not satisfied. Your Help Desk system may be able to do this automatically. You want to take all customer complaints seriously and look for trends. There could be a problem with a particular staff member not understanding or following procedures, or you could have problems with a specific customer who feels that his or her priority should be higher than anyone else's. Either way, the Help Desk manager needs to get involved to rectify the situation. A customer might need an explanation of the priorities, or a staff member might need an update on procedures or some training.

Planned Work

One of the first symptoms of an impending out-of-control problem cycle is unfulfilled objectives. When problems start to get out of control, planned improvements are often the first thing to be dropped, an action that pushes the Help Desk into an out-of-control cycle even faster. Amid all that is going on in the busy Help Desk environment, you need to make sure that your planned work is not buried under a pile of problems. Have weekly updates with the people doing the work so you are kept abreast of any roadblocks. Adjust your other Help Desk activities as necessary to make sure that your work gets done. This might involve some negotiations with management for more staff (this is a good place to make use of outsourcing extra help) or tools. If you have been logging all calls, you will have the statistics to back you up.

Improvement

In addition to making sure that your Help Desk is working as it should, you need to look constantly to improvements—to the future. Wherever possible, you need to stop problems before they happen:

Be part of the implementation and change management process. Know when new systems are being implemented and when existing systems are being changed.

Get involved in setting standards. Be on any standards committees that exist.

Be part of disaster recovery planning. Make sure that procedures are in place for short-term disasters, such as failure of major hardware or software.

Keep the Help Desk up to date on new tools, customer applications, and so on. Make sure that staff know what's happening in the Help Desk and the customer environments.

Keep the Help Desk staff trained.

Set up relationships with your vendors.

Keep an eye on trends, good and bad.

Listen to your customers and know what they need.

Change Management

Knowing when new systems are being implemented can prepare you for any initial problems. Better yet, you can be involved in the quality control of the new system. Get involved in any implementation meetings and make sure that the concerns of the Help Desk are heard. Also make sure that staff are available to support the application being put into place and that they understand and will follow Help Desk procedures. Once the new system goes in, monitor calls and give the application people feedback about how clean the system was. This will help them improve for next time and will give you ideas about what to bring up at the next implementation meetings that you will attend. The same goes for changes to existing systems. If you are part of the change management process, you will know when systems are being changed and can prepare accordingly and be part of quality control. Involve yourself and the Help Desk wherever possible—in acceptance testing if this makes sense and in any promotion meetings. Send call statistics back to the maintenance group for change so they can see what the quality was.

Standards

Standards generally make life on a Help Desk easier. They specify a finite number of products to support. Getting involved in setting and maintaining standards makes sense from a Help Desk point of view. You are close to the customers. You know the products they use and the problems they have with them, and you know what they want and need to do their jobs. You also know the problems that you are having with the performance of the hardware and software that you support. All of this information is extremely valuable for setting standards. You know what your customers need, what they do and don't like, and you know what technology is working and what is giving you problems. You will be able to help set standards that meet the needs of the customers, help ensure a stable technological environment, and help reduce Help Desk calls.

Disaster Recovery

When disaster strikes and a critical hardware or software component goes down, you will be on the line to get the problem fixed as soon as possible. You need to have recovery procedures in place for every critical component, and you need to make sure that everyone involved understands these procedures—Help Desk staff, other IT support staff, vendors, and customers. If this is not a Help Desk responsibility, you should still be involved in making sure that it happens. Critical hardware should be covered by stringent service-level agreements with vendors, or a backup should be available on site. Critical software and data should have easily accessible backups should it get corrupted. You should also be involved in disaster recovery planning to help ensure that everything is covered. Your Help Desk experience will give you an understanding of the impacts of outages, who is affected, and how long recovery takes. This kind of information is vital to recovery planning.

Keeping Up to Date

The technology environment changes very quickly; new products and processes are constantly being introduced. Keeping abreast of these will help ensure that the Help Desk is aware of and can take advantage of products that will improve service, solve a particular problem that the Help Desk is having, or cut costs. The Internet has made it much easier for everyone on the Help Desk (not just those few who get to attend conferences) to keep up to date. Make sure everyone on the Help Desk has an Internet ID and understands how to get information from the Internet. If people attend conferences, have them share what they learned with the rest of the team. As well as keeping up to date on the Help Desk environment, Help Desk staff should know what is going on in their customer environment. They need to know what their customers do, what business initiatives are taking place, and what systems are in the works. This information will affect what needs to be supported and may affect the selection of Help Desk tools. It will also give staff a greater understanding of problems when customers call in. They will have an idea of what the customer does, what the system does, and what impact problems have. If it is not possible for staff to meet with customer areas regularly, make sure you get them this information. Share it in team meetings. Have customers come into team meetings and explain what their areas do and how the Help Desk affects them.

Training

Training is just about the easiest thing in the technology world to put off. Yet lack of training is a great productivity reducer. If you don't get trained on how to use a software package properly, chances are that you aren't using it properly. If you don't get trained on how to handle customer calls, then maybe you aren't handling them as well as you could be. Make sure you don't fall into this trap with your Help Desk. Don't accept from people that they don't have time for training. It is their job to provide the best service possible, and they can't do that if they haven't been trained properly. Set training plans and make sure that they are adhered to.

Relationships with Vendors

Vendors can be valuable allies and resources. If you foster good relationships with them, keep them up to date on what is happening inside your company, and take the time to set up service-level agreements whenever possible, you will have a better chance of getting a quick response when you have a problem. If you don't do any of these things, then there is no guarantee that you will get any kind of response when you have a problem and need their help.

Trends

Trends are a good barometer for helping determine Help Desk direction. Keep a close eye on all Help Desk call reporting and constantly look for trends. Be aware of why calls are increasing or decreasing so you can do something to stop the trend or encourage it. If the number of calls increased significantly because of a software upgrade, find out why. Was it lack of customer training? Were customers notified? Was the quality of the upgrade poor? Was it installed properly? When you have your answer, you can make sure that the same thing doesn't happen again during the next upgrade. If the number of calls decreases because of a training program you sponsored, then you may want to consider sponsoring other kinds of training programs as well, or offering this one again for people who didn't take it the first time.

Listening to Your Customers

Finally, listen to your customers. If you give them a chance, they will tell you, loudly and clearly, what they need, what they're satisfied with, and what they're not satisfied with. You can use this information to improve your Help Desk, to make it more valuable to the business. You can also take this information to other areas—areas that develop or maintain systems, areas that train customers. If a system does not do exactly what a customer needs, or is too slow or too cumbersome, the customer may, in frustration, let you know. You, in turn, can take this information to the IT area responsible for the system. They may not be aware of the problem; they may be able to solve it without much effort. Customers might also be asking for expanded Help Desk services. Perhaps they are working later hours and need the Help Desk to be there for them during those hours. You can use their input to help justify the cost of additional Help Desk hours. If you listen to your customers, they will tell you how to improve service.

Figure 4.6 summarizes the components of improvement. Looking ahead, continuously planning for the future and for improvements, will help ensure that your Help Desk will be able to continue handling the support requirements of your customers and the business as those re-

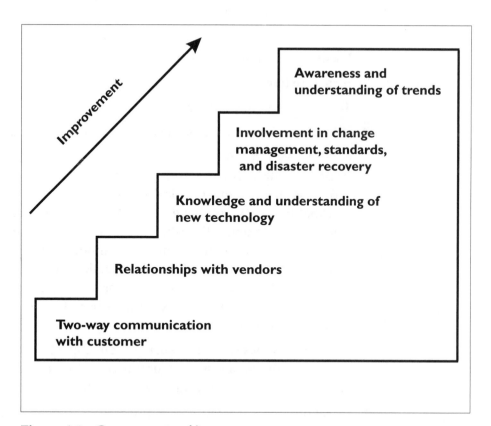

Figure 4.6   Components of improvement.

quirements grow and change. You will be improving the technological environment for your customers, making them more self-sufficient and more productive. The Help Desk will be recognized as an integral and essential part of the business.

Key Points Covered in This Chapter

You need effective problem- and work-management techniques on your Help Desk to ensure you are not being managed by your problems. The most important components of effective Help Desk problem and work management are as follows:

1. **Focus** (covered in Chapter 1).

2. **Structure** (covered in Chapter 2).

3. **Tools** (covered in Chapter 6).

4. **Priorities.** Know what is most important to the business and work on those things first.

    Priorities will help you ensure that your Help Desk resolves the problems that are most critical to the business before all others and that the work you have planned to improve service to your customers gets done. Priorities need to be established for problems, requests, and questions that cannot be immediately resolved by the front line of the Help Desk. They also need to be established for planned work and for work that has not been planned for but that has been made necessary by unforeseen growth or changes.

    Priorities are based on measuring their impact on the business. Impact on the business is determined by the importance of the component involved and the severity of the event.

5. **Procedures.** Set up and follow procedures to ensure correct and consistent service.

Establishing Help Desk procedures for each process involved in providing service to the customers will help ensure consistency of service and correctness of action. Procedures will also help customers make better use of the Help Desk, make automation easier, and make the use of Help Desk tools more effective. Procedures should be developed and documented by the people who currently perform them or who will be performing them. Documented procedures should be concise, reviewed regularly, integrated with Help Desk tools where possible, and created and understood by Help Desk staff. They should not duplicate information or attempt to train people in tool use.

6. **Evaluation.** Constantly evaluate the Help Desk's functioning to make sure that everything is working.

   Evaluating the activities of your Help Desk is an ongoing process that is necessary to ensure that your Help Desk is functioning effectively. It ensures that procedures are correct, understood, and being followed; priorities are balanced and are being followed; service delivered is accurate and accomplished within an acceptable time frame; and planned work is completed.

7. **Improvement.** Eliminate the need for as many of your calls as possible and stop problems before they happen.

   In addition to making sure that your Help Desk is working as it should, you need to look constantly to improvements and to the future to help ensure that your Help Desk will be able to continue handling the support requirements of your customers and the business as those requirements grow and change.

   Be part of the implementation and change management process. Know when new systems are being implemented and when existing systems are being changed.

   Get involved in setting standards. Be on any standards committees that exist.

   Be part of disaster recovery planning. Make sure that procedures are in place for short-term disasters such as the failure of major hardware or software.

Keep the Help Desk up to date on new tools, customer applications, and so on. Make sure they know what's happening in the Help Desk and the customer environments.

Keep the Help Desk staff trained.

Set up relationships with your vendors.

Keep an eye on trends, good and bad.

Listen to your customers and know what they need.

CHAPTER FIVE

Tracking

What is tracking? Call tracking means recording information about each Help Desk call and updating and monitoring its progress to closure. That's call tracking. But calls aren't the only thing you want to track on a Help Desk. You also want to track your hardware and software assets, your customer information, and your network performance. Tracking cannot be performed manually. The days of keeping lists on paper or in on-line files are gone—today's environments are just too large and too complex. You need tools to do the tracking for you. Tools range from standalone call-tracking components to completely integrated network management systems that take an ongoing automatic inventory of hardware and software assets, monitor all components of the network, notify Help Desk staff of any problems, and even recommend solutions.

Tracking information might seem time consuming at times, but the paybacks are tremendous. The information you can get from your Help Desk operation contains the blueprint you need to improve your level of service and to improve the technological environment of your customers. Tracked information can tell you everything from how many front line staff you need at any point during the day to how many and which PCs need to be upgraded to support a client/server system that is being planned for release on the network. If you want to operate a successful Help Desk in an environment of any appreciable size, you have no choice but to track. In a complex environment, you simply cannot know what is going on without tracking; tracking tools can see things that you need to know but that you cannot possibly see.

For example, a network management system can detect a faulty cable in a very complex network and tell you exactly where it is before anyone even notices a problem. If you were not tracking network performance, it might take significantly longer to find and resolve the cable problem. First, you would have to know that a cable was defective, and you could not know this until problems started occurring. You might not suspect that a cable was causing the problems—you might spend a significant amount of time checking other components. Once you realized that the cause was probably a cable, you would have to find out which cable was malfunctioning. You could be in the network for a long time, pulling cables, testing equipment, and wishing you had listened to your mother and become a doctor.

In This Chapter

Tracking brings benefits in (at least) four major areas. This chapter will look at each of these areas in detail. They are as follows:

- Asset control
- Problem control
- Help Desk control
- Customer effectiveness

The chapter will finish up with a discussion on integrating tracked data.

Asset Control

Asset control involves tracking hardware and software assets to facilitate their management and identification of trends in asset performance.

Manage Hardware and Software Assets

Organizations have a lot of money invested in their software and hardware assets. In order to safeguard this investment, they need to know what each asset looks like, where it is at any point in time, how much it is costing, and what value it is providing. They want to make sure that assets are maintained properly and upgraded when necessary so they are getting as much value as possible out of them. Asset management is not something that IT does for its own good—it is a business requirement.

Managing assets involves keeping track of hardware and software inventory. See Figure 5.1 for an example of the kinds of information asset management systems track. Since the advent of PCs and all the related hardware and software that came with them, managing assets has become a distinctly nontrivial task. PC equipment is small and light and can go wherever you go—which means that it can go out the door with a thief, who might even be an employee. If you aren't tracking it regularly, you won't know what you have, where it's supposed to be, and what might be missing. Stealing may go on for quite a while before you

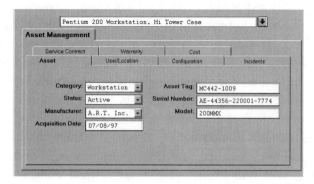

Figure 5.1   Asset management information.

notice it. Software is easy to install on PCs, and there is an abundance of it. It is also easy to copy. If you aren't tracking what is on your PCs, you could one day wake up to find your environment infested with viruses or your company charged with software piracy. The Internet has made this particular problem even larger. It is easier than ever to get software or documents. You can simply download or copy them from the Internet, if not at work then at home. Even simple documents can contain viruses, hidden in any macros that the documents might have associated with them.

Tracking hardware will provide you with information you need to plan for upgrades. You will be able to find all the PCs in need of memory, processor, or hard drive upgrades before a new system that needs these is installed. You can prevent people from running into problems that are caused by insufficient memory, disk space, or power. Tracking will help you manage the recycling of older PCs. You'll be able to see who is next on the PC replacement list, specifically, who has PCs in need of replacing, prioritized by factors such as install date and processor type.

Keeping track of the software in your systems will help you monitor and get rid of unauthorized software. You won't be in danger of having software in your organization that you are not authorized to use or perhaps have not even paid for. This has become a serious issue for software vendors, who are losing significant revenue through pirated copies of their software. They are serious about prosecuting offenders, and you want to make sure that your company won't be facing charges of software piracy—an expensive and embarrassing experience. Knowing your software and where it is will help you plan for upgrades and ensure that all occurrences of a version of software are upgraded. It will keep you aware of whether standards are being followed. It will also let you take advantage of volume to negotiate more advantageous licensing agreements. You can keep software costs at the absolute minimum for the number of users that you have.

Tracking assets will also help you with disaster recovery planning, purchasing and maintenance, and financial planning. For disaster recovery planning, you will know what your critical components are and where they are. Having a central database of hardware and software facilitates the centralization of purchasing and maintenance so that economies of scale can be realized. It also allows you to reconcile true inventory with cost and depreciation information from your company's finance area. This will give your company a more accurate picture of asset value and will make your budgeting easier.

Identify Trends in Hardware and Software Performance

If you are tracking hardware that is involved in problems, you will be able to identify the specific brands and models of the hardware that keep appearing as the causes of those problems. For example, if a specific type of monitor keeps appearing as a problem, you will be aware of it and will be able to do something about it. You can notify the vendor for some kind of resolution, and you can stop future purchases of this kind of equipment. Customers who have that specific brand of monitor but have not yet experienced a problem can be notified, and if necessary their equipment can be replaced. If you weren't tracking this information, each incidence of the problem hardware might be treated as a separate problem, and it might be a while before any trend was noticed. Purchases of the defective hardware would continue, and customers owning that hardware would not have any idea that it was defective until a problem happened. You couldn't take advantage of your statistics to negotiate a resolution with the vendor.

In the same way, software that is involved in problems needs to be tracked so that trends are identified. If a software release is installed with an undetected bug and several people start running into that bug, the Help Desk will know. The specific software will keep appearing in problem logs, and the trend will be noted in reports or queries. The vendor can be notified that the software needs fixing, and other customers can be notified that the problem exists and told what is being done about it. They can also be notified of any bypasses available. Customers won't have to call the Help Desk and won't be nearly as upset (if at all) about the problem because they were prepared for it. This would be true of software developed in house as well. The problem information could be fed back to the development group so they could make a fix and look at improving their testing and quality control. In fact, the number of calls logged against the software would be one measure of the quality of job that was done.

Trends can be positive also. If you're tracking hardware and software that are involved in problems, you will know, by default, which hardware and software were not involved in any problems. For software, this is positive feedback on the quality control of the implementation. For hardware, these are recommendations for components you might want to keep buying.

Problem Control

Tracking problems, problem resolutions, and system and network performance gives you valuable data to help keep problems under control. Tracking can help you manage network performance, build and maintain a problem/solution knowledge base, identify recurring problems, and identify major problems before they occur.

Manage Network Performance

Tracking network performance information will alert you to any changes that may put your network in danger. For example, network traffic might be increasing at a much higher rate than you anticipated. Your performance information will reflect this, and you can do something about it before the situation becomes an emergency and the network grinds to a halt. Without network monitoring statistics, you would have no easy way of knowing there was a problem until the network actually ground to a halt, inconveniencing the customers and the business.

Tracking network performance will help ensure that you aren't surprised by any major network problems. You can monitor software usage, storage usage, network traffic, and the performance of individual network components such as servers or cables.

Knowing how many people are using specific software on the network will help you plan for software license upgrades before they become an issue. You will know when the number of customers using a product is increasing so you can increase the licensing before people are stopped from using the product. If you notice that no one is using a piece of software, you can take steps to remove it and stop paying for any maintenance or licensing. Monitoring the use of space will allow you to plan for server upgrades before you run into space problems. If customers are putting more data on the servers than anticipated, you will be able to reorganize space or upgrade the server to prevent people from having problems when they try to store something there. If you notice that the number of users and transactions on your network is increasing faster than you expected, you will have the chance to do something about it before service starts getting degraded and people start calling in with problems. Monitoring network performance will also let you know when a specific component is malfunctioning so you can replace it before it becomes a major problem that affects the whole network. Sometimes you will be able to fix the problem before anyone even notices there was a problem.

Monitoring network information might not be a function of your Help Desk, but even if it is not it would be to your advantage to have constant access to the resulting data.

Build and Maintain a Problem/Solution Knowledge Base

If you keep track of how you solve specific problems, you will be able to use that information if other customers experience similar problems in the future. From the problem and solution information you collect from tracking calls, you will be able to create some form of problem/solution knowledge base. As Figure 5.2 shows, when a customer calls you can scan this data for information on similar past problems. This will help you resolve problems more quickly and for a wider variety of areas. For example, if someone is experiencing a problem where the display disappears from the monitor, the system might suggest that a loose power cord is the problem. Help Desk staff could suggest this solution to the customer even if they had never seen this problem before. They might not know a product very well, but if the problem has occurred before and its solution is documented, they can use that information to suggest a solution. Systems that store and retrieve problem/solution history can

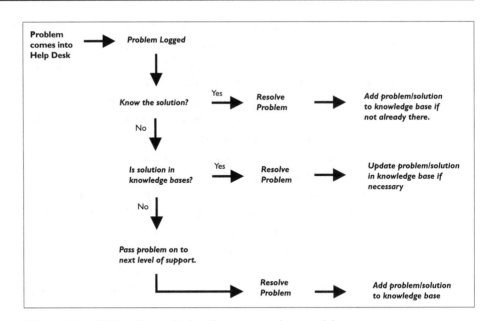

Figure 5.2 Using knowledge bases to solve problems.

range from simple relational databases to complex expert systems and can stand alone or be integrated with Help Desk management systems (see Chapter 6).

Identify Recurring Problems

If you have several people on the front line of your Help Desk all busy answering calls, you may not be aware of recurring problems unless you track problem symptoms and causes. Each person might, at different times, get a call about a different occurrence of the same problem. Because none of these people knows that the others are getting calls for the same problem, each person fixes a particular occurrence without addressing the fact that there is an underlying cause making the problem recur. The problem will just keep recurring, eating up valuable Help Desk time and costing customers time and inconvenience.

Tracking problem symptoms and causes will give a Help Desk management system the data it needs to identify problems that recur. Steps can then be taken to eliminate root causes of these problems so that customer inconvenience and calls to the Help Desk are reduced.

Identify Major Problems before They Occur

Being aware of trends in both problems and technology performance will allow you to stop more severe problems before they happen. As the graph in Figure 5.3 shows, early detection and correction of problems tends to lessen their severity.

If you notice an increasing number of problems with a specific software system, this may be an indication that the system needs to be replaced or rewritten so it will be more stable in the future. Perhaps limits in the software are being reached, and if something is not done to rectify the situation the software might just stop working altogether.

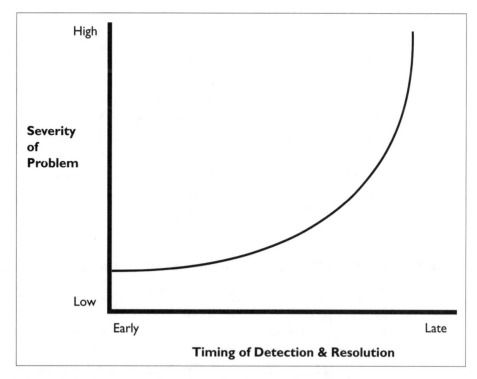

Figure 5.3   Early problem detection lessens impact.

If you are monitoring the performance of the network and notice degradation in any of the components, you can get them fixed before the degradation turns into complete failure and affects the whole network.

Help Desk Control

Data you gather from your calls can help you keep control of your Help Desk by showing you how its component parts are performing. Tracking call data will help you manage vendor performance, identify candidate processes for automation and outsourcing, measure Help Desk performance, and evaluate and manage Help Desk function. Tracking will also give you a solid basis for justifying improvements and provide the data necessary for charge back.

Manage Vendor Performance

If you track instances when vendor support is required to resolve problems, the corresponding resolution times, and the quality of the resolution, you can see how well the vendor is supporting you. You will have the statistics that will tell you whether the vendor is meeting any service-level agreements that have been set up. You can use these statistics to back up your discussion if you need to talk to the vendor about service. You can then continue to use them to monitor improvements, or lack thereof, and to justify breaking a contract with a vendor if that becomes necessary. You can also track overall performance of the products supplied by that vendor to see whether you should continue purchasing them.

Identify Candidate Processes for Automation and Outsourcing

Tracking the calls you get to the Help Desk will tell you what things people call the Help Desk about most often. This, in turn, will tell you what things you need to automate or outsource to get the largest decrease in Help Desk call load.

If people are calling the Help Desk frequently asking for terminal resets, then automation in the form of an interactive voice response (IVR) system that allows people to reset their own terminals would eliminate all of those calls. Automating as many of the routine calls you get as possible will have a big impact on the number of calls that your Help Desk receives. It will free up staff to focus on more complex calls and to make improvements to Help Desk service.

In the same way, information about the calls you get can also show you where outsourcing might help you. If you are getting a lot of calls for packaged applications—how to interface with other applications, how to perform specific complex functions, how to use an application—then you may want to outsource this support to an external organization that provides this kind of service. You could then integrate this service into your Help Desk in such a way that people wouldn't even realize they were accessing an external Help Desk.

Measure Help Desk Performance

You can use information that you track to measure the performance of your Help Desk. How many calls you handle, how you handle them, your rate of successful resolution, the number of users you are supporting, the hardware and software you are supporting, and so on—together, these will give you an excellent idea of how you are performing. You can communicate this information to management and customers to show the value you are delivering. If you are not doing well or are just starting up, you can use these same statistics to show what you plan to do to improve. For example, if you are taking too long to resolve calls but are planning to eliminate the causes of many of your calls, you can show the difference this will make in your call volume and how you will use that difference to resolve calls more quickly. (Staff will be getting fewer calls, so they should be able to spend more time on problems, and resolution time should improve.)

An important part of Help Desk performance is customer satisfaction. You may be doing everything right, but if your customers aren't happy, if they are going to places other than the Help Desk for support, then you are not succeeding. For example, your calls may be going down, but the reason may be that your customers don't think much of your service and have stopped trying to get help from you. They have found their own ways to get help—either by asking people around them who know more than they do (a very expensive use of people's time) or by going elsewhere. Tracking calls will tell you who is using the Help Desk, who is not using the Help Desk, and who is misusing the Help Desk. You can address the misuse and talk to areas not using the Help Desk to find out the reasons. You want to make sure that you are giving your customers what they need.

Call data can also be used to measure performance against customer service-level agreements to see whether those agreements are being met and what areas need to be addressed. See Figure 5.4 for an example.

Evaluate/Manage Help Desk Function

The more you know about what is happening with your calls, the better you can manage them. You can monitor staff performance, and you can ensure that calls are being handled efficiently, priorities are working, procedures are working and are being followed, and staffing levels are adequate. Tracking call data will allow you to do all this.

If Help Desk staff have access to logged call information, then they will know whether a problem coming in has been logged already. This will prevent a situation in which two or more customers call into the

Performance vs. Service Level Agreement

	Target	Achieved
• *Avg. call answer time*	*90% < 30 sec.*	*95% < 30 sec.*
• *1st level call resolution*	*75%*	*77%*
• *Priority 1 Resolution*	*100% < 1 hr.*	*91% < 1 hr.*
• *Priority 2 Resolution*	*100% < 4 hrs.*	*78% < 4 hrs.*
• *Priority 3 Resolution*	*100% < 8 hrs.*	*100% < 8 hrs.*

Figure 5.4   Using tracked call data in performance measurement.

Help Desk about the same problem and, because each speaks to a different Help Desk person, Help Desk staff do not realize that the same problem has been reported two or more times. As a result, the problem might be worked on by more than one Help Desk person—effort is duplicated, and valuable Help Desk time that could have been spent helping other customers is wasted.

If your Help Desk is receiving too many high-priority calls or logged calls are sitting in the assignment queue too long, priorities either are not being enforced properly or are out of balance. Information from your call-tracking system will make you aware of this situation and help you determine the cause. You can then, as required, either reeducate your staff and customers in priorities or adjust your priorities in order to balance them.

If logged calls are not getting allocated or completed, if problems are marked completed but customers call to complain that they have not been completed satisfactorily, then you might have a problem with your procedures. They may be incorrect or nonexistent, or your staff might be either ignoring them or ignorant of them. Looking at statistics for unallocated problems, outstanding problems, and reopened problems will make you aware of any of these situations and will give you the data you need to find the cause and come up with a solution.

Statistics pertaining to call volumes and times to resolve calls will tell you if there is just too much work for your Help Desk to handle. If the number of calls you receive in one day is constantly increasing and the number of calls you are actually resolving each day is decreasing, you know you have a problem. Your backlog is going to skyrocket if you don't do something about the situation. Call statistics will give you the data you need to find out why your calls are increasing and how you can get them down. Automation may be indicated, or you may have to ask for more staffing, but you will have the data to back you up. You can also check volumes for different times to see whether you are staffing appropriately for peaks and valleys. For example, if 9 A.M. to 11 A.M. and 2 P.M. to 4 P.M. are your busiest times and Thursday is your busiest day, you want to be sure that you have enough staff working during those times to handle the volumes. Call statistics will tell you when your busiest and slowest times are so you can staff most effectively for each.

If you keep track of who was assigned to each call, the resolution time, and the quality of resolution, you will have some good information about the quality of work that each person is doing. If poor quality is indicated, you can address it; if good quality is indicated, you can reward it. Your staff will appreciate this. They will also realize that their work is reflected in the statistics and may take more care to complete everything in a quality manner.

Justify Improvements

If you have the statistics to show how a lack of improvements is affecting the Help Desk you improve your chances of getting the funding you need to make them. You could show the current situation, what you would like to change, and how it will improve things. For example, if your problem is lengthy resolution times, then you can show the volume of calls, the resolution time, and the resulting backlog. You can project what would happen if you decreased the volume of calls or increased staff. You could also show how you could decrease calls because you would have already identified the most frequently occurring reasons for calling and how you could automate or get rid of them.

Keeping track of trends would show you unfavorable trends before they started to affect your service, so you could go after funding before the fact. For example, knowing that your call volumes were creeping up while your resolution times were also rising would give you an indication that you needed to either decrease calls or increase staff to prevent severe degradation of your Help Desk service. The same applies to trends in technology. If the business were planning to roll out client/server systems and your network monitoring and asset management systems told you that network equipment and PCs needed to be upgraded for this system to be able to run successfully, you could go after funding for the upgrades. You would know exactly what had to be upgraded, so you could make very accurate cost estimates and ensure that everything was in place before the system was rolled out.

Provide the Information Necessary for Charge Back

Call-tracking data will give you the usage information you need to bill your customers if your Help Desk charges back for services. Inventory information will also be required if you bill by PC or terminal. You can give each department an accurate breakdown of how it used the Help Desk over a specific period of time, including number of calls, types of calls, and so on. This information not only provides each department with billing information but can serve as a departmental audit of Help Desk use. Managers can see what their staff are calling the Help Desk for, if there is any misuse such as calling with questions that should be addressed by training, and if there is enough use. They can check to see whether staff who seem to be spending too much time trying to solve problems on their own are calling the Help Desk and then can address the situation as required. They can also check for trends in types and numbers of calls. If staff attended training, this information might give an indication of how effective the training was. If productivity was down, this information could show whether technology problems were contributing to the situation.

Customer Effectiveness

Data tracked from calls and network monitoring tools can increase the effectiveness of your customers. You can identify and help customers needing training, and keep customers informed of problems, unplanned maintenance, and other service interruptions.

Identify Customers Needing Training

A common complaint of Help Desks is that customers don't know the technology they are using. Rather than taking the training on how to use a software package or spending time looking for the information they need in a software manual, customers will call the Help Desk with their questions. Flooding the Help Desk with how-to questions is not the worst of their sins. Customers will use the software incorrectly because they don't understand it, and this can cause them to get incorrect results, to lose data, or to think that their computer isn't working properly. They waste a lot of their own time and the Help Desk's time.

Keeping track of these kinds of calls to the Help Desk will tell you whether there are any customers or groups of customers that need training in specific software. For example, say someone calls up with a spreadsheet problem and when you check the history for that customer you see that this is his or her fourth call about spreadsheets. This is a pretty good indication that this person needs some training. You can recommend training right on the phone. "I see that this is your fourth call about spreadsheets. There's a course being offered on that software. It will help you with your work and may save you some time." You can also do callbacks—that is, run reports against your call logs that highlight repeat calls and then call the customers highlighted with training recommendations. If you weren't tracking callers and call information, you might not be aware of this information. The customer might have spoken to a different Help Desk person with each call and, since the frequency of calls had not been noticed, would just keep calling, using up valuable Help Desk time. Decreasing these kinds of calls will lighten the Help Desk load and make customers more productive with their technology.

Another advantage of tracking this kind of information is that it will give you evidence to back up your assertion that these people need training. They can't really argue with you when you present statistics that detail how often they called and what they called about. They also know that you will be monitoring their future calls. They might just try to get some training before calling you next time.

Keep Customers Informed

If you are monitoring the network and tracking Help Desk calls, you can notify your customers of any problems, unplanned maintenance, or unscheduled shutdowns. In this way, customers can prepare for them rather than be logged off suddenly while in the middle of something important. You will be able to pass on information about trends to your customers. If you know that you are approaching license or storage limits, you can let them know so they can use both software and storage more judiciously while you get them upgraded. You can even use this data to help make customers more aware of the limits and costs of upgrading so they will use resources more carefully. The more your customers know about their technological environment, the more effectively they can use it.

Your call-tracking data will also allow you to keep customers informed of the status of their Help Desk calls. When they call to inquire, you will have the required information for them. Better still, if you are tracking this information in a database, you can give them the facility to get this information for themselves—via phone, by using an interactive voice response (IVR) system, or via a PC or terminal, by using an interface to your database.

Integrating Tracked Data

The information you track is most valuable when you can integrate it. The more that systems know about each other and can talk to each other, the more powerful they become. For example, if customer and asset information is integrated with the Help Desk management system, the Help Desk person can just key in the customer ID and all the customer information and asset information will come up automatically. In the call information, under "component," the Help Desk person just has to specify "monitor" and the system will fill in the rest because the system knows which monitor the customer owns. The monitor has been flagged as a problem and searches of call information looking for problems with monitors or that specific monitor will pick that call up. In this way, trends in monitor performance can be tracked. Help Desk staff can go into the asset database, select a component such as a brand of monitor, and ask if there have been any problems recorded against it. The system will be able to find all occurrences of problems with that brand of monitor that was cited as the component causing the problem. The integrated system knows asset information, customer information, and call information. You can get customer or asset information from a call; you can get customer and call information from assets; and you can get call and asset information from a customer, all without duplicating any information.

If the information were not integrated, recording a call would happen somewhat differently. The customer would call in, and customer information would have to be taken and keyed in. Things might be keyed in incorrectly. Then the customer would give the asset tags of the configurations being used. The Help Desk person would go to the asset system, check what the configurations were, then key them into the call-tracking screen. This presents more chance for error. Under "component" the monitor information would have to be rekeyed. If any information is keyed in incorrectly, searches will be useless. If a name is spelled wrong or a model number is omitted, valuable trending information can be lost. On top of all this, a lot of time was wasted by the Help Desk person to key everything in, especially compared to having it all happen automatically.

The more integrated a system is, the less data you have to keep duplicate copies of or rekey, and the less chance there is of error. Systems are talking to each other to get information; error-prone human intervention is limited. Systems know more, so they can be more intelligent. A network management system that can see all components of a network and how they interact, and can thus flag problems or potential problems, is much more powerful than several individual network tools that do not talk to each other but monitor their own network components in isolation.

When you are tracking data, the more integrated that data is, the more useful it will be to you. Keep this in mind when you are selecting tools for your Help Desk.

Key Points Covered in This Chapter

The information you can get from tracking can tell you everything from how many front line staff you need at any point throughout the day to how many and which PCs need to be upgraded to support a client/server system that is being planned for release on the network. Tracking information cannot be accomplished manually because of the complexity of our technology environments—you will need tools to help you.

Some of the things that you can accomplish through tracking are as follows:

1. Asset control

   Manage hardware and software assets. You will be able to improve planning for upgrades, ensure that software licensing is up to date, get rid of unauthorized software, provide more accurate figures for valuation and depreciation of assets, facilitate disaster and recovery planning, and facilitate the centralization of technology purchase and maintenance so that economies of scale can be realized.

   Identify trends in hardware and software performance. You can get the hardware or software fixed before it becomes a problem.

2. Problem control

   Manage network performance. You will be alerted to anything that might endanger your network and will have the ability to monitor software usage, storage usage, network traffic, and performance of individual network components.

   Build a problem/solution knowledge base. Keeping a history of problems and solutions will prevent you from having to rethink a problem each time a similar one happens.

   Identify recurring problems for elimination. Tracking the causes for calls will alert you to problems that keep recurring so you can get a proper solution put into place and reduce calls.

   Identify major problems before they occur. Negative trends, such as an increasing number of calls accompanied by increasing resolve times, can be noted and addressed before service grinds to a halt. Degradation in the performance of network components such as cables can be brought to light and resolved before network performance is significantly affected.

3. Help Desk control

   Manage vendor performance. You will know if your vendors are offering poor service or poor products and can take corrective measures.

   Identify candidate processes for automation and outsourcing. You can identify processes that will bring the most benefit by being automated or outsourced.

Measure Help Desk performance. You will know how effectively you are handling and resolving calls and which of your customers are or are not using your services. You'll know where you need to improve.

Manage Help Desk function. You can ensure that calls are being handled efficiently, priorities are working, procedures are working and are being followed, and staffing levels are adequate.

Justify improvements. Tracking will give you the statistics to show how a lack of improvements is affecting the Help Desk. This will improve your chances of getting the funding you need to make them.

Provide information necessary for charge back. You can provide each department with information on how often and how effectively it used the Help Desk.

4. Customer effectiveness

Identify customers needing training. You can make sure that customers are offered the training they need to use their technology properly and to best advantage from it.

Keep customers informed. You can provide your customers with information about problems, unplanned maintenance, and unscheduled shutdowns as early as possible to minimize impact on them.

Tracked data is most valuable when it is integrated. The more that systems know about each other and the more they can communicate, the more powerful they become. Errors will decrease, and rekeying or duplication of data will become unnecessary.

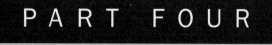

PART FOUR

Using Technology

Help Desk Tools

Help Desk tools give the Help Desk the ability to manage call traffic, track and control individual calls, resolve problems at point of call, and manage technology assets, as well as an infinite number of other tasks that might fall within an individual Help Desk's role. Given the complexity and range of technology being supported by most Help Desks, these tasks would be impossible without tools.

Since the first edition of *Running an Effective Help Desk*, there have been some major changes in the world of Help Desk tools:

The number of players has increased dramatically. There are now literally hundreds of vendors offering some flavor of Help Desk tool. For Help Desks, this means a wider selection, covering all budgets and all sizes of organization, and a better chance of getting exactly what you need.

The functionality and integration of the tools has increased. Each tool now performs more functions or allows for interfaces to tools that perform the functions. Tools are so integrated that it's sometimes difficult to tell where one begins and where another ends. Functionality can overlap.

The Internet has changed the way Help Desks support customers, solve problems, and do research on processes and tools. It has given customers the ability to solve some of their own problems. Chapter 7 is devoted to a discussion of the Internet.

A change that was expected but did not happen was huge growth in the use of expert systems. The reasons for this are discussed later on in this chapter in the section titled "Problem Resolution."

In This Chapter

In this chapter we will examine the types of tools available for the Help Desk. Depending on how widely you have defined the functionality of your Help Desk, you may use some or all of these tools, and you may use others that are not mentioned here.

The first two types of tools we will look at are as follows:

- Forums for learning and idea exchange
- Tools for communication

The remaining tools we will examine have become so heavily integrated that it's sometimes hard to separate them. The basic umbrella under which they all reside is the *Help Desk management system*. A Help Desk management system can be a very simple, basic system, or it can be extremely complex, interfacing with various computer telephony applications, network management systems, the Internet, and so on. The way we will approach discussion of the Help Desk management tools in this chapter is to first look at the very basic system, then at each of the plug-ins (see Figure 6.1). It is important to note that each vendor will typically package certain components into a basic system and offer other components as plug-ins. Components that a vendor does not supply can often be purchased from a third party and then plugged in to the system. The tools discussed in the remainder of the chapter are as follows:

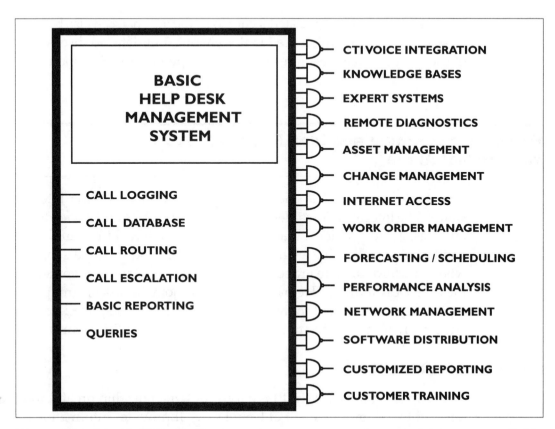

Figure 6.1 A basic Help Desk management system and some of the many available plug-ins.

- The basic Help Desk management system
- Telephone-related technologies
- Problem resolution tools
- Asset management tools
- Management aids
- Network management tools (including software distribution)
- Tools for customer training and self-help
- Selecting tools

The Internet, and the related technology, the intranet, can also be Help Desk tools. They are referenced in this chapter, but detailed discussions of each of these have been reserved for Chapters 7 and 8, respectively.

Forums for Learning and Idea Exchange . . . You Are Not Alone

The area of learning and idea exchange is one in which the Internet shines. The Internet allows Help Desk staff to exchange and get feedback on ideas, avoid problems that others have run into, and research tools and techniques. For those who prefer to exchange ideas in person, and who can afford to, there are several conferences available for workers in the Help Desk industry. Help Desk people can join discussion groups for topics they're interested in, hear lectures on various Help Desk topics, and simply find out what others are doing in the Help Desk world.

Help Desk Institute (HDI)

The Help Desk Institute (HDI) is a for-profit, membership organization devoted to the improvement of Help Desks. It provides information on methods, tools, technologies, and trends within the Help Desk industry; offers a wide variety of training given by experts in the field; and hosts the semiannual International Support Services Conference and Exposition. Membership in the institute, paid on a yearly basis, includes a subscription to a newsletter that deals with day-to-day Help Desk operations; a letter that deals with management issues; copies of HDI studies on Help Desk trends, salaries, and tools; and discounts on reference material, courses, and conferences. Membership spans eleven countries. HDI also helps set up local HDI chapters, which function as user groups—they meet to discuss Help Desk issues and bring in speakers.

The HDI Web site, which can be found at www.helpdeskinst.com, offers information about HDI and its services, profiles of current Help Desk industry issues and events, information on Help Desk technologies, and a moderated forum for the discussion of Help Desk issues. This useful Web site is always changing and should be referenced regularly.

Software Support Professionals Association (SSPA)

The Software Support Professionals Association (SSPA) is a for-profit, membership organization for service and support professionals in the software industry. It provides a forum for sharing ideas, discussing developing trends, and networking with peers. SSPA has over 700 member companies for which it provides training, seminars, and conferences; publications; networking opportunities; and special events and services.

The SSPA Web site can be found at www.sspa-online.com.

Support Services in Canada

Support Services in Canada is a nonprofit association directed at Canadian support professionals and organizations. It offers a wide range of information on various aspects of the support industry, including technology vendors and service providers, seminars, trades shows and conferences, associations and information exchanges, professional certification, and employment opportunities. It distributes a free electronic newsletter. (A paper copy can be ordered for a small fee.)

The Support Services in Canada Web site can be found at www .echo-on.net/~ssimpson.

Association of Support Professionals (ASP)

The Association of Support Professionals (ASP) is a membership organization exclusively for personal computer (PC) support professionals. There is a very small membership fee, which covers the expenses of the organization. The services that ASP provides to its members include industry research, a newsletter, discounts on publications and seminars, an annual Customer Support Conference, a network of ASP local chapters, listings of job openings, and various opportunities for networking with other support professionals.

The ASP Web site can be found at www.asponline.com.

Help Desk User Group (HUG)

The Help Desk User Group (HUG) is a U.K.-based for-profit organization that provides its members with a forum for sharing Help Desk ideas and experiences. It offers customer service professionals a variety of special events, exhibitions, seminars, consulting services, and reference publications. Members of HUG also receive discounts. HUG is guided by a steering committee drawn from its membership, which currently spans eighteen countries.

The HUG Web site can be found at www.hug.co.uk.

The Help Desk Frequently Asked Questions (FAQ) Site

Started by a dedicated Help Desk aficionado, this site has become the most recognized source of Help Desk information, resources, references, and links. You can find it at www.duke.edu/~pverghis/hdeskfaq.htm.

On-line Discussion Groups

There are several on-line discussion groups in areas that might be of interest to Help Desks. The Help Desk discussion group is one of these, and it addresses all aspects of Help Desk management. For information on how to use it, visit the Help Desk FAQ described in the previous section. If you sign up, be prepared to receive a lot of mail; and I mean a lot of mail.

Vendor Web Sites

Most technology vendors have their own Web sites. Services they provide include knowledge bases for self-help, product information, user groups, feedback opportunities, suggestions for more effective use, and so on.

Magazines on the Internet

Most computer magazines have Web sites on the Internet. You can do keyword searches to browse article archives and pick up information on products, events, and industry news. These sites are extremely valuable to Help Desks and offer management ideas, product comparisons, news of new technology, and so on. Some of the most relevant are the following:

1. *Service News*, at www.servicenews.com
2. *Support Management*, at www.supportmanagement.com
3. LTI Technomedia (*Computer World, Network World, Info World Canada, CIO Canada*), at www.lti.on.ca

4. *Network Computing*, at www.networkcomputing.com. This is part of a larger network of technical magazines, sourced at www.cmpnet.com

5. *PC Week*, at www.pcweek.com. This is also part of a larger network of technical magazines, sourced at www.zdnet.com.

Tools for Communication

Communication tools include those used to facilitate communication within the Help Desk and those used to communicate with customers and other support staff.

White Boards

Sometimes the simplest tools are the most effective ones. If Help Desk staff become aware of a serious problem, they might write a note on a central white board that is visible to all other Help Desk staff so everyone is made aware of the situation. Some Help Desk management systems have on-line white boards where staff can post messages. The challenge with on-line white boards is that staff members have to remember to check to see if there are new messages.

Voice Mail

Voice mail can be part of your Help Desk phone system. It can take messages when all Help Desk staff are busy and can be used to broadcast messages about the system. It must be used carefully on a Help Desk—if you don't get back quickly to people who leave messages, then people aren't going to use voice mail. They will find another way to get help, and it might not be through your Help Desk. Voice mail can be integrated with Help Desk software and/or other telephone technologies. For example, a customer might initiate a Help Desk call by using an integrated voice response (IVR) system that interfaces with Help Desk software to generate a call ticket automatically. As part of the problem initiation, the customer might leave a voice message describing the problem. The whole area of voice processing is discussed in more detail later in this chapter in the section entitled "Telephone-related Technologies."

E-mail

E-mail is not only a general-purpose communications medium, allowing communication with everyone who has a user ID for that system (usually all Help Desk customers), it can also be integrated with Help Desk software to allow customers to interact directly with the Help Desk system. Some Help Desk systems have interfaces that allow customers to log problems and generate call tickets automatically by sending an E-mail message into the Help Desk. In the same way, when a log is closed, an automatic notification can be sent to the customer. Other Help Desk systems allow for even more integration of E-mail into the Help Desk function. For example, when a Help Desk staff member enters a problem, it can be flagged as a problem relevant to another staff member's problem, and the details can be automatically routed to that person.

Electronic Displays

Electronic displays can be set up in customer areas to keep them up to date on system status. If there is a problem, the display will either flash or beep, and a message indicating the nature of the problem will be displayed. This will cut down on calls to the Help Desk. Customers will get information about system status when a problem occurs simply by looking up at the display.

The Basic Help Desk Management System

A Help Desk management system at its most basic level usually includes the following features:

- A function for capturing and logging call information
- A function for routing and/or escalating calls to the appropriate person or area

- A central database where all logged calls are stored
- Reporting and querying capabilities against logged data

A call management system may also have plug-in units for other functions such as asset management, forecasting and scheduling, knowledge base and expert systems, Internet access, and remote diagnostics. Call management systems can also have connections to E-mail systems, automatic call distribution systems, automated attendants, interactive voice response (IVR), pagers, and fax machines.

Capturing and Logging Call Information

When a call is logged into a Help Desk management system, some form of customer identification, such as a user ID, is keyed in, and the system fills in as much information as it knows about that customer—for example, name, phone number, location, department, time of call, and hardware and software configurations. The system also assigns the call a unique identifier, often called a call ticket or incident number. The Help Desk analyst can then enter details of the call. These might include description, components involved, and priority. A logged call contains all details of the call, its status, and any progress that has been made on it. Notes are entered on the logged call by the person working on it. Progress on calls can be monitored from call initiation to call close. Calls can be prioritized automatically based on several predefined variables.

Routing and Escalating Calls

Help Desk management systems allow analysts to route calls to specific people or areas. The calls are actually routed into queues where analysts can take ownership of a call by picking it off of the queue; that analyst's ID is automatically recorded against the call. The analyst fills in notes on the logged call as it is worked on to indicate what is being done and then enters a description of the resolution when the call is completed. Completed calls are marked as closed, and some systems even automatically send an E-mail message to the customer indicating that the call has been completed.

Call management systems also typically have a function for automatic call escalation. A predefined set of criteria is set up, and when an outstanding call meets this criteria it is automatically escalated to the next level. Automatic escalation can include messages, pagers, phones, alarms, or simply a flag against the call.

Central Database: Reports and Queries

Logged calls, and all of the notes surrounding them from beginning to end, are stored in a central database from which queries and reports can be run. Customers might be given access to this database so they can check on the progress of their calls. This database provides information that can tell Help Desk managers if their Help Desks are working as they should and point out problem areas. The data can be queried to find calls that have been outstanding for too long, calls that are receiving too high a priority, and calls that had to be reopened because they were not re-solved properly the first time. The Help Desk management software can usually be set up so that these kind of queries run automatically and ini-tiate some kind of alarms or notifications if certain predefined situations are encountered. Managers can use reports and queries to get informa-tion such as call volumes by type of call or reason for call, and they can also use them to sort data by Help Desk analyst. This data can tell the Help Desk manager if priorities are being used properly and are prop-erly balanced, if procedures are correct and are being followed, and if there are staff who appear to be having trouble getting calls resolved. It can also alert the Help Desk to trends such as problems with specific makes and models of hardware or recurring problems and can identify customers or groups that need training in a specific product.

Telephone-Related Technologies

The most significant advance in telephone-related technologies in terms of impact on the Help Desk is computer telephony integration (CTI). CTI is the integration of computer and telephone technology to allow greater and easier communication between the two. Many Help Desk manage-ment systems now have CTI components that perform functions such as simultaneous call and data transfer, which means that the Help Desk analyst gets not only the call but a display of caller information.

Telephone technologies for the Help Desk can manage phone traffic into the Help Desk, route calls, accept customer input entered via the telephone keypad, and interact with other technology based on input from the customer. Examples of these are automatic call distributors (ACD), automated attendants, and interactive voice response (IVR). The sophistication of these tools is increasing constantly, and functionality overlaps to the point that one tool will often include another. All of these tools can be part of CTI applications.

Computer Telephony Integration (CTI)

An example of a CTI application is an interactive voice response (IVR) application that allows the customer to perform a computerized function, such as information retrieval or terminal reset, by pressing keys on the telephone keypad.

The two major standards for the development of program interfaces for computer telephony are the Telephony Services Applications Program Interface (TSAPI) developed by Novell and targeted toward LAN-oriented applications, and the Telephony Application Program Interface (TAPI) developed by Microsoft and targeted toward desktop, Windows-based applications. TSAPI's applicability is geared toward corporate environments that can support a network. TAPI tends to lend itself to small office and home office applications. There are applications that support both standards.

One of the most important applications coming out of computer telephony from a Help Desk point of view is Caller ID database lookup. When a call comes into the Help Desk, the telephone switch identifies the caller (through automatic number identification) and passes the calling number to a Caller ID database. Information from the database is sent to the analyst taking the call, so that when the analyst picks up the phone the information for that caller is displayed on the analyst's screen. Information might include customer information such as hardware configuration, software used, records of previous calls and how they were resolved, and so on (see Figure 6.2). This means a significant time saving

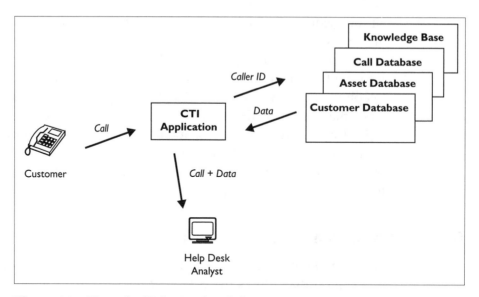

Figure 6.2   How the Help Desk might use CTI.

for each call. If necessary, the analyst can pass the call on, along with the screen full of information, to a second-level support person with a simple click of the mouse.

Other popular CTI applications include fax-on-demand; intelligent call routing, in which an auto attendant answers the call and routes it to a specific extension; and interactive voice response (IVR), which allows the customer to enter requests via a touch tone phone. The Help Desk might use an IVR that interacts with the customer to try to solve a problem by sending a fax, or by offering a selection of prerecorded solutions for the customer to listen to. Help Desk analysts can also initiate faxes from their PCs. If an analyst finds that explaining a solution is too complex or time consuming, it might be easier for that analyst to simply fax the information to the customer using a fax server on the LAN.

CTI can also provide call conferencing; call transfer via computer, which is as simple as dragging names onto a phone icon; multiple message types (voice, fax, E-mail) in the same mailbox; and intelligent call forwarding, an application that can find you and forward your calls to you.

A good source of information for computer telephony products is *Computer Telephony* magazine. You can find it at www.computertelephony.com.

Automatic Call Distributor (ACD)

At its simplest, an automatic call distributor (ACD) is a phone system, or software within a phone system, that manages the flow of calls coming into the Help Desk. An ACD typically routes calls on a first-come-first-served basis to the first available Help Desk analyst. If all analysts are busy, callers are put into a queue and played a recorded message, such as "All Help Desk staff are currently busy; your call will be answered as soon as a Help Desk analyst becomes available." The ACD monitors the queue and sends the caller who has been in the queue longest to the next available operator. Some ACDs allow the routing algorithm to be programmed so it can be customized to the requirements of each specific Help Desk and can vary according to traffic and time of day. The ACD monitors routed calls to make sure they are being distributed evenly among staff. More sophisticated ACDs ask customers to select from a list of options depending on the nature of their problem so that their call can be routed into the appropriate area. The ACD also provides statistics for calls such as number of calls coming in, number of calls abandoned, time on hold, and time per call. If the statistics provided by the ACD are not satisfactory—that is, not in the format required or not giving the information required—there are separate ACD reporting packages that will do the job. Some packages allow managers to pull ACD information up on their PCs and get the information in real time and in the desired form.

Automated Attendant

A basic automated attendant for the Help Desk answers a customer call with an automated greeting that offers a selection of options, then routes the call based on the option selected. The options usually include transfer to a human operator. Automated attendants can also be much more sophisticated. They can anticipate a caller's needs—based on where the caller is calling from, for example—and can be integrated with other technologies to use networking and voice-response features to route calls and give out information. Such integration can give customers the ability to check on the status of their Help Desk calls by entering their call ticket numbers. It can also give customers the ability to select an option and get prerecorded responses to frequently asked questions. While customers are on hold, the automated attendant can play prerecorded messages. Some automated attendants can make use of automatic number identification to pass calls on to Help Desk analysts who are servicing specific areas. Companies frequently use automated attendants to provide a reduced level of after-hours support.

Interactive Voice Response (IVR)

Interactive Voice Response (IVR) is a combination of hardware and software that allows a customer to interface with other technology, such as a mainframe, LAN, or fax machine, to get information or to perform a specific function. The customer typically makes a selection from a menu of options and then enters any data required via the telephone keypad. The IVR takes that data and acts upon it depending on the function requested. An IVR can fax selected documents back to the caller, provide prerecorded information on a specific topic, give the status of a job, reset terminals and printers, and reboot LAN file servers. The IVR can also be set up to interface with a call management system to allow customers to report problems or make requests and to check on problem or request status.

Problem Resolution Tools

The Help Desk tools involved most directly with the problem-solving process are knowledge bases, expert systems, and remote diagnostic software. Knowledge bases and expert systems are actually part of the problem-solving process, while remote diagnostic software enables the process by allowing the Help Desk analyst to view and control the customer's screen.

Knowledge Bases and Expert Systems

The Help Desk industry had high expectations for knowledge bases and expert systems, tools that were supposed to "put the knowledge of the experts into the hands of the novice," thereby making new analysts almost instantly productive and increasing the number of calls solved at point of call. Yet, according to the Help Desk Institute's 1997 survey results in their *Help Desk and Customer Support Practices Report*, only 17 percent of support organizations (of the 807 that responded to the survey question pertaining to technology used on the Help Desk) are using some form of expert system or artificial intelligence (AI). Why isn't there an expert system on every desk? The reasons are simple and involve both the fact that someone has to give knowledge to these expert systems and that technology is getting increasingly complex, with increasingly complex relationships between technological components. The specific reasons are as follows:

The knowledge in expert systems is time consuming and costly to set up and maintain. The technological environment supported by Help Desks will continue to change rapidly, necessitating high maintenance levels for any expert system.

The structure of the data is critical to an expert system. It's too easy to set up a poorly designed system that very quickly becomes useless. This is similar to setting up a database in which the segments are designed in such a way that the data you most often want is hardest to get. Most of us have experienced this kind of frustration. This will happen if the problem area in the expert system is not well understood.

Terminology and classifications can get very complicated to use and maintain.

In a very wide, complex environment many of the systems break down; they simply cannot handle all the relationships.

The systems sometimes require a certain degree of knowledge to use—you have to know what questions to ask.

Definitions

With respect to a Help Desk, a knowledge base is a database of diagnostic information that helps the Help Desk analysts solve problems.

Although often referred to as *reasoning* systems, expert systems are not really capable of reasoning, only of knowing. Humans find reasoning to be a time-consuming process, and what we tend to do is store the results of our reasoning for later reference. That stored information is what we put into expert systems. In his book *AI: The Tumultuous History of the Search for Artificial Intelligence,* Daniel Crevier illustrates this idea by comparing a biologist to a physician. Of the two, the biologist is better able to explain the workings of a human body but is unable to recognize a specific infection and prescribe the appropriate drug for it. Recognizing the infection and appropriate drug to prescribe is often not a matter of reasoning but of knowing which symptoms go with which infections and which drugs are effective in eliminating each infection.

An expert system is composed of a knowledge base and a shell. The knowledge base can be structured in various ways, but it always contains the knowledge—information that will suggest to the user of the system what to do or what conclusions to reach under a specific set of circumstances. The knowledge base is built by the experts who know how to solve the problems that might occur. The shell of the expert system is the part that contains the mechanism for accessing the knowledge base and the user interface. The knowledge base-searching mechanism is sometimes called the *inference engine.* Several vendors offer expert shells, which companies can customize to their own requirements by providing the information. The shells contain logic that is the result of years of AI research and that would take a significant time to re-create.

Approaches to Problem Solving Using Knowledge Bases and Expert Systems

There are several approaches to problem solving that use knowledge bases and/or expert systems. Nick Straguzzi of Advantage kbs offers a very interesting discussion of these various approaches in a white paper titled *Models, Cases, and Trees, Oh My . . . Which One to Use?* (it can be found at www.akbs.com). The paper defines four approaches to knowledge representation, and I will use the same (or similar) categorization here. I will discuss text retrieval systems, decision tree systems, case-based systems, and systems based on symptoms, causes, and corrections (often called troubleshooting systems).

In text retrieval systems, a search engine is used against a database of information, which may include common problems and solutions, documentation, or procedures. Help Desks typically build their own problem/solution knowledge bases by adding a new problem/solution to the base upon successful resolution (if it is not already there). It is very easy to add or remove information from a text retrieval knowledge base.

Numerous prepackaged knowledge bases are available for text retrieval systems. They provide solutions or technical information. Help Desks can plug them into their Help Desk management system and include them in their knowledge base searches when doing problem solving.

The limitations for the text retrieval technology are the search strategies. The performance of the Help Desk system can deteriorate rapidly as more text is added to the knowledge base. Speed of use has a huge impact on how quickly Help Desk analysts can solve customers' problems.

Decision trees work on the IF THEN ELSE principle. Gradually, through the process of elimination, they work down to the node of the tree that contains the problem. These systems are often implemented as hypertext documents. In a multiple choice, the customers select a choice and are instantly taken to the next level in the tree. Decision trees are useful for common, well-understood problems in a fairly simple area of knowledge. If the area becomes more complex, the tree becomes cumbersome and difficult to maintain. Design is also critical. If, for example, a key question is missed, then the poor Help Desk analyst may end up with a solution that has nothing to do with the original problem.

Case-based problem solving involves matching a current problem to one that has occurred previously and for which the solution is known. In such a system, the analyst typically enters the problem in free-form text, although some standards for keywords would make this easier. If the problem is not found then, when its solution is known it is added to the database so the next time it occurs, the solution will be there. The advantage to this type of expert system is that the analyst does not require expert knowledge to use it. Fairly new analysts can become productive using this system almost immediately. However, the analyst must know enough to make the final decision regarding the solution, choose between solutions, and test them.

The symptoms-causes-corrections approach focuses on identifying symptoms and causes. The system gathers symptoms, and when it has enough it suggests causes and tests them by asking questions. When it has gathered enough information, it suggests a specific solution. If the solution doesn't work, the system goes back to testing. This approach is not worthwhile for simple problems and does not work if the problem area is not well understood or the troubleshooting knowledge is not complete.

Selecting a Knowledge Base or Expert System

As you have seen, knowledge bases and expert systems can be complex. They can also be expensive. At the low end and middle are the text retrieval systems; at the high end are the case-based, decision tree, and troubleshooting type systems. Don't even think of purchasing these systems until you have spent a significant amount of time figuring out just what kind of problem-solving capabilities you are looking for, the expertise of your staff, the resources you are willing to assign to install and maintain the beast, and exactly what you are expecting from the system (as well as your budget). Don't buy without test driving. The specs are often the theory; the test drive is closer to reality.

In all the approaches to problem solving just described except the simplest one, a requirement for success is that the problem realm be relatively static and well understood. Think of how quickly technology is introduced and then, just as quickly, becomes obsolete. Technology is certainly not static, and the integration of technology, with all its components and various connective possibilities, is not well understood. Adding complexity to this situation is the fact that the technology itself is prone to problems (e.g., bugs) that are also not well understood. This is a tough environment for an expert system to keep up with. When you are considering purchasing an expert system, don't let your expectations run past what is reality.

Remote Diagnostic Software

Remote diagnostic software products allow Help Desk staff to take over a customer's local or remote PC session from their own workstations, so they can help resolve any problems the customer is experiencing. Help Desk staff can see exactly what the customer was doing at the time of the problem and what the customer's PC environment looks like, including configuration files. With remote diagnostic software, staff can watch the screens and operate the keyboards and mice of any node on the LAN. Privacy concerns from Help Desk customers are addressed by including varying levels of security, such as requiring the end customer to allow entry.

Remote diagnostic tools are a time-and-resource saver and should be part of the tool kit of all but the smallest Help Desks. They give the Help Desk staff the ability to perform fast and accurate problem diagnosis from their own workstations without asking too many technical questions that the customer might not be able to answer and without having to rely on the customer's version of what happened.

Internet Access

Various components of a Help Desk management system can be made available via the Internet through the use of Internet access software, which may take the form of a Help Desk system option or a third-party plug-in. This software typically gives customers access to external knowledge bases and internal documents, such as manuals in word processing format, so they can obtain their own problem resolutions. Customers can also create and inquire against call tickets. Remote Help Desk analysts can access call information, view call history, and perform other Help Desk management functions regardless of their location. Some versions of this software also offer the ability to create and distribute Web pages.

Asset Management Tools

An asset management system automatically tracks hardware and software that is connected to a network. It collects extensive information, including details on applications and system software, hardware configuration, memory, hard drives, boards, hard drive utilization, setup options, and configuration files. The information collected is stored in an asset database. The system can remove illegal software and keep track of software usage to help ensure that adequate (but not excessive) licensing is maintained. Warranty information and current ownership information can be maintained. Asset management systems may also include a financial component that does some book and tax value calculations against the database of asset information. Some asset software allows access to on-line vendor catalogs for ordering of new equipment or checking prices. Even details on user rights and spare parts can be tracked.

Reports from the asset database can be issued by node, customer, or type of equipment and can usually be heavily customized. Reports can be used to help solve network problems related to hardware and software configurations, plan upgrades, management of maintenance contracts, tracking of warranties, and managing of software licensing compliance.

Asset management software can be set up to run at predetermined times and can inventory the assets of some or all of a network at any one time. Some versions have the ability to inventory portions of a PC each time the user of the PC logs onto the network. The system remembers where it was last time and continues. This way, the customer does not have to wait while the software does a complete inventory. The software can also be used on individual workstations that are not part of a network to give the same information.

Management Aids

This section discusses the role of Help Desks in change and work order management, scheduling, and performance analysis.

Change Management

More and more, Help Desks are becoming involved in the IT change management process and some are actually leading it. Change management software enables control of the change management process across departments, with facilities for ensuring that the appropriate approvals are received and milestones are achieved before allowing any change to go into the production environment.

Work Order Management

The work order management plug-in typically allows a Help Desk analyst to create a work order right from the call record, automatically updates asset inventory with any changes, and keeps track of all time spent on on-site resolution.

Forecasting/Scheduling

Forecasting components include those that forecast customer demand and those that forecast staffing requirements. Software that forecasts customer demand can get very sophisticated, using historical data and neural networks to predict customer activity for a specific time period. If no historical data is available then information is gathered from the first day of use.

Components for forecasting staffing requirements typically use historical data, offer what-if analysis, and allow for fixed or variable multiple-staffing guidelines for each position. The software calculates the optimal staff coverage for any given time period. Staff guidelines are adjusted as business conditions change by special event, weekend, holiday, and so on.

Scheduling components allow Help Desk managers to schedule staff for a given period. Daily or weekly schedules can be created with input from factors such as employee preferences, availability, individual proficiencies, and work rules, including meal and rest breaks, overtime restrictions, and so on. Schedules are easily modified once they are created. Schedules can be created for rotating and split schedules, cross-utilization, and individual employees. The software can usually be set to warn of any scheduled overtime and to track days off. Various reporting and charting options are available.

Forecasting and scheduling software is typically designed for larger environments.

Performance Analysis

The performance analysis component of a Help Desk management system lets you analyze workload trends and compare staff availability to staff requirements. It can give you a customizable view, in report, chart, or record format, of exactly what is happening in your Help Desk at any time. It can show you how many calls are open, who has the largest queue, how the calls are distributed, how many calls are waiting, or any number of other activities.

Network Management Tools (Including Software Distribution)

Network management systems monitor the performance of all the components, or specific components, of a network and can flag occurrences of problems, degradation, or unusual activity. The more components your management system can monitor and the more information it can integrate, the more useful it will be to you.

Network activity can be watched from a workstation, and a graphic representation of the network will show where any problems, abnormalities, or degradations occur. Network management systems offer functions such as traffic monitoring, software distribution, storage management, and software license management. Some include components for managing assets and security, and others go even further and monitor workstation usage and application performance.

As a network management system runs, it continuously monitors a company's network looking for trouble spots. If it locates a problem, it can notify the appropriate person via E-mail or beeper and may even analyze the problem and use a case-based expert system to recommend a solution. Some network managers even take action to fix certain problems or allow staff to fix these problems from the network management workstation. Problems that can be detected include power problems, defective or broken cables, damaged connections, incompatible network interface cards, and nonfunctioning software routers.

Network management systems need to know what normal network behavior is so they can flag abnormal behavior. Staff can set thresholds defining normal behavior, or, in some cases, the system can watch the network for a defined period of time and define for itself what normal behavior is. After the definition period, the system will flag anything it did not previously encounter—for example, variations from normal network traffic volumes, virus activity, security breaches, and improper or damaged connections.

Network management systems allow potential problems or negative trends to be flagged and fixed before the network is affected, suspicious or unusual activity to be investigated before it becomes a problem, and problems to be identified as soon as they occur. They ensure that the network is running as efficiently as possible and that it is maintained and upgraded as necessary to handle any new software or increases in traffic. They make the network more stable and, as such, are a mandatory component of any mission-critical network.

Tools for Customer Training and Self-Help

Some Help Desk management systems include interactive computer-based tutorials that can be sent to customers via E-mail should a Help Desk analyst detect a training requirement in a call. Customers can view the tutorials at their own pace and keep them for future reference. Tutorials are available for many popular software products. Interactive computer-based tutorials can also be purchased separately. The possibilities for incorporating these tutorials into self-help applications are endless. For example, training can be incorporated into knowledge bases by including an option that lets customers download a tutorial on a specific topic that they would like more information on. Figure 6.3 illustrates typical Help Desk flow without any self-help options, while Figure 6.4 illustrates the flow that is possible once self-help options have been implemented. The following are some of the self-help options that can be offered:

Making knowledge bases or call databases accessible to customers so customers can find out the status of problems or can try to resolve their own problems

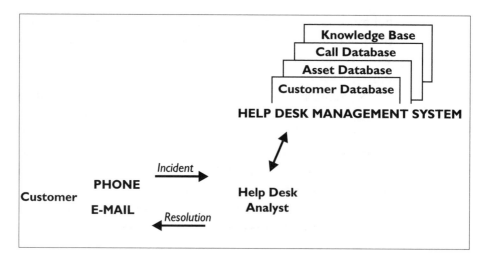

Figure 6.3 No self-help options.

Setting up interactive voice response (IVR) systems to let customers perform common requests such as terminal resets or to initiate fax-backs of problem resolutions or specific procedures

Making use of Internet or intranet Web sites to allow customers access to frequently asked questions or common problems and resolutions

Help Desk management systems also offer options for scheduling classroom training for those Help Desks that offer this service.

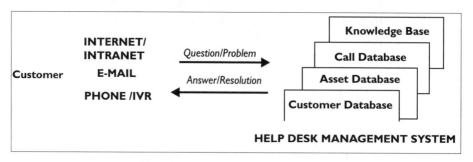

Figure 6.4 Self-help options for the customer.

Selecting Tools

Selecting Help Desk tools is not a trivial process. Some of the factors you need to take into account are as follows:

The information model for your Help Desk. This model identifies all of the information your Help Desk uses and how it is used. It shows the flow of information through your Help Desk and interfaces with other areas. It is tyically drawn as a flow chart. Your Help Desk tool must be able to support your information model, managing the information within it. If you don't have such a model for your Help Desk this might be the right time to create one.

What kind of reporting you need. If the Help Desk package you are considering does not meet your needs, can it be integrated with a reporting package? It is very frustrating to have all the information in a database and not be able to get it out in the format you need.

What functions you want to integrate (now or later) with your basic call management system. If you decide you want asset management, but not right now, you want to make sure that your system either offers an asset management component or will allow integration with someone else's asset management component.

The technical environment you have, including databases supported, operating environment, and so on. You need to understand how any tools you are considering will fit into your organization's technical architecture.

How many people will have access to the Help Desk tool. Some Help Desk management systems are designed for smaller Help Desks with one or a few users, others are more robust (and more expensive) and are designed for large support centers.

What price you can afford. The prices of Help Desk management systems usually reflect functionality and vary considerably. This might be your first level of constraint.

The *Microsoft Sourcebook for the Help Desk* (Microsoft Press, 1995) gives a good description of the process involved in selecting support software, including sections on establishing criteria and evaluating options.

Be prepared to spend a good three months in the process of tool selection. The phrase "select in haste, repent in leisure" applies with a vengeance. Take your time. Understand what you are getting. The wrong tool may do more damage than good. You can get feedback on specific tools from organizations that are already using these tools via one of the sources mentioned in the section "Forums for Learning and Idea Exchange" earlier in this chapter. Another good starting point is an article in the March 1997 issue of *Service News* by Cinda Daly titled "Help Desk Software Vendors, Understanding the Product Features Can Aid in Tool Selection."

Key Points Covered in This Chapter

Major changes in the world of Help Desk tools since the first edition of this book include the following:

- A dramatic increase in the number of vendors supplying Help Desk products
- An increase in the functionality and integration of the tools
- The emergence of the Internet, which has many aspects of support

A change that was expected but did not happen was major growth in the use of expert systems.

Forums for exchanging ideas and information include organizations such as the Help Desk Institute, the Software Support Professionals Association, Support Services in Canada, the Association of Support Professionals, and the Help Desk User Group. Each has a Web site. Also on the Internet are an FAQ site for Help Desk topics, various discussion

groups, vendor sites offering self-help, and magazine sites offering searchable archives of articles and information.

Tools for communication include a simple white board, E-mail, voice mail, and electronic displays hung in customer areas. Help Desk management tools offer, at the most basic level, facilities for logging, tracking, routing, and escalating calls; reporting features; and a call database. Various other functions might be part of the original system or may be purchased as plug-ins, sometimes from a different vendor.

Computer telephony integration (CTI) has given the Help Desk tools that allow it to make use of functions such as having customer data arrive on a Help Desk analyst's monitor at the same time that the actual customer call arrives. Other telephone-related technologies include ACD, automated attendant, and IVR. All of these may be part of CTI applications.

Problem resolution on the Help Desk is made easier with tools such as knowledge bases and expert systems, remote diagnostic software, and the Internet. Knowledge bases and expert systems include simple text retrieval systems, which can be built by the Help Desk and/or purchased prepackaged from various vendors, and the more complex decision tree systems, case-based systems, and troubleshooting systems.

Remote diagnostic software lets you take over control of a customer's PC without leaving your own desk. Many vendors of Help Desk tools provide software that allows their products to be accessed from anywhere via the Internet. This means that Help Desk analysts who were not local to the Help Desk can have access to the same tools as the local analysts. Customers could be given access to Help Desk tools such as knowledge bases, problem logging, or problem status inquiry via the Internet.

Asset management tools give the Help Desk the ability to control assets, monitor asset trends and quality, and pick up up-to-date asset information for a customer whenever that customer calls. Asset management tools automatically take inventory and gather information on almost all hardware and software assets that are part of a network. The software will also run on standalone units to give the same detailed configuration information.

Management aids for the Help Desk include tools such as change

management, demand and resource work order scheduling, forecasting, scheduling, and performance analysis. Change management tools allow the Help Desk to be actively involved in or to control the change management process, even when it crosses departments. Work order scheduling allows work orders to be automatically generated from a call and then put into the work order schedule. Forecasting tools can be used to forecast customer demand and/or the optimal number of staff required on the Help Desk for any period of time. Scheduling tools allow a Help Desk manager to schedule staff based on expected call load, various work restrictions, proficiencies, staff preferences, and so on.

Network management tools monitor the health of a network and warn of any impending or actual problems. These tools can include components such as those that distribute software, manage storage, and manage software licensing.

Customer training and self-help are important aspects of Help Desk service. Some Help Desk management systems include interactive computer-based training modules that can be E-mailed to customers. These modules are also available as standalone units and can be incorporated into many areas of self-help, such as knowledge bases. Other possibilities for self-help on the Help Desk include IVR systems that allow the customer to resolve common problems or request fax-back information and Internet or intranet sites that provide FAQs and knowledge bases of common problems/resolutions.

The Internet: Challenge and Opportunity

The Internet has been described as everything from the solution to most of the world's problems to a useless, overhyped waste of time and money. A large variance in opinion. The truth is, the Internet probably won't ever solve all the world's problems, or even most of them, but it is an incredible communication tool that provides endless opportunities for your Help Desk and for your customers. It's definitely worth your time and your money. The key word for describing the Internet is *tool*. Any tool can be misused. Take a lawn mower, for instance. If you don't know how to use it, or you are simply careless, it could cut your foot off. But that hasn't stopped millions of households from owning one and using it successfully.

Related to the Internet are two other types of networks, intranets and extranets. An intranet is an internal Internet, accessible only within the confines of an organization. For internal Help Desks, an intranet web site is an extremely useful communications medium that can bring a significant decrease in the number of calls and help customers make better use of their technology. Chapter 8 covers the topic of setting up a Help Desk intranet web site. Intranets often contain information that an organization does not want the public to see. Sometimes, however, some of the information on an intranet needs to be made accessible to some external resources or customers. An extranet is a network in which selected external customers of an organization are allowed access to a portion of the organization's intranet. An example is Federal Express's extranet, which allows customers to access information on the status of their packages. Customers actually access Fedex's own internal databases and systems.

In This Chapter

In this chapter we're going to explore the opportunities that the Internet opens up for your Help Desk and the associated challenges it presents. The topics that will be covered are as follows:

- Opportunities
- Challenges
- Getting the most out of the Internet

Opportunities

The Internet offers the Help Desk numerous opportunities for improving function and service. Among these are the following:

Access to a huge knowledge base of support information and a wealth of industry reference material and product information from around the world. Information can be referenced any time, anywhere. Vendor sites offer self-help for specific products and numerous technical sites offer suggestions, problem resolutions, and answers to frequently asked questions (FAQs).

Easy, quick, and (virtually) free communication with the rest of the world. Help Desk staff can talk to their counterparts in organizations all over the world. Discussion groups and news servers make it much easier to find someone in a similar situation or using a specific product. All Help Desk staff have the opportunity to exchange ideas and experiences, not only those few who are fortunate enough to be able to attend conferences.

Ability to transmit new software, updates, and fixes electronically and to download the same. If a problem requires a software update or patch, the software can be downloaded from the vendor site almost instantly. Similarly, if a remote customer requires an update or patch, it can be transmitted quickly via the Internet.

Ability to provide customers with on-line access to self-help and a central repository of information. The Web is a great publishing tool. You can make it easy for customers to access up-to-date standards, policies, procedures (e.g., steps to go through to order a PC), hints and tips, and lists of frequently asked questions. Organizations such as educational institutions find this feature a tremendous help in providing a widely distributed and large customer base (e.g., students and faculty) with the information and help it needs to make the best use of technology.

Ability to gather information from customers. Customer surveys or various other feedback mechanisms can be put on a Web page and input gathered as customers fill the information out and send it. Surveys can be included in any Web page to gather feedback.

Ability to access Help Desk software from anywhere. Many Help Desk management systems are now Web-enabled to allow access to the software via the Internet. Remote Help Desk staff, working anywhere, can access the software to log, track, assign, or escalate calls. Customers can access call databases via the Internet to check on call status. Customers and Help Desk staff can access knowledge bases to resolve problems.

Ability for support functions in even the smallest organizations to take advantage of all of the opportunities listed here. Owning a Web site can be very inexpensive. If you're a small company, many Internet access providers offer special packages based on your level of estimated traffic and will host your site for a very reasonable price.

All these opportunities translate into reduced calls to the Help Desk, improved service for the calls that do get through, and more information for improvement initiatives. Making use of the Web is inexpensive, largely because you are taking advantage of technology that is already in place. Web applications typically offer a fast and high return on investment.

Challenges

Of course, all this opportunity does not come without a price. As with any tool, there are certain caveats that you need to be aware of when using the Internet. Some of the challenges that Help Desks face in using the Internet are as follows:

Rampant growth, skyrocketing expectations. Help Desks are all of a sudden finding themselves with a new product to support, one that is rolling out at a rate beyond their control. A whole new set of customer service issues exist for Help Desks supporting Web sites. Addressing these can be tough when you are not prepared for the demand. For example, if you offer customers access to your Help Desk via the Web and you are suddenly inundated with E-mail, all requesting immediate responses, many of your customers are going to be disappointed.

Security/confidentiality of transmitted data. Anything that travels across the Internet is exposed to the danger of being tampered with. Anything you offer via the Internet must have a security component. Your organization probably already uses firewalls and encryption.

Unreliable information. Information taken from the Internet is "use at your own risk." Just as you can't believe everything you read on paper, you can't believe everything you read on the Internet. Opinions are often hard to differentiate from facts.

High volume of information. Finding what you want can be difficult. The information is there but getting at it can be frustrating. No nice indexing system (like in a library) exists, at least, not yet.

Licensing and validity issues for data/software downloaded by customers. It is so easy to download software from the Internet that people often forget the fact that some of it might not be legal, either because it may be a pirated copy, evaluation copy, or shareware that needs to be paid for. Help Desks that look after licensing have more to do now.

Exposure to viruses. Viruses are getting more and more clever and harder to detect, some even hiding in macros. The Internet makes it easy for people to download software and exchange documents, and they are doing so in incredible numbers. The risk of virus exposure gets higher with each item downloaded. A reliable source does not mean that the item has no virus. Extra precautions must be taken to prevent Internet users from accidentally accepting a virus.

Increased complexity for the environment being supported. The Internet, as another component to support, has added a level of complexity to the environment being supported. There's more software to support, and there is the service of the Internet provider to worry about.

I will not deal here with the issue of people running amok and using the Internet to access pornography or other information that you'd rather not have them looking at during business hours. That is a people management issue, *not* a technology management issue.

Getting the Most Out of the Internet

How well a Help Desk can take advantage of the opportunities the Internet offers and manage the challenges that go along with them depends on the specific relationship the Help Desk has with the Internet. Yours might have one or several. These relationships include the following:

1. **The Internet as another product to support.** Customers use the Internet along with other supported software and call the Help Desk when they run into trouble.

2. **An organization's Internet Web site to support.** Your organization has a Web site on the Internet. The Help Desk supports a Web site through which customers can log calls, ask questions, ask for help and/or get help themselves.

3. **A small business Web site to support.** You wear all the hats (including the Help Desk hat) for your business. A Web site allows you to do this.

4. **Internet access to support.** In this category are the Help Desks of Internet providers.

5. **The Internet as a knowledge base.** The Help Desk uses the Internet as a reference tool, a knowledge base, to solve problems and get information about products. The Help Desk might also need to support customers who are using the Internet as a knowledge base as part of their work.

6. **The Internet as a distribution tool** for transmitting and receiving software, upgrades, and documents. The Help Desk might need to support customers who are also using the Internet this way.

7. **The Internet as a means of accessing Help Desk management software.** The Help Desk uses the Internet to access the Help Desk management system from remote locations. Customers might also use this feature to log or query the status of their own problems.

8. **The Internet as a publishing tool.** The Help Desk uses the Internet to publish information and documents, for customers, for themselves, for other support areas.

We're going to take a look at each of these more closely to see how in each case you can take full advantage of the opportunities while managing the challenges. A word about management: Too often concern about misusing the Internet is so high that too many restrictions are put into place, effectively choking many of the benefits that could be realized. Don't suffocate your Internet users.

The Internet as Another Product to Support

Your customers use the Internet. As with every other product you support, it is in your best interests to make sure they know how to use the Internet and are aware of standards, security and virus issues, and any organizational rules governing Internet use. Your challenges are to ensure that customers have the information they need to make the best use of the Internet and to make customers aware of the potential for security infringements, virus contamination, copyright violations, and exposure of any data traveling the Internet. You also need to try to reduce the number of calls generated by the customers' use of the Internet.

Some suggestions to help you manage these challenges are as follows:

Create standards, or champion the process of standards creation, for Web browser software. The more standardized your customers are, the easier they will be to support.

Treat the Internet software as you would any other. Track its use, keep it up to date, and offer training for it. If you can't offer training, outsource it to someone who can or let people know where to get training. You might be able to purchase on-line computer-based tutorials for the topics you want to train in. Your customers could download these from your Web site.

Start one or more Internet focus groups so customers can share information about Internet use with their colleagues.

Offer people self-help via your Help Desk Internet/intranet Web site. Besides the tutorials just mentioned, this site could include the following:

- Answers to frequently asked questions

- Hints and tips for using the Internet more effectively or for resolving commonly occurring problems

- A series of how-to articles or tutorials on tasks that customers are able to perform in your environment, for example, how to download data

- Links to other sites that contain information or help that would be of use to your customers

- Security policies, procedures for virus checking, cautions about data exposure, and cautions about copyright infringements

- Any restrictions that your organization has placed on Internet use

See also the sections titled "The Internet as a Knowledge Base," "The Internet as a Distribution Tool," and "The Internet as a Means of Accessing Help Desk Management Software" later in this chapter.

Supporting an Organization's Internet Web Site

Your organization has a Web site, and your Help Desk supports some of the products that your company offers through the site. Your customers contact you via E-mail. The challenges for you include estimating the number of problems/requests you are going to have to answer, meeting any support response times you have marketed, and keeping up with the changing business. You want to make sure that customer expectations are in line with your service; otherwise, you may end up with irate customers, and your organization's business may suffer. The following paragraphs discuss some things you can do to manage these challenges.

If possible, set up an automated reply to each customer request letting customers know that you got their request and giving them an estimated response time. This really helps keep customer expectations in line with reality. Of course, your response had better be within the time promised on the automated reply message or you are back to irate customers.

Offer as much self-help as possible. Unload whatever support you can. Offer valuable links to other Web sites (if you don't have the answer on-line maybe someone else does), FAQs, hints and tips, procedures for specific tasks, even access to a knowledge base if this makes sense. You might even offer a library of tutorials that customers can download. The tutorials can be text only; or text and voice; or text, voice, and video, depending on what kind of equipment you and your customers have. You can develop simple how-to tutorials yourself or purchase prepackaged tutorials.

Whenever your organization wants to add a new service to its Web site, get involved. If it involves the Help Desk, pilot it first to see what volume of responses you can expect. You can offer the service to a select group of customers, giving them a special password and/or customer ID that they need to enter to gain access. They would simply click on some kind of pilot service icon and then be prompted for their password and/or ID. This would give you a good chance to get an idea of the response you'll get so you can prepare for it before releasing the service to all of your customers.

Do not promise what you cannot deliver. Take time to research expected customer traffic and the load you can handle so you do not set unrealistic customer expectations. If you have a heavy workload, let any promised response times reflect that workload. A poor reputation, once earned, is hard to get rid of.

Keep Help Desk staff trained in all the products you support. Don't let training lapse because of time constraints.

If you have service-level agreements with your customers, your response times have already been set for you. You should be using a solid Help Desk management system that will automatically log each customer's problem or request, tell you what the target response/ resolution times are, warn you when you are getting close to missing response times, and track and measure your response and resolution times.

Supporting a Small Business Web Site

You are the Help Desk (and probably the salesperson, the president, and employee) of a small business. You have a small budget. The Internet can work as your employee for almost nothing. You can set up a Web site where customers can get support and order your products. Even if you aren't there to answer the phone, you can still be offering support and taking orders.

Talk to your local Internet providers about setting up a domain name (your company's identifier on the Web) and a virtual Web site. The address of your Web site will typically be www.your domain name. Internet providers offer all kinds of services specifically geared toward small businesses. Be careful about selecting a provider. Don't select solely on the basis of cost. You want to go with a provider who offers good service and support and who is going to be around for a while. Ask business associates and friends for references.

Some of the challenges that face a small business Web site include keeping it up to date, handling unexpected volumes, and managing customer expectations. Some suggestions to help you manage these challenges while taking advantage of opportunities your Web site offers include the following:

> Schedule time near the end of each month (or more often if possible and if it makes sense) to update your Web site. Make sure it actually happens.

> Offer as much self-help as possible, via FAQs, procedures, or training documents, for each product or service you support. Make use of training material and problem-solving information that already exists. Have a list of links to other Web sites that customers might find useful.

> Respond to all customers. If economically feasible, purchase technology that will automatically acknowledge each E-mail you receive.

> Be very careful about keeping your promises in line with what you can actually deliver. Don't set false customer expectations. If you have a heavy workload, let any promised response times reflect that workload. A poor reputation can ruin your business.

> If you are considering offering a new service, pilot it first to a select group of customers so you can estimate the E-mail volume it will generate.

For small businesses, an Internet site is often the whole business. It is worth taking care of.

Supporting Internet Access

You are the Help Desk for an Internet provider. Your customers are all external. Some of the challenges you face are the following:

> **Volume of calls.** Your organization is always looking to increase the number of subscribers. Chances are you're going to hear from a large percentage of them.

> **Wide range in the knowledge/expertise of callers.** Some of your customers know nothing beyond how to turn a PC on; others know a lot more about the technology than you do. You must service both extremes.

Range of problems/calls. When customers call, the problem may not be with their access setup or software. It could be a problem with the modem or modem setup, it could be a problem with PC configuration, it could be a compatibility issue—it could be just about anything. You are sometimes left trying to solve a problem that really belongs to another vendor.

Lack of any standards in the hardware and software the customers are using. The customers are external, and you have absolutely no control over what kind of computers they have and what software, such as Web browsers, they are using.

The best thing you can do to manage these challenges and keep your customers satisfied is to eliminate, as much as possible, the need for them to call you. Some suggestions for doing this are as follows:

1. **Give the customers as many self-help options as possible.** Your customer base is growing, and you want to eliminate as many calls as you can. On your organization's Web site, offer a support area for customers. This support area can include information such as:

   how and what to do to get Internet access up and running

   FAQs about Internet access

   links to sites with information on various things you can do on the Internet (e.g., write HTML [Hypertext Markup Language] code, use search engines, etc.)

   instructions or procedures for performing some tasks such as downloading software, setting up a Web site (some providers offer customers free Web sites), registering a domain name, setting up a virtual E-mail ID, setting up a virtual Web site, and so on. For a good example, check out the Interlog Web site at www .interlog.com.

2. **Offer training courses.** If you don't want to be in the training business, outsource this or make some kind of deal with various training providers that already have the kind of training you need. You might be able to have them offer training to your cus-

tomers for special prices. The more your customers know how to do, the less they will need to call you.

3. **Offer a newsletter that lets customers know about new services.** Don't expect them to keep checking your Web site. E-mail it to them. Explain any service interruptions. If they feel you understand what caused an interruption, they will be more confident about it not happening again. If they know about upcoming service interruptions they might not call about them when they happen.

4. **Don't skimp on Help Desk staff.** Hire top-notch people who are good communicators. It is not easy to tell someone that the problem is with the modem they just purchased rather than their Internet access.

5. **Don't skimp on staff training.** Keep Help Desk staff trained on all new Web technology.

6. **Don't promise what you cannot deliver.** If you've just had an unexpected influx of customers (e.g., another provider has gone out of business and you have received some of their abandoned customers) adjust your promised response times accordingly. Keep a close eye on the business so that, wherever possible, you do not make promises that you just cannot keep.

7. **Track and use call statistics religiously.** Know your volumes so you can plan your support staffing. You might consider investing in demand forecasting and staff scheduling software.

8. **Pilot new services to selected customers.** Get an idea of likely response so you can staff up accordingly.

Be on a constant lookout for ideas. Check out competitors' Web sites to see what they're offering their customers, especially those services that will reduce calls. You might get some good ideas.

The Internet as a Knowledge Base

Your Help Desk uses the Internet as a knowledge base to search for problem resolutions and information on new products. Your challenges include the sheer volume of information available (i.e., how do you find what you need?) and discerning between fact and opinion.

The following are some tips to help you make the best use of the information on the Internet:

Register with discussion groups that deal with topics of interest to you. If the volume of mail proves to be too great, check out other means for getting the information, for example, news servers, digest versions of the discussions, or searchable archives.

Register with Web sites that provide information of interest to you so you get regular updates or newsletters.

Gather all the sites that you find most useful and make them part of your team reference site (see Figure 7.1) so they are not lost and are easily accessible. You can organize them in any way that makes sense to you. You can even set your browser software to make your reference site your home site so you start off your Internet session with your most useful links. Formalize and rotate the responsibility for gathering information and updating this site.

Check out the "new and interesting sites" listed in the various online and paper computer journals that you read.

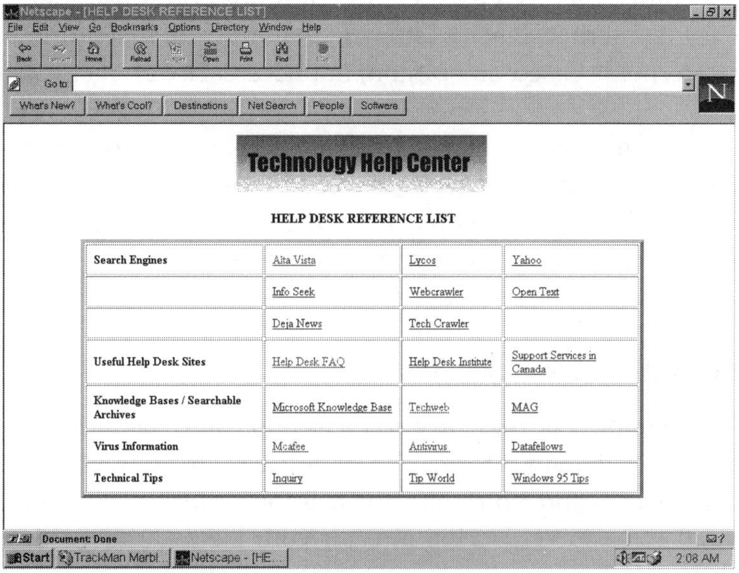

Figure 7.1 **Set up your most useful links on a reference site.**

Make sure everyone on your Help Desk is well trained in using the Internet, specifically, how to use search engines, what common search tools are available, and what they are capable of (strengths, weaknesses). This will be a small time investment for a large payback.

Set up some guidelines for using information based on how credible it is. Don't completely discount sources that are opinion only; you might get some great ideas from these, but mark your favorite sources as either factual or opinion.

The following are some tips to help your customers make the best use of the information on the Internet:

Create a list of useful Web sites (based on input from customers) and put it on your Help Desk Web site. Encourage customers to contribute to this list.

Offer short tutorials on how to search for information, what search engines are available, where they are, and how to use them. This might be as simple as documents that customers access from your Web site, or it might involve classroom training (you could outsource this activity). Include cautions about using information from the Internet. Teach customers that much of the information on the Internet is based on opinion, not necessarily on fact.

The Internet contains much valuable, free information that could contribute significantly to the productivity of your organization. You should do whatever you can to take best advantage of this opportunity. Make sure that you and your customers know how to get the information you and they will need.

The Internet as a Distribution Tool

Your Help Desk regularly receives and/or sends software updates. You might download information or software from other sites to use on the Help Desk, and you might pass information on to customers. This instant accessibility is a big plus for your Help Desk, making it possible to decrease the time it takes to resolve problems. Your customers might also have this capability. Your challenges include the security of confidential data, the licensing of downloaded software, copyright infringement, and viruses.

To ensure that you are getting/sending what you need without getting into trouble with bugs, hackers, or the law, you may want to do the following:

Understand the security measures and infrastructures your organization has in place for information coming in from the Internet. Follow all rules and procedures.

Set up policies on your Help Desk to use virus checkers consistently. Make them easy to access. You might even set up a download area and have the virus checker run off of that automatically.

Keep virus-checking software up to date. Some vendors of virus-detecting software allow you to register at their Web sites to receive automatic notification of new virus information and any software updates that are available. Check to see if the vendor of the software you are using offers any of these services.

Set up policies regarding licensing. Treat downloaded software as purchased software. If you need to buy a license, do so. You should be setting an example for your customers, and getting caught with licensing violations is embarrassing for the whole company.

Don't publish indiscriminately information that you find on the Internet. Check copyright concerns with your legal department. Rather than publishing the document, give the location on the Web or simply include a link to the location if you are publishing on-line.

The following suggestions will help you ensure that your *customers* are getting/sending what they need without getting into trouble with bugs, hackers, or the law:

If your customers have the ability to download information and software from the Internet, get and use asset management software if you don't already have it. It will find (and eliminate, if you wish) occurrences of illegal software.

Work with your organization to set up policies for your customers for downloading information from the Internet. You don't want to take potential benefits away from customers but neither do you want to expose your organization to legal action due to unlicensed software, copyright infringement, or data destruction caused by viruses.

Work with your organization to set up policies for the kinds of information that can be shared with other organizations and the kinds of information that is confidential and needs to be kept within the organization. If your customers have Internet access, they can share documents or information with anyone else on the Internet. They need to be made aware of what they can and cannot share so they don't inadvertently give away confidential data.

Work with your organization's legal department to set up some policies regarding the distribution of information published on the Internet. Customers may be distributing information that belongs to someone else and may be infringing on copyrights.

Publish a "getting started on the Internet" package for your customers (see Figure 7.2). Include it on your Help Desk Web site. Information in the package could include the following:

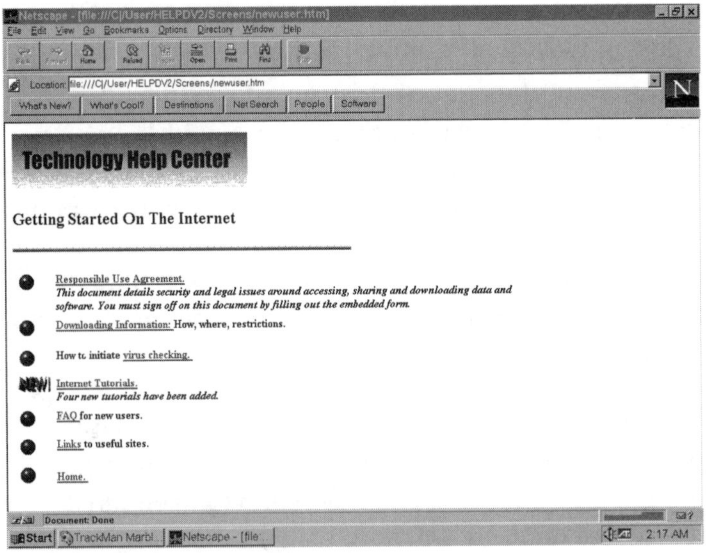

Figure 7.2 Publish "getting started on the Internet" information for your customers.

- Security measures and infrastructures your organization has in place for information coming in from the Internet and any associated rules and procedures.

- Rules for downloading information. These will depend on how tightly your organization wants to control this activity.

- Information on where viruses can occur and procedures for virus checking.

- Information on licensing issues. Let people know that licensing violations are a punishable offense and that your asset management software will uncover any such violations (if you have asset management software).

- Information on the legality of distributing information downloaded from the Internet.

- Information on confidentiality of data, on what they can and cannot share with people outside of the organization.

The Internet is a great resource, and you want to make sure that, where possible, you do not cut off access to this resource in your attempt to control it.

The Internet as a Means for Accessing Help Desk Management Software

Several Help Desk management software vendors offer options that will allow you to access the software via the Internet. This means that you can access the software from anywhere. If you have remote Help Desk analysts who may travel from site to site, they can update call information as they go and make use of all the tools the Help Desk management system offers. Customers can access this software also to log their own calls, to check on calls, and to use the knowledge base to try to solve their own problems. This means fewer calls to the Help Desk.

The challenges to your Help Desk here stem from the fact that you are giving customers access to Help Desk management information. In order to ensure they make best use of it, you will want to take the following steps:

Ensure customers know how to use the software, especially the knowledge base. Have them attend training or send them simple tutorials via E-mail.

Ensure customers understand security restrictions, password usage, and the potential exposure of any information they're passing on.

Have some kind of automated response to acknowledge your receipt of a log or an E-mail from the customer. The customer will be sure the information was received.

The more your customers understand how to use the system, the more confidence they will have in it and the better use they will make of it, meaning fewer calls for you.

The Internet as a Publishing Tool

Information publishing is probably the biggest win for the Internet and intranets. The return on investment is proving to be very quick, and returns of one thousand percent are not uncommon. People simply become more productive when they know more about what they're doing. Publishing can also be used for Help Desk marketing, to communicate performance, and to teach customers about their technology. Information that a Help Desk might want to publish includes the following:

Technical hints and tips and/or FAQs

Information about the technological environment, for example, upcoming changes, updates, and so on

Policies and procedures, such as how to order a PC and security policies

Short training tutorials—these can be as simple as a library of how-to documents.

Forms that customers may need to fill out to order equipment—you can even make these on-line forms so no paper needs to change hands

Customer surveys and survey results

Help Desk performance

The challenges here are understanding what customers need in terms of what to publish, organizing information, and keeping information up to date.

Following are some suggestions for publishing information for Help Desk customers:

Create a Help Desk Web site as a central source for information. It doesn't matter where on the Web the information is actually stored; you simply include a link to it.

For information such as hints and tips, or FAQs, have a "New this month" option (or whatever time period makes sense for you) so that people can see what you have added most recently.

Organize information in ways that people would naturally access it. Go to your customers to get this information. For example, if you are building an FAQ list, don't just build one humongous FAQ; break it down by subject. Check the distribution of your calls, or ask your customers to find out what these subjects should be.

If you need to publish a very important and/or time-sensitive piece of information, don't count on people going to your site to read it. Send them an E-mail letting them know that an important update has been made.

Wherever you have control over content of information, be concise. Just because the information is on-line doesn't mean that people should be forced to wade through pages of garbage or fluff just to get to the key information.

Keep the information up to date. Don't leave the responsibility open ("Update the FAQ whenever you run across an interesting question") or it won't happen. No one will have time. Assign the responsibility on a rotating basis. Have the assigned person collect data from Help Desk stats, from customers, and from fellow Help Desk employees; organize it and perform the Web site update.

The Web is full of examples of Help Desks that have published information. A good starting point is the Help Desk FAQ, described in Chapter 6. It includes links to the Help Desks of several educational institutions. Chapter 8 also includes examples and screen shots from a Help Desk Web site.

Key Points Covered in This Chapter

The Internet is an incredible communication tool that provides endless opportunities for your Help Desk and for your customers. Related to the Internet are two other types of networks, intranets and extranets. An intranet is an internal Internet, accessible only within the confines of an organization. An extranet is a network in which selected external customers of an organization are allowed access to a portion of the organization's intranet.

Internet opportunities for Help Desks include the following:

Access to a huge knowledge base of support information and a wealth of industry reference material and product information from around the world

Easy, quick, and (virtually) free communication with the rest of the world

The ability to transmit new software, updates, and fixes electronically

The ability to provide customers with on-line access to self-help and a central repository of information

The ability to gather information from customers

The ability to access Help Desk software from anywhere

The ability for support functions in even the smallest organizations to take advantage of all the opportunities just listed

The challenges of the Internet for the Help Desk include the following:

Rampant growth, skyrocketing expectations

Security/confidentiality of transmitted data

Information taken from the Internet is "use at your own risk"

Finding what you want can be difficult

Licensing and validity issues for data/software downloaded by customers

Exposure to viruses

Increased complexity for the environment being supported

Some key tips for managing challenges while taking advantage of the opportunities include the following:

Create a Help Desk Web site and update it regularly.

Offer customers as much self-help as possible (via your Web site), including tutorials on specific tasks, FAQs, links to sites that might help customers with their problems, and perhaps even access to your knowledge base.

Work to standardize Web software.

Make sure both you and your customers understand how to use search engines.

Keep track of useful Help Desk sites for both you and your customers.

Join relevant Internet discussion groups and/or register with Web sites that will send you information updates on any topics you are interested in.

Keep Help Desk staff trained and up to date on Web technology and use.

Work with your organization to define policies for security, downloading data, distributing information taken from the Internet, and virus control. Market these to your customers.

Manage expectations of customers being supported via a Web site. Don't promise what you cannot deliver. Adjust your response times to reflect reality. Respond to each customer.

CHAPTER EIGHT

Setting Up a Help Desk Internet/Intranet Site

Typically, a Help Desk intranet site is accessible only to the customers within an organization while a Help Desk Internet site is accessible to anyone outside the organization. The implementation(s) you choose for your Help Desk will depend on the nature of your organization and the technology it has in place. For example, educational institutions typically choose to implement Help Desk Internet sites because of the large and scattered customer base they support. Anyone can access the information without any kind of ID or password or registration process—representing a huge administrative savings for the institution and an advantage for students and staff, who can access the Help Desk site anytime from anywhere, without any special permission. The principles behind intranet and Internet sites are similar.

In This Chapter

In this chapter we will discuss the process of setting up a Help Desk site on the Internet or an intranet. The following topics will be covered:

- Benefits of a Help Desk Web site
- Planning your site
- Information and functions to include
- Designing your site
- Marketing your site
- Maintaining your site
- A few references

The purpose of this chapter is to give you ideas for your Web site and to make you aware of the opportunities a Web site offers, not to teach you Web design or to go into any technical detail. I will refrain from spouting HTML code at you.

Chapter 15 contains an example and explanation of a Help Desk intranet site. Many of the ideas in this chapter are illustrated there.

Benefits of a Help Desk Web Site

Ultimately, the purpose of a Help Desk Web site is to eliminate calls. You want to give your customers as much information and help as you can via your Web site so they don't have to call you. A Help Desk Web site can do the following:

Help customers use technology more effectively via hints and tips, options, and tutorials.

Offer customers the opportunity to solve their own problems via FAQs and access to knowledge bases.

Help ensure that customers understand all organizational policies, standards, procedures, and cautions for technology use (especially true for internal customers). Information on licensing violations, copyright infringements, and virus exposure can all be communicated to the customer.

Increase the information and knowledge available to customers by offering links to helpful Web sites.

Allow customers to log service requests and problems.

Measure customers' perspectives on Help Desk performance by gathering customer feedback from Web site surveys. Results can be published on the site. The Help Desk can use this information to improve service and performance.

Keep customers informed of events in the technological environment. This might include upgrades, fixes, scheduled service interruptions, and so on.

Market new or changing Help Desk services.

Market Help Desk performance.

Planning Your Site

Unless you are a very small organization, you probably have your own Web server where you store all of your Web site information. If you're adding a Web site, you may need to get Web support or network groups involved. They will want to look at your design and see your traffic estimates.

If you're a small organization and don't have your own server, you will use the server of your Internet access provider. The access provider will give you instructions on how to upload your Web site to its server and how to make any future changes. The provider will also charge you a basic fee, which gives you a certain amount of space on the server and allows for a certain amount of traffic to your site. Should you exceed either of the limits your fee will increase.

The security of the data you store on your Web server should be a concern. Even if the data isn't confidential it wouldn't do to have someone come in and destroy the server configuration. If your organization is using its own server, it should have stringent security measures in place. If your web site is on an intranet, your network or web support people need to make sure that the intranet is not accessible from the Internet. A reputable Internet provider storing your web site on its server will have a high level of security to protect the data from unauthorized access. In both cases, security considerations will most likely be out of your hands, but if you are concerned about the safety of your data you need to ensure adequate security measures are in place. If your Internet access provider does not offer adequate protection then find a provider that does.

Who Should Be Involved

There are several factors that determine who needs to be involved in getting your Web site up and running:

Where the Help Desk site is—intranet or Internet. There are generally fewer restrictions on intranet sites since they will only be seen by employees. Once your site is open to the public, more people may want to get involved since the reputation of the organization may be affected.

Whether or not the Help Desk site is linked to any other site, such as an organization's home site. If your site will be linked to another site, chances are you will have to follow some kind of standard design template, and actual page design will be out of your hands. You may have to work through a Web support group.

Whether or not the Help Desk site is supporting products the company produces. If the Help Desk does support products the company produces—such as software—management, marketing, and development groups may want to be involved. Support of the product is a product in itself, and careful thought needs to be given to its design, content, and marketing. These things may need to be integrated with other initiatives the organization is carrying out.

Whether or not the Help Desk site is providing a chargeable service. If the site does charge for service (e.g., you may enter only if you have an account) you may need extra security measures, and you may need to get finance, management, and marketing groups involved.

In all cases, you want to get your customers involved in the design and content of your site. Customers can tell you what kind of help is most important to them, and the best way to flush out all of the problems with a site design is to give it to a few customers for a while. Web sites are so easy to update that you can go through several design iterations in no time at all.

Information and Functions to Include

You want your site to eliminate the need for customers to call your Help Desk. Your call management system statistics will tell you the reasons for most of your calls. Try to put resolutions for these on the Help Desk. Talk to your customers to find out what information they would like to see on your Web site, but be very careful not to promise (or to give the impression that you promised) something you cannot deliver.

You may want to use your site to do the following:

Publish documents and updates.

Provide or suggest training.

Help customers resolve problems.

Communicate changes.

Market performance.

Accept problem/request logs.

Gather customer feedback.

Gather information about your customers.

Tell customers about your Help Desk.

See Figure 8.1 to see what one Help Desk Web site (from Interlog Internet Services) offers.

Publish Documents and Updates

The kinds of documents you may want to publish include the following:

1. **Policies,** such as

   Security policies that lay out your customers' responsibilities in protecting technology assets and confidential data.

Internet use policies that describe any customer responsibilities and specific restrictions such as distribution of data found on the Internet.

2. **Terms and conditions for product use** (see Figure 8.2).

3. **Standards.** The hardware and software standards for your organization.

4. **Procedures.** Steps a customer has to go through to perform specific functions, such as ordering a PC.

5. **Service-level agreements.** You may also want to include your performance against service-level agreements.

Provide or Suggest Training

There are several ways to make training accessible to customers via your Web site:

Online tutorials. These could be simple documents that you create or buy, that deal with specific problems or how-to questions. Customers could select whichever one they wished to see, then simply view it. You could also add photos, sound, and even video depending on your environment. For an example of a simple but excellent six-part tutorial (on HTML tables), see www.canlink.com/helpdesk/.

Computer-based interactive training. Vendors offer a variety of prepackaged training modules on many aspects of the most popular software. You could make these accessible from your Web site so that customers could select the module they wished to view.

Tutorials. You could include links to other sites that offer tutorials and how-to information (see Figure 8.3).

Schedules. Offer schedules and course descriptions for classroom training that you (or an outsourcer) provide. You could even offer a registration option so that customers can sign up from your Web site.

Help Customers Resolve Problems

You can help customers solve their own problems on your Web site in a variety of ways:

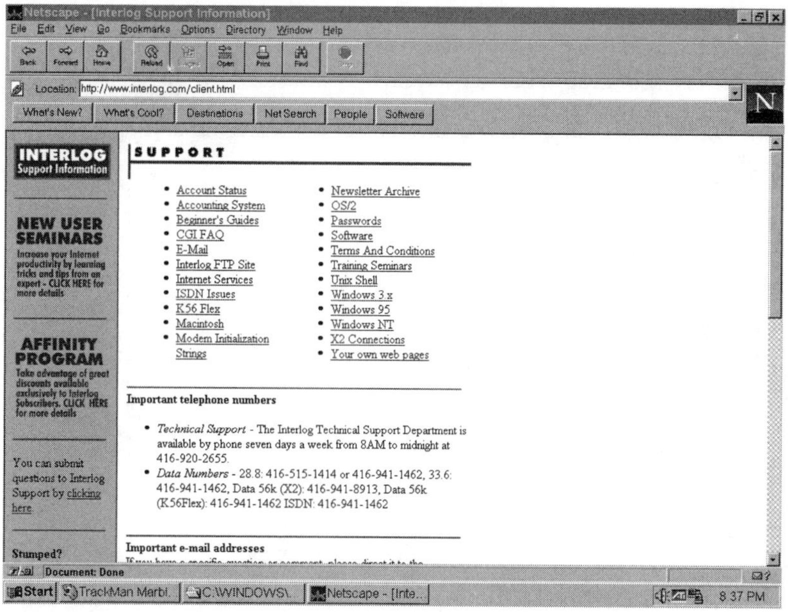

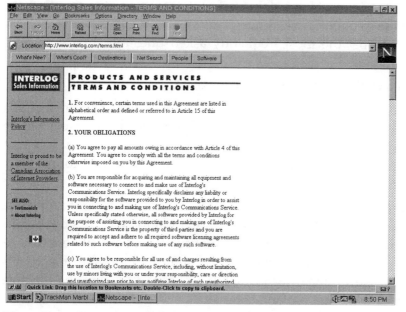

Figure 8.1   Sample Help Desk Web site offerings.

Figure 8.2   You can publish documents such as "Terms and Conditions for Product Use" on your Help Desk Web site.

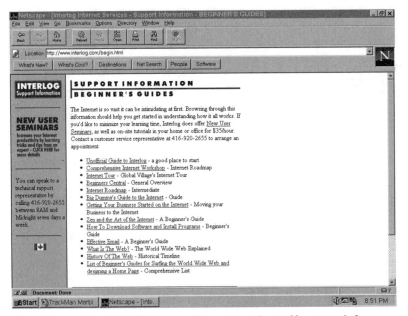

Figure 8.3   Include links to other sites that offer tutorials.

FAQ sites. Look at your Help Desk management statistics to find out what the frequently asked questions are. Divide these up by subject area, and list the most frequently asked questions first. This will make it easier for customers to find what they are looking for.

Hints and tips sites. Set up much like FAQ sites.

Knowledge bases. Your Help Desk Management system may include one or more knowledge bases. If you can, give your customers access to these so they can try to solve their own problems. You may need to set up some tutorials to teach customers how to use your knowledge base(s).

Links to other sites. Don't reinvent the wheel. If you find a Web site that has great problem-solving information for your customers, include it as a link from your site so that customers can take advantage of it. (A caution: Many ownership-of-information issues for the Internet are still being thrashed out. If you have a concern about pointing your customers to someone else's site, check it out with your legal department.)

Communicate Changes

Things you may want to tell people in your Web site include the following:

Product updates. You can post news about upgrades or new software or hardware.

Scheduled service interruptions. You can post a schedule, then issue reminders.

Changes in Help Desk services. You may include new Help Desk hours, new tutorials available, or any new functions you offer.

Operational changes. You can post changes in the way customers have to perform a specific function, for example, logging into the network or logging onto the Internet.

Changes in any procedures, policies, or standards. You will want to change the source for these kinds of documents on your Web site, but you will also want to let people know that changes are imminent or have happened.

This information can all be part of a "What's New" or news option on your Web site. People will get used to going there first to see what has changed (see Figure 8.4).

Market Help Desk Performance

A Web site is a great medium for letting customers know what kind of value they're getting. You can showcase information on the following:

The environment you support. Show, via charts and/or graphs, how your call distribution is changing and how the number of customers you support is changing.

Resolution times. You can show how the "percentage of calls resolved per time interval" pie chart is changing (see Chapter 9, "Measuring Performance").

Accomplishments. Things you may have done to prevent service interruptions or reduce the number of calls.

See Chapter 9 for more ideas on what information to include.

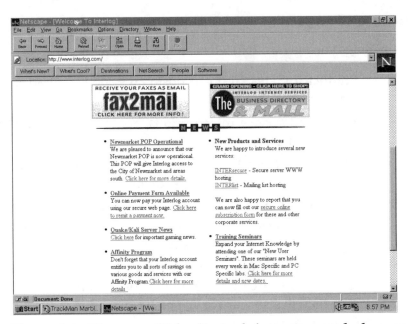

Figure 8.4   Use your Web site to bring news and changes to your customers' notice.

Accept Problem/Request Logs

You may want to give your customers the ability to log calls themselves, either through a form from your Web site, through direct access to your Help Desk Management system from your Web site, or via E-mail. Whichever option you choose, you need to make sure of the following:

You do not create more work for yourself. Have a direct interface from your Help Desk management system to the medium that the customer uses to enter the problem. Don't get into the situation where you have to rekey the data that the customer is sending you.

Customers understand how to log problems and requests. A tutorial might be called for or, more simply, enough instructions so the logging process is very clear.

You acknowledge receipt of the customer's log in some way. Use an autoresponder to let customers know the log was received.

It would be a good idea to also give customers the ability to check on the status of the problem or request from your Web page. To do this, you would need to give them access to your Help Desk management system.

Gather Customer Feedback

Your Web site provides an excellent medium for gathering customer feedback. Customers are there anyway trying to get help or picking up information. You can collect feedback in several ways:

Have a customer survey as one of your Web site options. You might send E-mails to targeted customers encouraging them to visit your Web site and fill out a survey.

Set up a "Before you leave this site" button. Have it bring up a short survey form or embed a question or two right into your site so customers don't have to be taken to another page (see Figure 8.5).

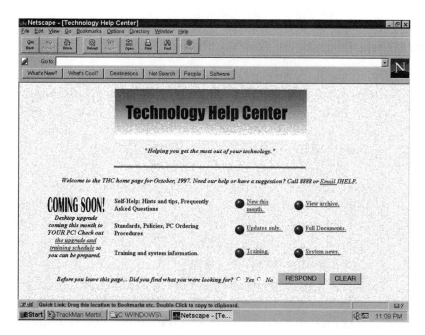

Figure 8.5 Embedded customer survey.

Target specific areas for surveys. For example, put survey questions in areas where you want to check feedback, for example, tutorials: You may want to get feedback on how useful customers think the tutorial is. At the end of the specific tutorial, include, in an embedded form, a question about the survey. Alternatively, you could have a button labeled "What did you think of this tutorial? Help us make it better," which initiates a short survey.

Give customers the ability to send you an E-mail from your site to give feedback. Assign someone the responsibility for answering E-mail to make sure it actually happens.

For each type of information gathering you do, you should know exactly what kind of information you are looking for. Having surveys that are too general is a waste of customers' time. You also need to feed survey results back to customers. Summarize customer feedback and let them know what you plan to do based on that feedback. You can do that on your Web site also. See Chapter 9 and Chapter 10, "Marketing," for more information on collecting customer feedback using surveys.

Gather Information about Your Customers

If you are interested in knowing more about your customers, your Web site can help you do this. You might be particularly interested in this if your customers are external and you do not have as many communication pathways to them as you would to internal customers. To gather information about your customers do the following:

Get customers to register. Registration would involve filling out a form on your Web site. The form could collect the information you are interested in. Incentives to register might include access to information such as article archives. The site would allow customers access any time once they register.

Offer a free newsletter. A newsletter or some piece of information such as a free tutorial could be offered to people who register. Make it something worthwhile, but remember, you're going to have to deliver it, so don't try this unless you have the time to follow through.

Use counter software. Counter software will count the number of hits your Web site gets. This will tell you how many people actually visited your site.

Tell People about Your Help Desk

A Web site is a great place to post information about Help Desk services. You could include information on Help Desk hours of service, what happens during off hours, and details about any chargeable services the Help Desk provides.

Customers don't often get to meet the people on a Help Desk. The Help Desk Web site can provide them with this opportunity. You could have an "About the people on the Help Desk" option that brings up photos and names of each person working on the Help Desk.

You may want to share some (tasteful) humor with your customers in the form of cartoons or quotations (see Figure 8.6). Always make viewing cartoons an option. Customers may not appreciate waiting for a possibly complex cartoon to load up.

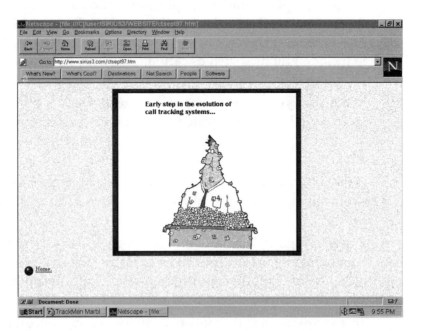

Figure 8.6   Customers might appreciate some Help Desk humor.

Designing Your Site

When you're designing your Help Desk site you need to work under the premise that your Web site will be visited by busy people who are looking for help in a hurry. Don't waste their time. Bear in mind the following rules of thumb:

Be concise. Don't just fill pages with data. Give customers the important information they're looking for.

Make your main Web page no more than one screen long. This way, customers can see all of the options at a glance. If the number of options you offer gets too high, offer a Web site map option.

Make your site easy to navigate. Be careful with frames. Web sites using frames can be very frustrating if they don't allow you to go where you want to without starting all over again. Don't nest hypertext to infinite depths. People can get lost.

Keep it simple. Complex graphics and photos take time to load, as does animation. Leave these out of your site. Test your site on a variety of modems so you can see how quickly it loads up. If you want to include graphics such as cartoons, include them as an option so people who have the time can have a look at them.

Make sure your screens are easy to read. Dark text on light backgrounds is best. Complicated backgrounds interfere with text. Do not use blinking text. It becomes extremely annoying after a few seconds.

Have a "What's New" feature. Such a feature enables visitors to avoid having to wade through information they may have seen before.

Put your logo or identifier on each page. Inserting a logo or identifier and having each page follow a standard template or set of templates ensures that your customers are always aware that they are still within your Web site. Each page will have the same "look."

Test your site. Test the site on a variety of screen sizes, resolutions, and Web browsers. If your customers are all internal, you may have standards. If your customers are external, you will have to assume that "anything goes."

Marketing Your Site

Your Help Desk site won't do anyone much good if people don't know it's there.

If you are a small business, include your Help Desk site address on all promotional material, including business cards and flyers. Include it everywhere you include your phone number. For the first few months of your Web site's life you may want to include a "Visit Our New Web Site!" announcement wherever you can.

If your Help Desk serves internal customers, you can send out an E-mail announcing your new site or use company newsletters or any customer gatherings or organizational meetings to spread the word. Again, include your Web address wherever you include your phone number.

If your Help Desk services external customers, your organization's marketing department will most likely take care of your site's marketing. Your site will probably be an option on the organization's main site.

Register with Internet search engines so your Web site will come up when people use specific keywords during a search. Most search engines have options on their home pages that allow you to submit a URL (uniform resource locator—the address of your Web site), which will be included in the index of their search engine. You may be asked to submit a short description or keywords that the engine can index. You can also use the META tags in your HTML code to control how your page is indexed. The META tag will allow you to specify both keywords and a short description.

Check out the "Search Engines and Directories" option at the Web Designer Help Desk, which can be found at www.canlink.com/helpdesk/ as well as the "Add/Remove URL" option at www.altavista.digital.com (home of the Alta Vista search engine) for more detailed explanations.

Another way of registering your Web site with search engines is through sites such as Submit It! (www.submit-it.com/) and Net Creations (www.netcreations.com/postmaster/). These sites will submit your URL to a number of the most popular search engines for free. They also offer various other Internet marketing services for a fee.

Maintaining Your Site

Update your site on a regular basis or people will stop visiting it. Information that is outdated, that people have seen time and time again, has lost its usefulness. If your FAQ only covers Windows 3.1 but your customers have upgraded to Windows 95, your site won't be of much use to them.

Tell people when the most recent updates were made. If you group all your updates and perform them monthly, let your home page reflect the month, for example, "ABC's Home Page for December," so visitors will know the site has been updated for that month (see Figure 8.5 for an example). Another way to do this is to include a "Last updated" date on your site and/or on the particular option that you updated.

Maintain a "What's New" section so visitors can see immediately what things have changed (see Figures 8.4 and 8.5). If your site has links to other sites, check these on a regular basis to ensure they are still valid. If they aren't, get rid of them. It is very annoying to follow a link that looks interesting, only to find it doesn't exist. Review FAQs and hints and tips options. If the lists are getting too lengthy you need to weed out the defunct information and/or reorganize.

Review all information regularly for relevance and validity. If your system news includes scheduled service interruptions for January and it's now May, you are wasting space and people's time. Policies and procedures that don't exist should be removed. Those that have changed should be updated. If something such as a policy or standard has changed, put it in your "What's New" section, but also include a NEW! icon (or some similar indicator) with a short description of what has changed next to the option containing the changes.

A Few References

There are virtually an infinite number of Web sites that have suggestions to help you set up, market, and manage your Web site. As mentioned, a good place to start is the Web Designer Help Desk, at www.canlink .com/helpdesk/. The site offers information on site design and marketing, HTML coding (the tables tutorial is excellent), and an explanation of search engines and the use of META tags. To find other sites, use your favorite search engine to look for the specific topic you want more information for.

You should also check out other Help Desk sites so you can pick up ideas and see what you do and do not like. Look in the Help Desk FAQ site (www.duke.edu/~pverghis/hdeskfaq.htm) for some good links to Help Desk Web sites. Interlog's *Beginner's Guide*, which can be found at www.interlog.com/begin.html and in Figure 8.3 (only part of the Beginner's Guide is shown), is a list of links to some great sites for beginner Internet users. You may be able to use some of this information if you are supporting new Internet users.

Chapter 15 in this book contains a sample Help Desk intranet site. Most of the ideas in this chapter are illustrated there. A book I highly recommend is *Customer Service on the Internet* by Jim Sterne (John Wiley & Sons Inc., 1996). The book offers many useful ideas on Web site design and management.

Once you start searching the Web for information to help you set up and run your Help Desk Web site, you may find yourself overwhelmed. Pick up all the ideas you can. They're absolutely free.

Key Points Covered in This Chapter

Ultimately, the purpose of a Help Desk Web site is to eliminate calls. When you're planning your Web site, make sure security is addressed, and get the right people involved: one or more of management, marketing, finance, Web support, and network support. Always involve your customers. Information you may want to put on your site includes published documents and updates, news about the technological environment, Help Desk performance information, and general information about the Help Desk and its services. Functions your site may want to allow are various forms of training, problem resolution, problem logging, and customer feedback. You may also want to gather information about your customers.

Some tips to help you design your site include the following:

Be concise.

Make your main Web page no more than one screen long.

Make your site easy to navigate.

Keep it simple—avoid anything that takes too long to load.

Make your screens easy to read—dark text on a light background.

Have a "What's New" feature.

Put your logo or identifier on each page.

Test your site on a variety of screen sizes, resolutions, and Web browsers.

You need to market your Help Desk if you want people to know about it. Some ways to do this include the following:

Include your Help Desk site address on all promotional material.

Send out an E-mail or use newsletters to promote your site.

Register your site with Internet search engines.

Update your site on a regular basis:

Tell people when updates were last made and maintain a "What's New" section.

Check links to make sure they're still there.

Reorganize and/or delete any documents that are getting too lengthy or are out of date.

PART FIVE

Optimizing Performance

Measuring Performance

"It is wise to keep in mind that no success or failure is necessarily final."

—Unknown

As a Help Desk manager, you must keep a vigilant eye on the performance of your Help Desk. You need to take on the role of auditor and be constantly checking for cost-effectiveness, business value, and the satisfaction of your customers. You can't afford to let performance slip. Corporations are less tolerant today of unsatisfactory performance than they ever have been.

In This Chapter

In this chapter, we will look at the components of performance, and how to get accurate measures of each. We will cover the following topics:

- What is performance?
- Measuring return on investment (ROI)
- Measuring the effectiveness of call load management
- Measuring proaction

- Tips for Help Desks that are just starting up
- Reporting on performance
- Communicating performance
- Measurement as a control

What Is Performance?

There are three main aspects of performance. All three are necessary to get a complete picture of performance:

1. **Return on Investment (ROI).** The dollar value of what the Help Desk is delivering to the business balanced against the dollar value of what the Help Desk is costing the business (see Figure 9.1).
2. **Effectiveness of call load management.** How well the Help Desk is handling its call load within the changing environment it is supporting.
3. **Level of proaction.** Existence and effectiveness of improvement and planning initiatives to meet current and future business demands.

These three items are not the same. A Help Desk might be doing a great job managing call load, but if a Help Desk outsourcing company can do the same job for less money, then the Help Desk does not have a good ROI. A Help Desk might be doing a good job managing call load for less cost than an outsourcer, yet doing almost nothing about planning for the future, about making sure it is prepared to handle changes in the organization it supports. This Help Desk is heading for a fall. If things are left as they are, all three aspects of performance will be negatively impacted.

A Help Desk that is just starting up will not be looking at these same performance measurements. It will be focusing on developing and defining its measurements and making adjustments. This is discussed later on in this chapter in the section titled "Tips for Help Desks That Are Just Starting Up."

Figure 9.1   ROI: Costs are weighed against value.

A Moving Picture

Performance is more than a snapshot. A snapshot tells you only where the Help Desk is at one instant in time. It does not tell you where a Help Desk is going or where it is coming from. As Figure 9.2 shows, looking only at a performance snapshot may give you a falsely positive reading when the Help Desk is really on a downward spiral. Similarly, a snapshot could give you a falsely negative reading when a Help Desk is really on a path of rapid improvement and success. Performance is a moving picture and must always be considered in terms of change,

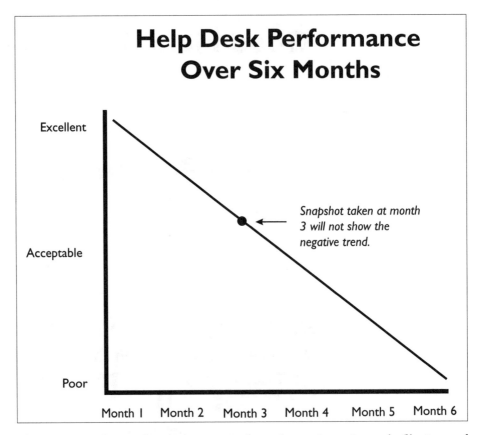

Figure 9.2 A performance snapshot is not a true indicator of performance.

trends, and comparisons with previous data. We must look at where performance is coming from and where it is headed.

Different Perspectives

Performance also means different things to different people. For example, if you ask your customers how your Help Desk is performing, they might think that you're doing a fabulous job. You're answering all of their WordPerfect questions quickly and correctly. They've started calling you more and more because your answers are so reliable. In fact, your call volumes are increasing because you are so good at answering these questions. If all you looked at was customer satisfaction, you'd think you were doing a pretty good job as a Help Desk. But that's just one point of view.

Your staff might have something different to say about it. They might be getting pretty tired of answering WordPerfect questions—especially since the kinds of questions customers are asking show they haven't bothered to take any training. They're using the Help Desk to learn the software. A Help Desk manager might have a different perspective again: The Help Desk won't be able to achieve its objectives this quarter because too much time is being spent on WordPerfect support. The senior management view won't be positive either. Managers will not be quite as impressed as your customers. For what the Help Desk is costing in terms of people and tools alone, it should be delivering a lot more than WordPerfect support. What management is looking for is evidence that your Help Desk is adding value to the business. And they aren't seeing it—WordPerfect support just doesn't cut it.

In order to get all perspectives on performance, you need to look at performance from the viewpoints of the customer, the Help Desk staff, the Help Desk manager, and senior management. Together, these different perspectives on Help Desk performance provide a complete picture of the situation. In this case, they show a Help Desk that is not meeting objectives, is not adding value to the business with its current focus, and is not an interesting place to work—a dysfunctional Help Desk that has specific areas needing improvement.

Customer Perspective

A customer is most interested in how the Help Desk is managing its call load, particularly in the kind of service the customer is receiving:

Are Help Desk staff knowledgeable and polite? Can the person on the phone usually resolve my problem?

Are problems followed up on and resolved, or do I have to keep calling back?

Are problems resolved quickly? Am I able to get a high priority in an emergency?

Are things done when promised—for instance, does a service technician arrive within the time promised?

Am I given training opportunities when I need them?

Am I kept informed of the status of problems?

Am I kept informed of system changes and scheduled service interruptions?

Are the services I need being provided?

These are things that are important to most Help Desk customers—things that will help ensure minimum downtimes and make dealing with the Help Desk a pleasure rather than a frustration. The more "yes" answers you have to these questions, the more successful your customers are likely to consider you.

Customers won't call the Help Desk to say "You're doing a good job," but neither will they necessarily call to say that you're not doing a good job. Don't believe that everything is fine just because you don't hear from them. They may have given up and began getting their support elsewhere, or they may have decided to go higher up to complain. Either way, your Help Desk isn't going to benefit. You have to go after customers for their feedback. The sooner (and more often) you get it, the sooner you can start to adjust your service to better meet their needs.

Staff Perspective

Help Desk staff are interested in how effectively they feel they are able to manage the Help Desk workload and how proactive they are allowed to be. The factors that will tell them this include the following:

Do callers appear confident in our ability?

Do we have a reasonable workload?

Are repetitive, uninteresting tasks automated? (Or do we keep spending time on the same mundane, reactive work?)

Are we given time to work on improvement initiatives?

Are we getting the amount of training we need?

Do we have the tools we need to do the job? Are the tools working properly? (For example, is our Help Desk software fast enough to allow us to log calls as they occur?)

Are we getting the support we need to do the job? Are second-level support areas handling passed-on calls effectively?

Are vendors providing adequate service?

Staff will feel they are performing well when customers trust and respect them; when their work is interesting and challenging; when they are allowed to spend time to make improvements; and when they have the tools, training, and support they need to do a good job.

Help Desk Manager Perspective

The Help Desk manager needs to be interested in all three aspects of performance: ROI, effectiveness of call handling, and proaction. A Help Desk manager needs to ask the following questions:

Are staffing levels appropriate? Is the Help Desk able to handle peak loads without being overstaffed for times of lighter traffic?

Are priorities working? Are the most critical issues being resolved before all others?

Are there any negative/positive trends in the calls, by type? Are there improvement initiatives we can put into place to make sure we change/continue the trends?

Are response and resolution times acceptable? Is the Help Desk meeting its service-level agreements?

Is the Help Desk meeting its objectives?

Are staff performing well? Are they managing workloads? Do customers speak positively about staff?

What is the trend in technology purchase and use? Is the Help Desk going to be able to handle growth in the environment? What needs to change to meet the future?

Senior Management Perspective

Senior managers are also interested in all three aspects of performance, but they will be looking most keenly at ROI. They will be asking the following questions:

Are objectives for improvements and preparation for future initiatives being developed and met?

Is the Help Desk managing its call load? Are service-level agreements being met? Are customers satisfied?

Is the Help Desk bringing value to the business? What is its ROI?

Senior management will probably always be assessing the Help Desk for cost-effectiveness: Can they get the same or better (especially if they don't feel you are performing well) service elsewhere for a better price, without giving up anything of importance? If they think they can, then they will. Don't wait for them to come to you. Go to them with the information that will let them evaluate the performance of your Help Desk. Better still, make sure your Help Desk is delivering the business value, the ROI, they're looking for.

Measuring Return on Investment (ROI)

Help Desk ROI can be defined as the dollar value of the gains, advantages, and services the Help Desk is bringing to the business (the return) divided by the operating cost of the Help Desk (the investment). Because the services and benefits of the Help Desk are not always tangible, putting a value to return is a challenge.

Return

Possibly the easiest way to calculate return is to base it on replacement value, or the market value for the services the Help Desk is providing. In other words, what would it cost someone else to do what your Help Desk is doing in today's market? Help Desk outsourcers could help you greatly in this calculation. Ask a few outsourcers what they would charge for the services you perform. Take care to ensure that the fees they quote include exactly what your own Help Desk is giving you now, including service levels. This is going to involve significant work on your part, especially if you haven't gone through the exercise (in Chapter 1) of getting focused. You'll have to define all the responsibilities you have, the services you perform and the levels required, and the hours and locations you cover. To help keep outsourcers honest, do not divulge any information about your current Help Desk costs.

If, for example, the cost of running your Help Desk is $1 million per year and the outsourcers come back with costs of $900,000, then, even if your Help Desk is meeting or surpassing all service levels, your Help Desk ROI does not look very good. It would appear that your organization is paying $1 million for $900,000 worth of services. If your Help Desk was performing poorly (e.g., poor response times, low customer satisfaction) then the ROI becomes even lower. At this point, senior management would be very tempted to outsource your Help Desk.

Investment

Investment is the Help Desk's operating cost. This should include the following:

1. Staffing costs. Remember to include the cost of benefits and other overheads. Your human resources department can give you this information.
2. Expenses such as outsourced contracts.
3. Training costs for Help Desk staff.
4. The cost of any training material distributed or made available to Help Desk customers.
5. Office supplies.
6. The cost of Help Desk software and associated maintenance. You need to figure out what your purchase plus maintenance costs are on a yearly basis. In other words, if you purchase the software in year 1, maintain it in year 2, and upgrade it in year 3, you will want to estimate those total costs and spread them out over the three years.
7. Cost of Help Desk hardware and associated maintenance and depreciation. Include computer and telephone equipment and peripherals and office equipment such as fax machines and photocopiers. Hardware may also include any telephone-related equipment such as interactive voice response (IVR) units. The

costs a Help Desk is responsible for will vary from organization to organization.

8. Facilities overhead (e.g., rent).

An example of Help Desk operating cost over one year is shown in Table 9.1. Hardware is leased rather than purchased in this example.

Expressing Investment/Operating Cost

Investment, or Help Desk operating cost, is most useful when expressed as a cost-per-unit basis, for example, cost per workstation. You cannot expect your Help Desk costs to remain the same, no matter how many workstations you add. If the cost per workstation decreases, then even if your overall Help Desk costs increase you know you are more cost-effective than you were before, when the overall Help Desk cost was lower. A Help Desk in start-up mode will typically have a very high cost-

Table 9.1   Example of Yearly Operating Cost, or Investment

Item	Yearly Cost
Salaries, benefits	$ 880,000
Contract for outsourced hardware maintenance	$ 210,000
Contract for leasing computer-based training for customers	$ 110,000
Training for Help Desk staff	$ 40,000
Office supplies	$ 5,000
Yearly Help Desk software maintenance costs (purchase is prorated over a three-year cycle with cost distributed equally over the three years)	$ 5,000
Help Desk hardware leasing costs	$ 30,000
Yearly IVR hardware and software maintenance costs (purchase is prorated over a three-year cycle with cost distributed equally over the three years)	$ 50,000
Facilities overhead	$ 18,000
TOTAL	$1,348,000
Number of workstations supported	2,000
OPERATING COST PER WORKSTATION	$ 674

per-workstation figure. As more workstations are added and Help Desk services are stabilized, economies of scale will be realized and the cost per workstation will go down.

Operating cost expressed as cost per call, although popular, is a much less useful figure. It starts out with the premise that the lower your cost per call, the more successful your Help Desk is. This is a false premise. Consider the example of a software firm that manufactures complex engineering software and hires expensive, highly skilled professionals to staff its Help Desk. Calls involve questions about how to apply the software to engineering techniques. The cost per call might be $200 or higher. Each call can take from one hour to half a day to resolve. Consider the other extreme: A Help Desk that costs only $10 per call but that is spending its time answering questions that are the result of customers not bothering to take training. The Help Desk is unable to do any proactive work because it spends all its time answering repetitive, mundane questions. Customers with more complex problems must fend for themselves because the Help Desk is not staffed to answer them, and they probably couldn't get through to the Help Desk anyway. Which offers better value? The answer: the $200 per call Help Desk. It is supporting its business. The $10 per call Help Desk is a gross misuse of resources.

According to the Help Desk Institute's 1997 *Help Desk and Customer Support Practices Report*, the cost of support calls among those Help Desks actually having a handle on this cost (roughly 40 percent) varies from less than $10 to more than $100. This variance is in itself an indication that this measure should be used with caution.

ROI Calculation: A Good Exercise

Calculating ROI is a very good exercise for Help Desk managers to go through every year or so. It is a great way to audit the cost-effectiveness of the Help Desk and also a good way to find out if an outsourcing company can offer you any options that might help the performance of your Help Desk (see Chapter 12, "Outsourcing"). This process is also more effective than trying to compare yourself against so-called industry benchmarks that may be totally unsuitable for your Help Desk.

A prerequisite to being able to calculate ROI is to truly understand how your Help Desk is performing—what service levels you are meeting—so costs can be compared on an equal footing. ROI by itself is not an adequate measurement. To understand how your Help Desk is performing, you need to understand the other two components of performance: the effectiveness of call load management and proaction.

Measuring Effectiveness of Call Load Management

To measure how effectively you are managing your calls within your changing environment, you're going to have to look at a number of measures, both qualitative and quantitative:

- Objectives
- Service-level agreements
- Customer evaluation
- Staff evaluation
- Help Desk management statistics, specifically:

  Change in environment and in call load—number of calls, by type; number of supported workstations; number of calls per workstation

  Change in resolution times—percentage of calls resolved at point of call; resolution times, by percentage per interval for remaining calls

  Change in customer wait times—abandonment rate; customer wait times, by percentage per interval

A Note about Measures: Qualitative versus Quantitative

In order to determine how your Help Desk is performing, you'll need both quantitative and qualitative measures. Quantitative measures give you actual quantities or numbers, while qualitative measures give you the characteristics or qualities of what you are measuring—the things you can't put a number to. For example, consider a Help Desk that is measuring itself against a service-level agreement. The Help Desk manager looks at the numbers and thinks things look pretty good. Response times are being met 100 percent of the time. The manager decides to get some qualitative measures as well and goes to customers and Help Desk staff for feedback. Customers think the Help Desk is doing a great job and is meeting all aspects of the agreement. Staff, on the other hand, think it's failing. The response times aren't reasonable, and staff are working themselves into exhaustion trying to meet them. The Help Desk manager now has a very different picture of performance and can address the situation before service is degraded or the staff drop from exhaustion.

Another example is a Help Desk that has a problem resolution time that looks good on paper but is completely unacceptable to a specific group of customers who need a faster resolution time. They are doing critical work that the Help Desk might not know about, and the existing resolution times are affecting the business.

A third example, and somewhat more drastic, is the Help Desk that is quite pleased to see the quantitative measure of number of calls decreasing. Customers, however, are simply fed up with inadequate service and have found another source of support. In each of these examples, just looking at the numbers would give a false impression. In the same way, just looking at qualitative measures would not give the whole story. Customers and Help Desk staff might be quite happy with the way the Help Desk is working, but the numbers might show that a large percentage of calls are of a training nature. This would indicate that customers are not using the technology properly or to its full potential and are wasting their own time and Help Desk time with problems and questions that could be eliminated with the appropriate training.

Objectives

When you're measuring your Help Desk against your objectives, you might be measuring the effectiveness of changes or improvements you have made or the stability of existing service levels. For example, one of your objectives might be to reduce calls to the Help Desk by 20 percent. In order to achieve this reduction, you need to make some kind of change, such as installing an interactive voice response (IVR) application to handle specific types of calls or eliminating recurring problems that are causing extra calls. Another of your objectives might be to maintain an average problem resolution time of four hours. You're already at the four-hour level, but you want to ensure that you stay there. Regardless of whether your objectives measure change or stability, they should be focused on the business.

Quantitative measures that you may want to use in your objectives include the number (or percentage) of calls resolved at the point of call, the number (or percentage) of a specific type of call, resolution times for problems not resolved at point of call, number of calls left unresolved, delivery time for services, and promised versus actual times for service or solution delivery.

Number (or Percentage) of Calls Resolved at Point of Call

Help Desks typically want to increase this number so they can offer more of their customers total service with one call. Improvements that can increase the number of calls resolved at point of call include using tools such as interactive voice response (IVR), remote diagnostic software, or expert systems and giving staff training that will enable them to handle a wider variety of calls. This number can be measured easily by just about any Help Desk call management system. An example of an objective using this measure would be to "Increase number of calls resolved at point of call from 50 percent to 60 percent."

Number (or Percentage) of a Specific Type of Call

Your Help Desk might be trying to decrease the number of certain types of calls: calls of a training nature, for example, or requests to handle tasks such as terminal resets. In the former case, you might be planning to initiate a marketing campaign for training and offer several training courses; in the latter, you might be planning to automate terminal resets through an interactive voice response (IVR) unit. To know that your training campaign worked, you would need to see a decrease in the number of training-type calls into the Help Desk. Similarly, to know that your automation of terminal resets has been successful, you would need to see that calls for terminal resets were all being handled by the IVR system—none of these calls should be coming into the Help Desk. Call statistics from your call management system would tell you whether you achieved your target decreases. Examples of targets are "Reduce the number of training-type calls by 10 percent" and "Reduce number of calls into the Help Desk by 30 percent," where 30 percent of the calls were terminal resets.

Resolution Times for Problems Not Resolved at Point of Call

If resolution times are too high for problems that cannot be resolved at point of call, one of your objectives might be to reduce them. You might expect to do this through training, additional tools, improved procedures, outsourcing, or additional staff. Help Desk call management systems typically collect information on problem resolution times and show whether you have been successful in reaching your target: "Reduce average problem resolution time for calls not resolved at point of call to forty-eight hours from seventy-two hours."

Number of Calls Left Unresolved

If your Help Desk is finding that problems are being left open too long or are somehow falling through the cracks, one of your objectives will probably be to reduce or eliminate the number of calls left unresolved after a specific time—say, five days. In order to achieve this, you may be creating new procedures, providing training for staff, or purchasing new Help Desk software. Your objective might be to "Reduce the number of calls left unresolved after five days to less than 2 percent." Your Help Desk call management system can give you the data to tell you whether you've succeeded.

Delivery Time for Services

For whatever services you provide, such as the purchase and installation of PCs, you may be hoping to improve delivery time. Your objective might be to "Reduce the average time between PC order and installation to fourteen working days." Your solution may be to outsource the whole activity to a vendor. If the vendor is using your call management system, you can check your performance there, or you may ask your vendor to provide service-level information that you can check.

Promised versus Actual

If the estimates your Help Desk is giving customers on when a service or solution will be delivered are consistently too low, you will want to set an objective for improving them, perhaps through training or improved procedures. As an example, if currently you meet your promised delivery date only 45 percent of the time, your objective might be to "Meet promised delivery dates 90 percent of the time." If your call management system tracks promised delivery time, it can tell you how successful you've been.

Other measures that you use will depend on your own individual Help Desk. Performance against objectives isn't always as simple as "Yes, we achieved this" or "No, we didn't." Your achievements might look different from your objectives for various reasons:

Circumstances can change quickly, as can the demands of the business. You may have had to change your focus to something of greater business value.

You may have underestimated the time required to achieve the objective. The objective may not have been realistic.

You may have failed in some part of your change initiative.

Staff may not be performing up to expectations.

In each of these cases of objectives not met, there is something your Help Desk can learn from and improve upon. You can improve your knowledge of what is required for a good estimate so that future objectives will be more reasonable. You can find and correct what went wrong in your change initiative and avoid the same mistakes in the future. You can identify and correct staff performance problems. You can turn any failures you have into learning experiences.

Table 9.2 is an example of a set of objectives and Help Desk performance against them.

Table 9.2 Example of Performance versus Objectives

Objective	Accomplished	Problems (if any)	Information for Improvement and Planning
Increase number of calls resolved at point of call to 85 percent by using remote diagnostics software.	Achieved 85 percent.	Customer survey indicated that some customers are afraid that Help Desk staff can monitor their sessions at any time.	*Need to communicate the fact that the software requires that users allow access. A marketing effort is needed here.*
Upgrade all machines with less than 32 megabytes of memory to prepare for client/ server	85 of 110 machines upgraded.	Taking longer per machine than planned. Ran into scheduling difficulties with customers.	*Next time, need to take this into account. This was an unrealistic objective.*
Install fifteen PCs into the sales area for the new sales promotion project.	Done on time; no major problems.		
Install new release of word processing software.	Network operating system required an emergency upgrade to fix response problems that happened when the 950th user came on-line. This was successfully completed. Word processing upgrade was postponed.		
Research and select asset management package.	Not done.	Support load was too high.	*Have to get this done. Need to reduce the load or get help.*

In the example in Table 9.2, not all objectives were achieved. The reasons for this included a problem with the support load, unrealistic objectives, and the way in which a specific tool was implemented. There are (at least) three ways in which this Help Desk can improve from this information:

It can improve its estimation skills. It has learned something about the time required to carry out PC upgrades.

It can focus its attention on the support load it is handling. The load is interfering with improvements, and an investigation into the reason for the increased load and ways of decreasing it is required.

Even though an 85 percent first-level call resolution was reached, customers are fearful of the remote access technology. This can cause problems in the near future. The Help Desk has learned that it can improve the way it is handling the rollout of automation. More time must be spent with customers to make sure they understand it and are comfortable with it.

The installation of the word processing upgrade was not accomplished, but instead the focus was switched to a network operating system upgrade, which had much greater business value at the time. This can be considered a successful accomplishment.

Service-Level Agreements

A service-level agreement (SLA) can be characterized in the following ways:

It is a two-way agreement between the Help Desk and a specific group of customers. The agreement specifies services the Help Desk must provide and targets it must meet. It also specifies the responsibilities of customers using the services.

It measures both Help Desk performance and customer compliance with the agreed-upon responsibilities.

It is created through a joint effort between Help Desk representatives and customer representatives. All items specified in the agreement must be agreed upon by both groups.

SLAs not only define a Help Desk performance measurement but also clarify both customer and Help Desk expectations. Each party understands what its responsibilities are and what to expect from the other party. The agreement contains both qualitative and quantitative measures. SLAs are based on those services that provide the best value to the business, and defining these was part of the exercise of getting focused on the business discussed in Chapter 1.

A Help Desk might have a separate agreement with each customer area, agreements only with critical areas, or one agreement with all customers. In creating an SLA keep the following rules of thumb in mind:

Don't forget about the people you rely on for support. Their performance affects your ability to meet measures. Spend time defining and agreeing on who is responsible for what. Don't expect this to be trivial. It will be time consuming.

Each item in the SLA must be measurable. If you can't measure the item, don't include it.

Each item in the SLA should be very specific. For example, if performance reports are required, a layout of the report should be included and frequency and recipients stated. The more specific each item is the less chance there is of misunderstandings and of expectations not being met.

Ensure everyone affected by the SLA is represented in the creation and negotiation process.

The creation process is an iterative one. A draft SLA is created by a work group of representatives. The representatives then take the draft back to their groups for changes, additions, or clarifications. The process continues until all groups are satisfied with the result.

Items that might be included in an SLA are as follows:

Description and location of customer group—you may need different levels of service for different groups and therefore different SLAs

Period covered by the agreement—usually one year

Services to be provided by the Help Desk

Help Desk hours of operation and after-hours service options

How customers can access Help Desk services

Customer responsibilities

Definition of call priorities and required response times

Service measures to be met

Escalation procedures

Reporting to be generated by the Help Desk

Components supported

Components considered critical

Support fees, if any

Pay-for-use services, if any—in this section include any services that are available to the customers at extra cost, for example, training

Service-Level Agreement Example

The following is an example of an SLA between a Help Desk and a marketing department.

Service-Level Agreement

Between:
The Corporate Help Desk and Marketing
For:
January 1, 1998, through December 31, 1998

1. **Services to Be Provided by the Help Desk**

    Perform first-level support for all standard software applications and all hardware that meets corporate standards.

    Manage second and third level of support.

    Log and track all customer calls.

    Carry out quarterly customer satisfaction surveys to rotating client base, 100 at a time. Publish results (see section 8, "Reporting").

    Carry out customer callbacks to 50 percent of customers daily. Publish results (see section 8, "Reporting").

---

2. **Hours of Operation**

   Regular Business Hours:

   7 A.M. to 7 P.M., Monday through Friday, nonholiday

   After-hours support via pager: 111-222-3333, priority 1 only

   7 P.M. to 7 A.M., Monday through Friday, nonholiday

   24 hours Saturday and Sunday

   24 hours holidays

3. **Service Access**

   Help Desk Service Is Accessible via:

   Phone—Call 123-HELP

   E-mail—Send a message to EHELP

4. **Customer Responsibilities**

   Use only specified phone number or E-mail ID to get support. No other support requests will be processed.

   Customers who are new to technology must attend two half-day LAN and PC familiarization seminars before receiving a workstation.

   Attend training on all software used. (Percentage of training-type calls will be tracked.)

   Read and abide by the Corporate Security Policy and Corporate Standards Policy documents.

5. **Call Priorities and Response Times**

Priority	Impact	Response	Resolution
1	Critical component down	15 minutes	As required
2	Critical component degraded	45 minutes	4 hours
3	Noncritical component	4 hours	8 hours
4	Other request, question	8 hours	12 hours

6. **Service Measures to Be Met**

   By the Help Desk:

   First-level call resolution—85 percent or greater

Average call answer time—90 percent in thirty seconds or less

Percentage of calls reopened within two weeks—2 percent or less

By Customers:

Percentage of training-type calls to be less than 10 percent

7. **Escalation Procedures**

Level	Initiate when:	Call:	Phone/Pager
1	Agreed-upon response time not met.	Help Desk Manager	123-222-222 111-999-999
2	No response two hours after level 1 escalation.	Director, Local Operations	123-222-333 111-999-000
3	No response three hours after level 2 escalation.	V.P., Local Operations	123-333-444 111-999-111

8. **Reporting**

Weekly Reporting:

Distribution—

- Manager and Director, Marketing
- Director and Vice President, Local Operations

Content:

Number of calls

Call breakdown by percentage for training-type calls, hardware, software, communication, service requests, abandoned

Percentage of first-level call resolution

Average call answer time

Percentage of calls reopened within two weeks

Percentage of calls meeting agreed-upon response times for each priority

Percentage of calls meeting agreed-upon resolution times for each priority

Results of callbacks to customers to check work quality—show number of callbacks as percentage of total calls

Show percentage of callbacks with positive response

Quarterly Reporting:

Distribution—

- Manager and Director, Marketing
- Director and Vice President, Local Operations

Content:

Results of quarterly customer surveys

Change from previous quarter in number of workstations supported

Operating costs

Note:

All weekly reporting must show current week compared to three previous weeks. All quarterly reporting must show current quarter compared to previous quarter.

9. **Systems and Components Supported**

Critical Systems/Components Supported:

Price flow system

Server T1AD

Catalog system

LAN ring 006

All PCs on ring 006

Noncritical Components Supported:

Marketing Search, Competitor System, Marketing Performance. All standard desktop software as per Corporate Standards document.

Hardware Supported:

All hardware that meets corporate standards (as per Corporate Standards document) will be supported.

10. **Support Fees**

    Cost will be allocated at the rate of $60 per workstation per month.

11. **Pay-for-use Fees**

    Training of standard desktop packaged software is available and will be arranged by the Help Desk for the cost of $300 per half day. Course dates and times are available from the Help Desk intranet web site and are distributed to all customers quarterly.

12. **Signatures Denoting Agreement**

    Manager, Help Desk:

    _____

    Director, Local Operation:

    _____

    Manager, Marketing Liaison:

    _____

    Director, Marketing:

    _____

Responsibility for revising this agreement on an annual basis lies jointly with the Manager, Help Desk, and the Manager, Marketing Liaison.

Measuring Performance versus Service-Level Agreement

Performance must be measured against each category in the agreement and any recommendations for improvements made. Performance against an SLA is a two-way measurement. In one direction, it measures how the Help Desk meets its responsibilities; in the other, it measures how customers meet their responsibilities.

Performance against the SLA can be checked using the following:

1. **Customer surveys or callbacks.** You are checking customer perception of service, as per section 1 of the agreement presented in the previous section, and you will report on this as per section 8 of the agreement. You can use these surveys and callbacks to find out if customers were able to get access as per sections 2 and 3 of the agreement.

2. **Call statistics from your Help Desk management system.** Information your call statistics will give you includes response and resolution times for specific priorities, as per section 5; percentage of calls resolved by the first level and average call answer time, as per section 6; and percentage of calls by type, which you can use to measure the percentage of training-type calls, as per section 6.

3. **A survey of staff.** Help Desk staff will be able to give feedback on whether customers fulfilled their responsibilities (section 4 in the agreement): Did they go through proper channels, or did they try to cajole Help Desk staff away from their other calls to do work for them? ("Can you help me with this? It will just take a minute.") Did they abide by corporate standards? Did they take any security risks?

Table 9.3 shows a sample of SLA measures, and indicates several areas for improvement:

Customers aren't following regular channels when reporting problems. This must be stopped to prevent valuable statistics from being lost and to prevent disruption in priorities and staff workload. This might mean that a marketing initiative could be included in future objectives.

Customers are wasting their own time and Help Desk time with training calls. At 30 percent of calls, this is an area that has room for significant improvement if customers take the required training. The Help Desk could be looking at why customers aren't taking the required training, and if there is any type of training that could be provided (such as just-in-time on-site training) that would be more convenient.

Table 9.3   Example of Performance versus Service-Level Agreement

Item	Performance	Information for Improvement and Planning
Customer Responsibilities: *Use only specified phone number or E-mail ID to get support. No other support requests will be processed.*	Feedback from Staff: *Customers try to get support from staff who are en route to fix another problem.*	*Need to market the cost of stolen support to customers. Revisit terms of the SLA with marketing liaison.*
Service Measures to Be Met: *Percentage of training-type calls to be less than 10 percent.*	From Help Desk Statistics: *Percentage of training type calls = 30 percent.*	*Revisit terms of the SLA with marketing liaison. Make sure customers are being kept informed of available training. Are there any types of training we could be providing that would be more convenient to customers?*
Service Measures To Be Met *First level call resolution to be 85 percent or greater.*	From Help Desk Statistics: *First level call resolution is 72 percent.*	*It appears that the standard desktop upgrade was rolled out before Help Desk staff were as adequately trained. This needs to be addressed for this and all future releases.*

Staff are not being trained before software is rolled out. This has affected first-level call resolutions. Training needs to be incorporated into plans for all future upgrades.

Customer Evaluation

A customer evaluation is a report card on the Help Desk's performance from customers. It is not a onetime thing but an ongoing process in which the Help Desk goes to the customers for feedback. Customers evaluate the Help Desk against those things that are most important to them. These include:

Speed and accuracy of service. Customer perception may be different from the quantitative measures supplied by a call management system.

Provision of emergency service when required. Measuring customer perception would give an indication of whether the definition of emergency in Help Desk priorities was adequate.

Quality of Help Desk staff (how knowledgeable they are). Just one customer who feels that the Help Desk doesn't know anything can do significant damage to the Help Desk's image and its success.

Quality of training. How appropriate was it for the customer and environment? Was the topic covered adequately? How timely was it?

Quality of services, such as PC purchase. Was the equipment delivered appropriate for the job being performed? Was it delivered when promised? Was it set up properly?

Quality of communication. Are customers kept informed of the progress on their calls? Are they informed of the occurrences and durations of system outages or planned downtimes? Are they informed of the training available, the services available, how to use the services?

Getting customer evaluations of Help Desk performance can mean meeting with customer representatives to gather input on each of the preceding performance categories, sending out short customer surveys, or calling customers back to ask them to evaluate their service experience. Specific areas, such as training and PC purchase, can be targeted separately for feedback. Perhaps all training attendees could be surveyed a few months after receiving the training so they could give feedback on its relevance after having had some time to apply it. Each person who received a PC might also be asked to fill out a quick survey form to give feedback on the whole process.

Customer surveys are most effective when you follow a few guidelines:

Target a specific incident or a specific aspect of service. Don't try to cover too much in one survey. Be very focused.

Be prepared to make changes based on survey results. If you are not, don't survey.

Explain the purpose of your survey to customers.

Include no more than five questions per survey.

Always give the customer room for comments.

Survey customers on an ongoing rotating or random basis rather than everyone once a year. This will give you a much better idea of how things are changing throughout the year and will let you react to problem areas or suggestions more quickly.

Always, always, report on survey results. If customers hear nothing and see no changes, they'll stop responding.

Measuring Performance versus Customer Evaluation

Table 9.4 shows an example of a customer survey.

Table 9.5 shows the results of the survey in Table 9.4. Observations and areas for improvement are also indicated.

The survey results in Table 9.5 point out a few areas for improvement. The Help Desk needs to assess these and make plans for improvement as follows:

The Help Desk is not delivering on promised workstation visit times. The workstation visit scheduling procedure must be revised. The current process is "make a best estimate." A solution involving a new process has been suggested and approved. The new process will involve an on-line scheduling and dispatch system that will schedule the appropriate on-site analyst and then send that person a page to indicate the addition of a new on-site visit. The new process will be in place at the start of next quarter.

Problems are not being resolved in a timely manner in almost one-third of Help Desk calls. This indicates either that the Help Desk is simply too slow, that is, not meeting our service-level agreement, or the service-level agreement is not adequate. An examination of the Help Desk resolution times indicated that the Help Desk is meeting

Table 9.4   Example of a Help Desk Customer Survey

Survey Objective:	To check on the quality of service, as perceived by customers, being provided by the Help Desk.
Vehicle:	E-mail.
Audience:	For every fifth call that is closed the Help Desk management system will automatically send the survey to the customer involved.
Survey Header:	*Dear Recent Help Desk Customer,*
	Please help us check the quality of our work by taking a few minutes to respond to the survey below. You may return the survey via E-mail, or, if you prefer to remain anonymous, print it out and send it via internal mail to HELP DESK, 12th Floor. Thank you!

Survey:
For each question below, please choose the appropriate response and enter any comments you may have.

Did you feel the Help Desk analyst who served you was knowledgeable?	__Y __N
Comments:	_____
Was your problem resolved in a timely manner?	__Y __N
Comments:	_____
If someone had to visit your workstation, did they arrive when promised?	__Y __N __No-one had to visit my workstation.
Comments:	_____
1. Was the problem resolved to your satisfaction?	__Y __N
Comments:	_____
2. Please rate your Help Desk experience on a scale of 1 to 4, 1 being highest and 4 being lowest.	__1 __2 __3 __4
Comments:	_____

Table 9.5 Survey Results and Observations

Question	Results by Percentage	Observations, Areas for Improvement
1. Did you feel the Help Desk analyst who served you was knowledgeable?	Y: 95% N: 5%	
2. Was your problem resolved in a timely manner?	Y: 71% N: 29%	*Is this a result of the late workstation visits? Also check resolution statistics and SLA requirements.*
3. If someone had to visit your workstation, did that person arrive when promised?	Y: 10% N: 22% N/A: 68%	*Check workstation visit scheduling procedures.*
4. Was the problem resolved to your satisfaction?	Y: 97% N: 3% *One comment mentioned that "the problem was solved eventually."*	*Check resolution statistics and SLA requirements.*
5. Please rate your Help Desk experience on a scale of 1 to 4; 1 being highest and 4 being lowest.	1: 32% 2: 53% 3: 15% 4: 10%	

agreed-upon service levels. Phone calls to several of the survey respondents revealed that customer expectations were higher than the service levels agreed upon. A meeting with customer management reaffirmed the agreed-upon response times. A marketing initiative is necessary to make sure that all customers understand the response times that the Help Desk is expected to meet. This issue will be mentioned on the survey response cards and will be added to the Help Desk intranet site.

Once you decide what improvement initiatives you are going to undertake, you need to let customers know the results of the survey. Don't leave this too long or customers will forget what was in the survey and will be less likely to fill out another one ("No one ever reads these things so why should I bother filling them out?"). Figure 9.3 illustrates an example of a postcard sent to customers showing the results of the survey.

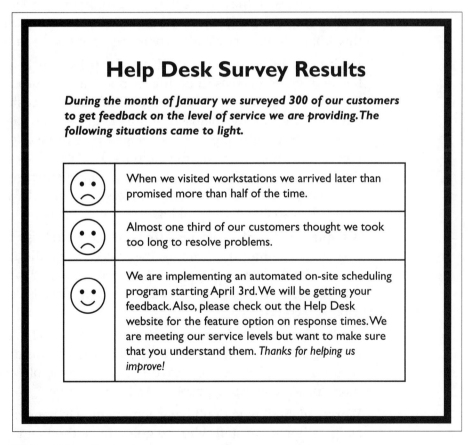

Figure 9.3   Customer survey results.

The example is of a paper postcard, but an electronic one might be more appropriate in your environment.

Help Desk Staff Evaluation

Factors that Help Desk staff will use to evaluate Help Desk performance include the following:

Customer attitude. Help Desk Staff are close to the customers. They talk to them all day, and they will notice if and when attitudes change. Customers calling the Help Desk aren't always in the best of moods, but staff can gauge changes to identify whether customers are satisfied with the service they are getting. If your Help Desk has a callback program to check on the timeliness and quality of tasks, this will tell staff very clearly whether customers are satisfied.

Legitimacy of customer calls. If the Help Desk is being misused, business value decreases, so this is not a trivial measure. If Help Desk staff notice an increasing number of calls that customers could have resolved easily themselves, this could signal misuse. If customers aren't bothering to look things up or to take training, then they are wasting time that the Help Desk could be spending doing things of greater value, such as making improvements. In addition, those customers probably don't understand the software, so they could be misusing it and making expensive mistakes.

Adequacy of training received (for staff). If Help Desk staff feel that they aren't getting the training they need to handle the calls that come in (to deal professionally with the customers or to use the tools they have), then they won't feel that the Help Desk is doing as good a job as it could.

Availability and performance of tools. If staff don't have the tools to do their jobs properly, performance will suffer. In this measure, staff will indicate whether they have the necessary tools and whether those tools are working properly and are effective.

Workload. Staff who don't have enough time to handle all the work assigned them are staff who are going to be tired and stressed and not nearly as effective as they could be on the Help Desk. Call statistics might not show this. Reports might indicate volume of calls, but if the staff are doing something else besides calls the reports won't show this.

Availability and function of second-level support. Help Desk staff will also evaluate interfaces with other support areas that they may have to pass calls to. If staff have to do a lot of calling or reminding to get the calls handled, then their jobs are more difficult, and they are wasting time unnecessarily.

Vendor performance. Help Desk staff might have a lot of contact with vendors and will be able to report on qualitative measures such as responsiveness, quality of service, willingness to help out in the case of problems, how warranties are honored, and so on.

Value of tasks performed. Besides quantity of work, staff are going to look at the value of the work they do. If they find themselves doing simple tasks over and over or are constantly interrupted in their work by time-wasting administrative tasks, they aren't going to attach much value to their jobs. This measure can also identify candidate processes for automation or outsourcing—are the staff doing something that should be automated?

These factors (see Figure 9.4) all impact the performance of your Help Desk, and the sooner you know about any problem areas the sooner you can fix them. You need to discuss these issues with your Help Desk staff at regular (and frequent) intervals. A good forum is your weekly/monthly staff meeting. Turn the issues just listed into questions, E-mail them to your staff before your meetings, and then discuss them during the meetings. If you make this a regular part of your meetings, people will start to gather and prepare this information automatically.

Instead of, or in addition to, staff meetings you may want to simply E-mail questions to staff and get feedback that way. You can get further feedback as required on an individual basis. A discussion of the issues, especially value of work performed, should also be included in any performance appraisals you have with your staff. Staff who are really interested in improving the Help Desk will give you good feedback. Staff who are just putting in time may not (although a Help Desk seems a

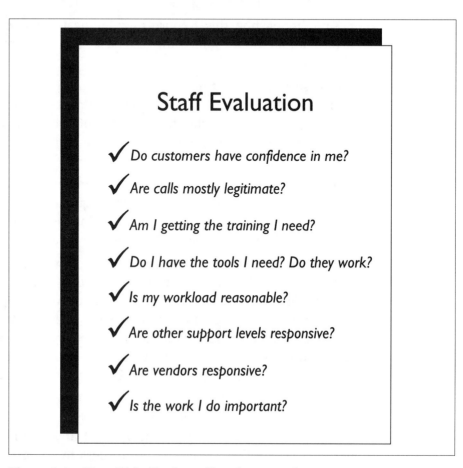

Staff Evaluation

✔ *Do customers have confidence in me?*

✔ *Are calls mostly legitimate?*

✔ *Am I getting the training I need?*

✔ *Do I have the tools I need? Do they work?*

✔ *Is my workload reasonable?*

✔ *Are other support levels responsive?*

✔ *Are vendors responsive?*

✔ *Is the work I do important?*

Figure 9.4   How Help Desk staff evaluate performance.

rather torturous place to be putting in time). You will have to recognize this and sort it out.

Help Desk Management Statistics

Your Help Desk management system provides you with endless statistics about the performance of your Help Desk. You need to keep a sharp eye on these, for if you get too busy and ignore them, they're apt to change by leaps and bounds before you notice. Remember, performance is a moving picture, and you need to be looking at change. Some of the most critical changes to watch for include the following:

Change in Environment and in Call Load

Statistics to watch include number of workstations supported, overall number of calls, daily call distribution, number of calls by type, and number of calls per workstation. Your asset management package should give you information about changes in software supported, change in type and complexity of hardware supported, and so on.

Number of workstations supported will tell you whether you are supporting more or fewer customers.

Overall number of calls will tell you only what is happening to the number of calls. It won't tell you if the increase or decrease is due to changes such as an increase in customers or specific call types.

Daily call distribution will tell you if your peak and off-peak hours are changing and may explain decreases in service during new peaks that you are not staffed up for.

Call breakdown by type will tell you whether or not any specific type of call is increasing.

Number of calls per workstation will tell you whether any call increase/decrease is due to an increase/decrease in workstations or whether your customers are actually calling you more/less often.

Change in Resolution Times

You need to look at the percentage of calls resolved at point of call to make sure your front line is at maximum effectiveness. If this percentage has gone down, you need to look at other statistics such as number of calls by type to find out why.

Some Help Desks report on average resolution time, but this can be a very deceiving measure if there is a wide variance in your resolution times. Better than reporting on an average would be to select intervals that make sense in your environment and report on these. Figure 9.5 shows an example in which selected intervals are the percentage of calls resolved in less than one hour, between one and four hours, between four and eight hours, and more than eight hours. You would have to pick intervals that make sense in your environment. Experiment to see where the bulk of your calls lie and which intervals are the most meaningful.

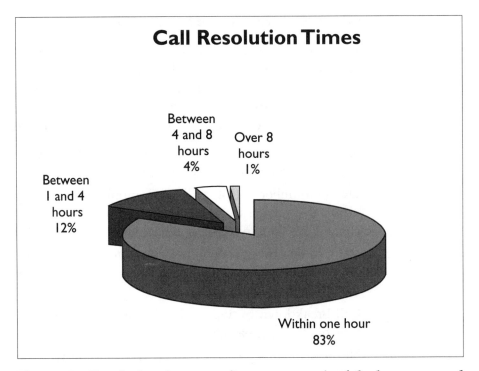

Figure 9.5   Resolution times are often more meaningful when expressed as a percentage of interval.

Another important statistic is resolution times, by percentage per interval, for calls passed on to other areas of support. This would tell you how well second and third levels of support are doing in terms of response times. This statistic is especially important if your resolution times are increasing and you want to know why and where.

Change in Response Times

Customer wait times and abandonment rate will tell you whether your customers are having to wait longer to get service and whether they are actually waiting or just hanging up.

Interpreting Help Desk Management Statistics

Figures 9.6 through 9.12 show examples of Help Desk management statistics. We will analyze these in terms of Help Desk performance.

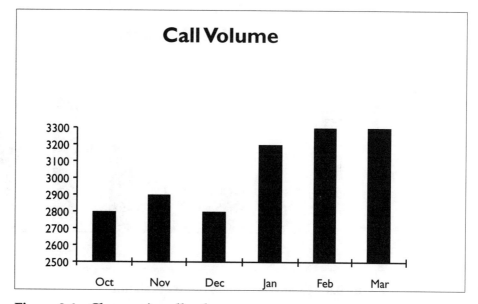

Figure 9.6   Changes in call volume.

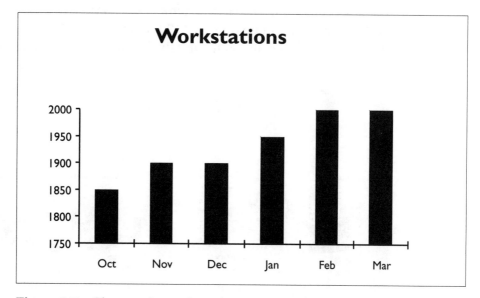

Figure 9.7   Changes in workstations supported.

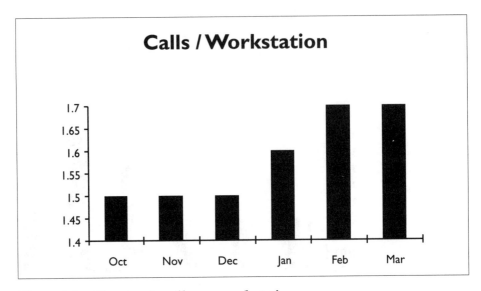

Figure 9.8   Changes in calls per workstation.

Figures 9.6, 9.7, and 9.8 show that there has been a 15 percent overall increase in calls from one quarter to the next, an 8 percent increase in the number of workstations from the beginning of one quarter to the end of the next, and an increase in the number of calls per workstation from 1.5 at the beginning of one quarter to 1.7 at the end of the next. Looking at the calls and workstations separately doesn't tell you much. But looking

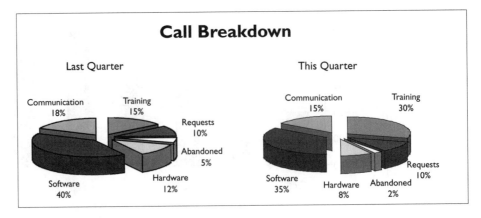

Figure 9.9   Call breakdown.

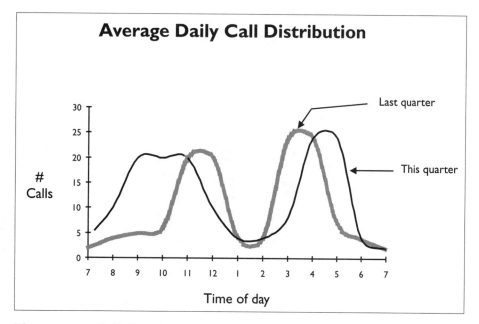

Figure 9.10   Call distribution.

at the calls per workstation tells you that your calls are not just increasing because you are supporting more workstations. You are actually getting more calls per workstation. You can go to other statistics to find out why. Figure 9.9, which shows call breakdown by type, might hold the answer. Your training-type calls have increased from 15 percent of calls

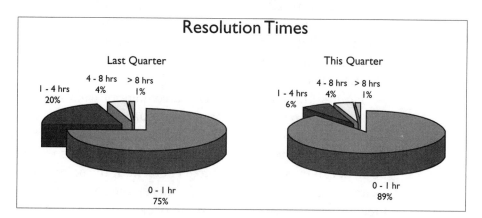

Figure 9.11   Call resolution.

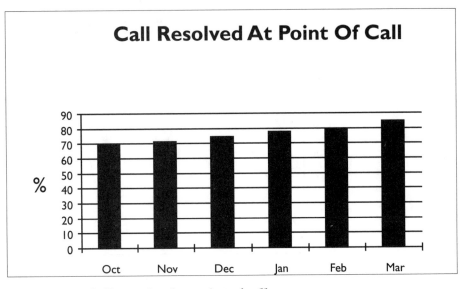

Figure 9.12   Calls resolved at point of call.

to 30 percent from one quarter to the next. You will have to address this if you want your calls per workstation to come down. The good news is that your abandonment rate is down from 5 percent to 2 percent.

Figure 9.10 shows changes in average daily call distribution from one quarter to the next. Your call peaks have shifted. Fortunately, you have been watching this on a weekly basis and have adjusted your staffing accordingly, so your call management has not been negatively affected. Figure 9.11 shows that you have increased the calls you resolve within one hour, from 75 percent to 89 percent. This is probably due to the increase in the percentage of calls that you are resolving at point of call, which is shown in Figure 9.12.

Figure 9.12 shows you the percentage of calls resolved at point of call, over the past six months (two quarters). You don't have a lot to worry about there. From the beginning of the first quarter to the end of the next, you have increased the percentage of calls that you resolve at point of call from 70 percent to 85 percent. If the service-level agreement example presented previously in this chapter was yours, you would be meeting the calls resolved at point of call dead on.

In summary, what the statistics illustrated in Figures 9.6 through 9.12 show is the following:

1. **Your calls per workstation are increasing,** probably due to the fact that the percentage of training-type calls you are getting has doubled. This is a dangerous trend. You want to eliminate anything that is causing the calls-per-workstation figure to increase. Improvement initiatives you may want to consider are as follows:

   Making basic PC and LAN training mandatory for all customers, to be taken before they get their PCs. You have the data you need to go to customer management with this proposal. You may want to do some calculations to show how much this increase is costing in customer time and Help Desk time (see Chapter 11, "Cost-Benefit Analysis").

   Offering various training options to customers. You need to do some investigation to find out why customers aren't taking training. Perhaps it just isn't convenient enough. You might suggest having a trainer come into customer areas on a regular basis to work with customers as they go about their daily tasks. This just-in-time training might be just the thing to reduce calls to the Help Desk. Customers may be very willing to pay for this kind of help.

2. **Your call distribution has changed.** Your morning peak starts earlier and lasts longer, and your afternoon peak starts earlier. You need to keep an eye on this to make sure you're staffed to handle it. You also need to talk to your customers to see if their requirements are changing. You may have to add hours to your Help Desk to start earlier.

In the preceding examples we looked at statistics from one quarter to the next. We were probably preparing a quarterly performance report. In reality, you would probably want to look at these figures from month to month, or even more frequently if your Help Desk is just starting up, if you want to watch a potential problem area more closely or if you want to check if an improvement is working.

Measuring Proaction

When you are measuring proaction you are checking whether your Help Desk is standing still or whether it is moving ahead with the business— working to eliminate calls, making improvements, and getting ready for future technology or customer requirements. How do you measure this? Your primary measurements for proaction are your objectives. You may also look to unplanned work that you did to prevent problems or meet a sudden business need.

The first question you must ask yourself when you look at your objectives is "Are we doing anything to eliminate calls?" If your Help Desk is to be proactive, the answer to this question must always be "yes." You may have an ongoing call elimination project in which analysts are assigned to find and eliminate the reason for the most frequently occurring calls. This becomes a cycle like the following:

1. Find most frequent reason for calling.
2. Eliminate it.
3. Go to 1.

You might add or improve monitoring tools so you can look for trends and find problems before they start. You can also ask yourself, "Are we doing anything to decrease resolution times or increase calls resolved at point of call?" Positive answers to these questions are also indications of proaction. Initiatives toward achieving these ends might include the following:

- Remote diagnostic software to allow analysts to see and control the customer's screen so more calls can be resolved at point of call, with no need to go on site to the customer's PC.
- Knowledge bases or expert systems to increase the knowledge that an analyst has access to while resolving a call.

"What is the organization I am supporting doing? Am I preparing to meet it?" is another question you need to ask yourself when measuring proaction. To answer the latter part of the question you would need to look at the following:

Are your networks and your assets ready for any improvements that are coming?

Do you provide the software the business needs? Are your updates timely?

Are there services you should/should not be offering?

Are your support hours adequate?

Are your staff adequately trained? Do they need to pick up different skills?

Proaction isn't really an option. If you want to be able to measure up to your competition—if you want to be able to support your organization effectively—you absolutely must be proactive.

Tips for Help Desks That Are Just Starting Up

Help Desks that are just starting up need to plan their measurements carefully and understand what they mean before they publish them.

Spend some time getting to know your Help Desk management statistics:

Learn all your Help Desk tools well (e.g., ACD, IVR, Help Desk management system) so you know what your full capabilities are for gathering and reporting on Help Desk data.

Play with measurements such as call resolution by interval (Figure 9.5) until you find intervals or scales that are relevant to your Help Desk.

Understand your measurements before you try to do anything with them:

Keep measurements simple at first and make sure you understand them. Add new measurements slowly. Don't try to do everything at once.

Don't share measurements until you are absolutely sure what they mean. Don't be in a hurry to publish.

Lay whatever groundwork you can to save time preparing for more complex measures:

Service-level agreements take a long time to set up. Resolving responsibilities takes a large chunk of the time. Try to iron out responsibilities with all of the areas you interact with to get a good understanding of who does what. This will help you no end when it comes time to set up service-level agreements.

Don't work for even one day without objectives.

Get a handle on your costs as soon as possible.

Reporting on Performance

Management will make its evaluation of Help Desk performance based on the information it receives from you, the Help Desk manager. You need to ensure that the information is accurate so that any misconceptions that they may have picked up elsewhere are cleared up and you have recommendations for resolving each identified problem. Don't try to hide poor performance. You won't be able to do it for long. Focus your efforts on recommending good solutions for any problems that you do have. Even departments that are functioning well will have problems—but they will make sure the problems are resolved quickly and permanently. Using the data you gather to identify problems and trends, reporting them honestly, and recommending well thought out solutions will help gain you and your Help Desk the respect and support of management.

The way you present information is important in that it could determine whether the information even gets read. Be clear and concise. You can always have more detail ready should anyone require it—or you can present it as an appendix. Graphs can communicate a lot of information in a relatively small space.

Management will want to know the following:

Operating cost. ROI is not usually included in a quarterly performance report; it is typically part of a separate process, but it can be included if it's available and if it's fairly current.

Effectiveness of call load management.

Level of proaction.

Based on these three aspects of performance, you need to put together a formal quarterly performance report. The report will include

Summary of Help Desk management statistics, including changes in the environment. You want to show the environment the Help Desk is working in and how it is performing within this environment.

Performance against objectives.

Performance against service-level agreements.

Summary of customer and Help Desk staff evaluations. You might use these only to support other statistics.

Help Desk operating cost (investment) expressed as cost per workstation. If you have it, you may also want to include the dollar value of services being provided (return), also expressed as cost per workstation.

Summary and recommendations. Summarize performance strengths and weaknesses and make recommendations for addressing weaknesses.

A few points about the format of the report:

1. Be brief. No long lists or long paragraphs. Cover the main points only.
2. Use graphs and charts.
3. Have detailed calculations available for reference should someone ask. Don't include them in the report.

The following is an example of a performance report that the Help Desk might give to management for evaluation.

Help Desk Performance Report

Period: January–March 1996
Services Added/Changed
Remote diagnostic capabilities added.
Change in Workstations/Calls

	Oct	Nov	Dec	Jan	Feb	Mar	Percentage Change over Qtrs.
Workstation	1850	1900	1900	1950	2000	2000	8%
Call volume	2800	2900	2800	3200	3300	3300	15%
Calls per Work-station	1.5	1.5	1.5	1.6	1.7	1.7	13%

Call Breakdown by Type

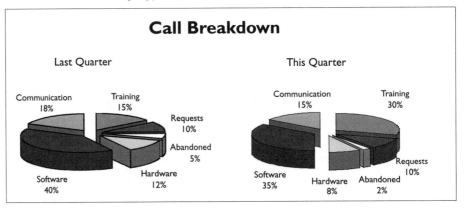

Call Resolution

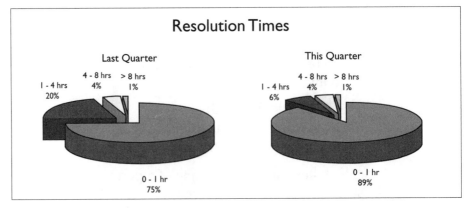

Objectives/Accomplishments

Accomplished:

Increased resolution of problems at point of call from 78 percent to 85 percent.

Prevented significant production response problems by installing new version of network operating system. Network monitoring software identified the problem, and we were able to respond quickly, preventing major service interruptions.

Not Accomplished:

Did not implement automated asset management. A 15 percent increase in calls precluded this activity.

Service-Level Agreement

Levels Met

Average call answer time:	97 percent in thirty seconds or less
Percentage of calls reopened within two weeks:	0
First-level call resolution:	85 percent
Priority 1 response achieved:	100 percent
Priority 2 response achieved:	100 percent
Priority 3 response achieved:	98 percent
Priority 4 response achieved:	100 percent
Customer satisfaction:	91 percent of callbacks received positive ratings.

Levels Not Met

For customers:	Percentage of training-type calls = 30 percent (limit was 10 percent)

Operating Cost

Salaries (including benefits, overhead):	$293,000
Contract for outsourced hardware maintenance:	$70,000

Contract for leasing computer-based training for customers:	$36,000
Training for Help Desk staff:	$13,000
Office supplies:	$1,600
Help Desk software maintenance costs:	$1,600
Help Desk hardware leasing costs:	$7,500
IVR hardware and software maintenance:	$16,600
Facilities overhead:	$6,000
TOTAL:	$445,300
Number of workstations supported:	2,000
Cost per workstation: This quarter	$223
Cost per workstation: Last quarter	$225
Return per workstation: Calculated July 1996	$229

Last return calculation based on input from ABC Help Desk Outsourcing and XYZ Help Desk Services.

Summary/Recommendations

This quarter saw a 15 percent increase in the number of calls per month. The number of calls per workstation has increased from 1.5 to 1.7. The increase appears to be due largely to training-type calls that have doubled this quarter (as a percentage of total calls), exceeding the limit of 10 percent laid out in the terms of the service-level agreement. The number of calls must be reduced and contained so that support costs do not increase needlessly and improvement initiatives may continue. Recommendations to achieve a decrease are as follows:

Bring training on site for customers, at the customers' cost. Work with customer management to put together and market a policy that outlines training that the customer must take before getting PC equipment and any new software.

Offer just-in-time training, at customers' cost. Trainers can tutor customers as they work.

Market terms of service-level agreement to customers.

Charge back for all training-type calls. Each quarter, the number of training-type calls could be totaled and charged back to customer management.

Communicating Performance

You've gone to a lot of trouble to evaluate your performance. Who needs to know how you are performing?: Your customers, your staff, and management.

Customers

You want your customers to understand the environment you are supporting and some of the challenges you face. This will help them have more realistic expectations and will help correct any misperceptions they have about Help Desk service. Customers need to be aware of how well they and the Help Desk are meeting service-level agreements so customers can see how such agreements impact Help Desk performance when customers don't meet their responsibilities. Customers can also see how the Help Desk plans to improve when it does not meet its responsibilities.

The customers' management will probably be getting a copy of your quarterly performance report, but most customers will not. You need to communicate to them frequently and more informally (see Chapter 10, "Marketing," for some ideas). Information they should know includes the following:

- Changes in the technological environment (e.g., new software)
- Total calls, total workstations supported, calls per workstation
- Call breakdown by type
- Call resolution, percentages by interval
- Major accomplishments
- Performance versus service-level agreements
- Results of any surveys

Individual components of this information can be communicated separately (e.g., newsletters), but the performance information in its entirety should be accessible to them at any time. A Help Desk intranet site would be a great place to keep this kind of information.

Help Desk Staff

Staff should see the results of all performance measurements that you do. The more Help Desk staff know about their environment, the more informed they will be in any decisions they have to make. The more feedback they get, the more they can improve. If you give them all the information, they will be able to see for themselves how they are performing or where any problem areas lie. Posting this information will reward positive performance and encourage improvement of less than positive performance.

Tell your staff specifically what you plan to do based on their feedback (staff evaluations) and on the results of your other performance measurements. They will know that you take their input seriously and value their opinions. It is, after all, Help Desk performance that you are evaluating, and they are the Help Desk.

Management

There is much valuable information in the performance report you have created for management. Rather than just send it out, meet with managers and make a presentation, if possible. You could answer questions and concerns as they come up and provide more details as they are asked for. If you have to send the report, follow up a week later to see if each recipient has read it and if there is any feedback.

You can and should communicate performance to management less formally at more frequent intervals than quarterly. Information such as call volumes by type, resolution times, and environment growth will be of interest to them, as will any specific accomplishments that demonstrate the business value you provide. The information doesn't necessarily have to be sent directly to them, although you may find that they request it. You can put performance information on posters and in newsletters—places where they are likely to see it. If they do request monthly updates, or if you feel it is appropriate, put together the same information in report format and send it out at each month's end.

Measurement as a Control

Measuring the performance of your Help Desk thoroughly and regularly will give you more control over its success. You will have the information necessary to make improvements, address problem areas before they get out of control, and do informed planning for the future. You will know what the organization you support needs and will be in a good position to provide it. Your Help Desk will be difficult to compete with.

Key Points Covered in This Chapter

There are three aspects of performance that must be considered when measuring it:

Operating cost versus value returned, or return on investment (ROI)

Effectiveness of call load management

Level of proaction

There are also four perspectives on performance:

Customer

Senior management

Help Desk staff

Help Desk manager

Performance is a moving picture. You must measure change rather than a single moment in time.

The "return" in ROI can be measured by taking the time to find out what it would cost for someone else (e.g., a Help Desk outsourcing company) to do the job. The "investment" in ROI can be calculated by simply adding up Help Desk operating costs.

To measure how effectively you are managing your calls within your changing environment you're going to have to look at a number of measures, both qualitative and quantitative:

Objectives. Proactive initiatives. You can learn and improve from the objectives that you do not achieve.

Service-level agreements. A two-way measurement between Help Desk staff and a specific customer area.

Customer evaluation. A qualitative measure, usually gathered from some form of survey and dealing with factors such as knowledge and responsiveness of the Help Desk. It's very important to give customers the results of surveys and what you plan to do to address any issues.

Staff evaluation. Includes information such as customer trust, legitimacy of calls, reasonableness of workload, adequacy and timeliness of training, availability and usefulness of tools, quality of support received from other areas and vendors, and value of work performed.

Help Desk management statistics. The most useful statistics include number of calls per workstation, percentage of calls resolved at point of call, resolution times by percentage per interval, call breakdown by type, and daily call distribution.

To measure proaction you look to your objectives. You may also look to unplanned work that you did to prevent problems or to meet a sudden business need. If you are proactive then you are always working to eliminate calls.

A performance report for senior management should include the following information:

Summary of Help Desk management statistics, including changes in the environment. You want to show the environment the Help Desk is working in and how it is performing within this environment.

Performance against objectives.

Performance against service-level agreements.

Help Desk operating cost (investment) expressed as cost per workstation. If you have it, you may want to include dollar value of services being provided (return), also expressed as cost per workstation.

Summary and recommendations. Summarize performance strengths and weaknesses and make recommendations for addressing weaknesses.

A few tips for new Help Desks:

Learn all of your Help Desk tools well.

Keep measurements simple at first.

Play with measurements until you find intervals or scales that are relevant to your Help Desk. Understand them before you try to publish them.

Do the groundwork to prepare for more complex measures.

Share performance with customers, senior management, and Help Desk staff. Do it frequently and informally and use a variety of communication vehicles. Formal performance reports should be given to, and discussed with, senior management.

CHAPTER TEN

Marketing

Your Help Desk is a business. You have products and services to sell, and you have customers to sell them to. Customers aren't going to buy from you just because you're there. Management isn't going to fund you or support you just because you're there, either. You need to show customers and management what the Help Desk offers, what it can do for them, and what it can do for the business. You need to market.

Consider the legendary vacuum cleaner salesperson. Marketing is his bread and butter. He must constantly worry about image, about showing you that he is reputable and his company is not fly by night. He must sell you the value of the vacuum cleaner he is trying to get you to buy. He might just pour a bucket of dirt on your rug and then vacuum it up to show you how his company's vacuum cleaner sucks up every last dirt particle. He will also teach you how to use the vacuum cleaner. If you should buy one, he doesn't want you calling him with questions. He's very busy, and he doesn't want to have to come back to show you how to do things. He needs to be out selling more vacuum cleaners. The salesperson will also give you information about upcoming sales, new models, service center shutdowns, new accessories, and so on. In other words, the vacuum cleaner salesperson must worry about image, selling value, education, and communication—the four components of marketing. You can pick up some valuable tips from him because each of these elements applies whether you're marketing a vacuum cleaner or marketing a Help Desk.

As an illustration, consider the Help Desk that does no marketing:

No focus on image. Customers base their opinions of the Help Desk on an occasional, poorly written communication that they might happen to see. This may cause them to avoid using the Help Desk and even to pass their own unfavorable opinions on to their colleagues. They are passing on a negative Help Desk image, even though they may never have used the Help Desk themselves.

Little or no selling value. Help Desk successes go unnoticed and unrecognized, so customers and management only remember problems. If cost cutting or outsourcing comes up, the Help Desk will be on the "endangered department" list.

Little or no education. Customers aren't aware of any policies or standards that are in place. They may introduce nonstandard products, which would increase the complexity of support, and they may inadvertently breach security, perhaps allowing a virus into the system.

Little or no communication. Customers don't know that the Help Desk is there or what it offers. They don't really know what's happening in the technology environment. They might waste time struggling with a problem on their own or they might go to a colleague for help, wasting the colleague's time as well as their own. Two people who should have been focusing on their jobs and contributing to the business have instead gone into another time-consuming business: support.

If this same Help Desk were to practice the four components of marketing, things might look different:

Image. The Help Desk has a professional, service-oriented image. Its members took the time to attend some writing courses and now check each other's memos and documents before sending them out to the customers.

Selling value. Customers and management receive formal quarterly performance reports and frequent, informal updates. They are kept informed of Help Desk performance and understand the business value that it is delivering. They consider the Help Desk a valuable part of the organization.

Education. Customers are aware of policies and standards, are offered regular training, and have access to on-line information such as technical hints and tips and answers to frequently asked questions. They are using technology effectively. As a result, the Help Desk is getting fewer calls.

Communication. Customers are kept up to date on the range of services that the Help Desk offers and all changes in the technological environment. Their feedback is encouraged, and they give it. They're pretty satisfied with their Help Desk.

The four components of marketing can have a significant impact on the success of your Help Desk. Two words of caution, however.

First, it is sometimes easy for internal Help Desks to become complacent and think "We don't have to worry about marketing. We have no competition." Wrong. Whether you realize it or not, you are competing. You may be an established internal Help Desk, but that is not a guarantee that you will get the company's business. Outsourcing is almost always an option and one that is becoming more popular as organizations are forced to cut costs. If you want to continue to do business, you must market your value and your accomplishments. It may be the case that you offer better service and better value than a third-party service provider, but if your customers and management don't know this or aren't reminded of it on a regular basis you might lose out to your competitors, who aren't afraid to market their value. You need to pull out your suitcase of samples and start pounding the pavement.

Second, marketing is important to Help Desk success, but it will not replace or hide poor Help Desk performance—at least, not for very long. Your marketing can be only as effective as your Help Desk is. It should be considered a showcase for your services and your performance, not a substitute. If you are performing well, your marketing can spotlight the value you are adding to the business. If you are performing poorly, any marketing efforts will be greeted with cynicism and ridicule, and people's already poor perception of you will get poorer. Don't try to market something that you don't have.

In This Chapter

This chapter will explore the four components of marketing:

- Image
- Selling value
- Education
- Communication

We will also look at marketing vehicles and creating a marketing plan. The chapter will finish up with some marketing ideas for new Help Desks and for established Help Desks.

Image

Image is how you're perceived, all the things your words and actions are saying without you necessarily verbalizing them. You project image with every customer interaction you have. Consider the following very simple example.

Mary A and Mary B (not their real names) work on a Help Desk. Mary A gets a call. She picks up the receiver and gives a big sigh. "What can I do for you?" she asks in a slow, tired voice. "Hmm . . . " thinks the customer, "I don't think this person is interested in my problem."

Mary B answers her call a little differently. "Help Desk, Mary B speaking," she says, in a brisk, cheerful voice. Mary B's customer thinks "Oh good. Here's someone who wants to help me."

The image projected by Mary A is that of a Help Desk analyst who is bored and not really interested in her customer's problems. Worse, Mary A's behavior has tainted the image of the whole Help Desk. Her customer probably thinks the Help Desk isn't as effective as it could be. That image will stay with Mary A's customer until something happens to change it. With no extra effort, by simply following Mary B's example and adopting a more enthusiastic greeting, Mary A could have avoided the results of poor marketing and conveyed the same, positive image as Mary B.

Why Worry about Image?

If the Help Desk has a poor image, if customers don't have confidence that Help Desk staff can solve their problems, if customers don't like to speak to Help Desk staff because they're rude, then customers may try getting support elsewhere or wait longer than they should. "I really don't want to talk to those people. I'll try solving it myself first." The business value offered by the Help Desk decreases. Customers become less effective employees.

A poor image also tends to lower morale. It is not easy working on a Help Desk when customers don't think you're very good. Their perception of your service will come through in comments and attitude. A poor image means improvements will be more difficult to implement. Customers won't be as eager to cooperate. You won't have their support.

Where Does Image Come From?

Image comes primarily from the quality of your services. If you aren't doing a good job supplying Help Desk services, if you are not meeting promises or are delivering upgrades that don't work the first time, then no amount of marketing will help you. You need to clean up your act. Even if you are doing a good job, however, your image won't automatically be perfect. It will still depend on a number of factors. These include the following:

You. Your voice, your body language. If your voice or body language are saying "I don't care about you or your problem" then it really matters little what your words are saying. As you've probably heard a million times before—but is worth thinking about again—in a face-to-face situation, customers will take 55 percent of the meaning of what we are saying from our body language, 38 percent from our tone of voice, and only 7 percent from our actual words. Over the phone, the percentages are 14 percent for words and 86 percent from tone of voice. If you sound uncaring, the customer will think you are uncaring, even if your words say "I want to help you."

Your communications. If your memos or documents are sloppily written, with spelling mistakes and errors, then your customers will think "They can't even write a decent memo. They're probably incompetent." If your messages are tactless or rude, blaming other people, you will be labeled unprofessional, unwilling to take responsibility for your actions. If you are giving seminars or holding meetings and are unprepared, customers will think "this guy doesn't know what he is talking about!"

What Can You Do about It?

If the quality of your Help Desk services is good, there are things you can do to establish or improve your image:

Make yourself more customer-friendly. Be aware of your customers and of the image you are projecting at all times. A customer service course will help you. If you can't take a course, read (and practice) a customer service book. There are many good ones. My favorite is *Customer Service for Dummies*, by Karen Leland and Keith Bailey (IDG Books, 1995).

Make your communications more customer-friendly. Let your communications imply "I care about my customers so I took the time to do this properly." Set standards and templates for documents and memos to leave less room for creative writing and generate a more professional image. You might consider some kind of logo or "look" that shows that this product is from the Help Desk.

Monitor image constantly. Have peer reviews so staff can get feedback from each other on the kind of image they project. Use customer surveys to get a reading on your image and for suggestions on how you might change it. Make image problems a team issue to be discussed at team meetings.

A good image cannot cover up poor service—customers will soon see through it—but a poor image can cloud good service. Image is worth looking after.

Selling Value

It's cost-cutting time again. Senior management is looking over each department searching for ways to improve efficiencies. They look at the Help Desk.

"Hmm . . ." they say, rubbing their chins in unison, "What does the Help Desk do, anyway?"

If you aren't selling your value, people may not be aware of it. Your products are not always tangible, and your value is not always obvious. Many of your successes are quiet—preventing disasters rather than delivering a flashy and highly visible result. For example, much of the value you offer might come from the problems you prevent. Management, especially in the current economic climate, is always looking for ways to deliver increased value at decreased cost. If they don't understand where your value lies, they may make decisions that hurt the business and your Help Desk. If you're constantly selling, people become aware of and appreciate your successes, your value to the business.

What Do You Sell?

Marketing means selling the value your Help Desk offers. Value involves Help Desk performance and successes.

Performance

Help Desk performance is a complex entity involving several perspectives (customer, management, Help Desk staff, Help Desk manager) and countless measures, both qualitative and quantitative. What you need to market is not performance per se but change in performance. If the change is positive, you market your success. If the change is not positive, you market acknowledgment of the cause and recommendations for improvement (see Chapter 9, "Measuring Performance").

Successes

Much of the value of a Help Desk lies in its ability to prevent problems. You upgrade hardware to accommodate an increase in network traffic; you eliminate a virus before it spreads. This work typically goes unnoticed yet offers significant value to the business and should be marketed or management may not see it.

How Do You Sell?

You sell value in two ways: formally, via regular performance reports, and less formally whenever you have something specific to market, such as a decrease in response time or the prevention of a major problem.

Formal Reports

Formal performance reports need not be paper based. You may want to use on-line reports, videos, or presentations, depending on your audience. Performance reports should appear on a regular basis (e.g., quarterly), be concise, and be easy to understand (use charts and graphs). See Chapter 9 for a description of the information you should include in your report and for an example of a quarterly performance report.

Informal Updates

You achieved a reduction in resolution times. Market it. Make it into a fun poster, or put it in a newsletter. Successes can also include work done to prevent problems and new tools or services. Don't leave the marketing of successes for quarterly reports. You need to keep reminding management and customers of your value in the following ways:

Updates in newsletters. Updates might include success stories or growth in environment.

Help Desk report cards, detailing results of customer feedback.

Meetings with customer departments.

Options such as "What's Great" or "What's New" on your Help Desk intranet/Internet Web site.

Figures 10.1 through 10.4 illustrate different ways of selling value.

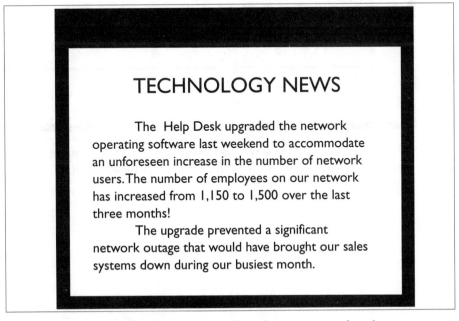

TECHNOLOGY NEWS

The Help Desk upgraded the network operating software last weekend to accommodate an unforeseen increase in the number of network users. The number of employees on our network has increased from 1,150 to 1,500 over the last three months!

The upgrade prevented a significant network outage that would have brought our sales systems down during our busiest month.

Figure 10.1   Example of an informal performance update in a company newsletter: The facts speak for themselves.

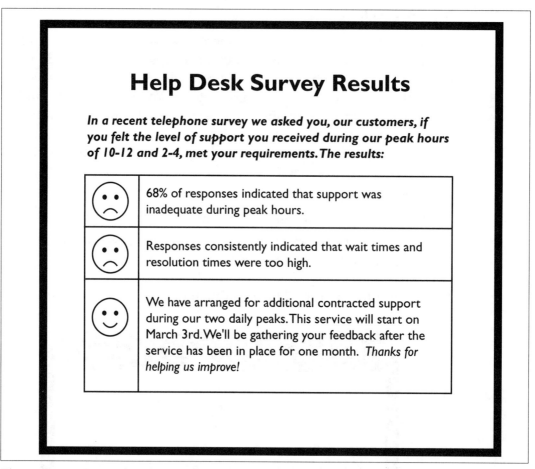

Figure 10.2   Example of a survey response card sent to customers: The card acknowledges there is a problem and states what will be done about it.

Figure 10.3 Example of an informal performance update, using a poster.

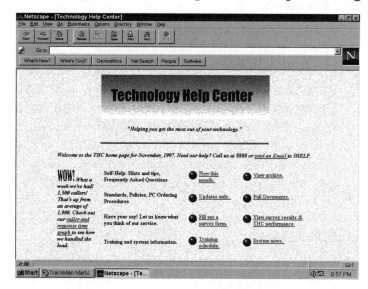

Figure 10.4 Example of selling value via a Help Desk intranet web site.

Education

No one wants to cause a disaster. No one wants to be inefficient. Ignorance, not intent, is the cause of many disasters and inefficiencies. For example, "Oh . . . was I supposed to check for viruses?" is not something the Help Desk wants to hear, but it is probably not what the customer really wants to be saying either.

The more your customers understand about using their technology, the more effective use they can make of it. They will make fewer calls to the Help Desk, make better use of their own time, and cause fewer mistakes and disasters.

Time

Education can help customers make better use of their own time and prevent them from wasting the time of their peers. They won't be stopped by simple mistakes ("Yikes, my icons have disappeared!"), and they won't be making life difficult for others ("Who the #$@! put a carriage return after each line in this document?").

Minimizing Mistakes

Although much technology is very simple to use, it is also simple to misuse. People who don't understand the software they use can make expensive mistakes. Some of these mistakes are very visible, such as data lost when files are inadvertently deleted or work is not saved properly. Other mistakes are less visible, such as the incorrect use of formulas in spreadsheets. A customer who does not understand how formulas in a spreadsheet work might end up creating a successful cost justification for a project that has inadequate payback. As a result, a project with poor payback for the business goes ahead, while other more viable projects sit and wait.

Preventing Disasters

"I didn't know that installing this software on my PC would bring down the network!" (and keep it down for two hours) suggests the kind of disaster that can be prevented with a little education. Spilling coffee on a PC is another, albeit smaller, disaster that education can help prevent. People don't generally come to work with the intention of doing damage. Disasters are usually the result of ignorance. The more customers understand about the impact of their actions, the less damage they are likely to cause.

What Do You Teach?

What can you teach as part of your overall marketing initiative? Begin with "the rules" and the effective use of technology.

1. "The Rules"

   Standards

   Security policies

   Priorities

   Procedures (e.g., purchasing a PC, reporting a problem)

   Terms of service-level agreements (SLAs)
2. Technology Use

   Training/seminars

   On-line tutorials

   Hints and tips

   Answers to frequently asked questions (FAQs)

The Rules

Your goal is to make your customers aware of the fact that policies, procedures, priorities, and standards do exist and need to be followed. Your challenges are to keep these policies and procedures in the forefront of people's minds and to communicate updates. Some suggestions for doing this include the following:

Avoid paper documents as they become obsolete very quickly and get lost easily (except for severely out-of-date versions. These seem to stay around forever).

Keep information on-line and easily accessible by your customers. You can set up a Help Desk intranet or Internet Web site so customers always know where to find documents (see Chapter 15 for an example).

Inform customers of updates. Customers will not keep checking on-line documents to see if policies or procedures have changed. Use E-mail, notes in newsletters, posters, and your Web site to let people know that something has changed. Try not to inundate people with information. Hit them with the highlights and tell them where to find the rest. For example, "Staff found with unlicensed software on their PCs are subject to immediate dismissal. Drives will be scanned each night" will catch your customers' attention. If you include "See Help Desk Home Page for other new technology-use policies" you can bet people are going to have a look.

Effective Use of Technology

Marketing initiatives that will help customers make better use of their hardware and software include the following:

A regular technology hints and tips column in your company newsletter. You can provide the same (or more) information in your Help Desk Web site. Figure 10.5 shows an example of a Help Desk FAQ on an intranet web site.

Dramatic posters to emphasize the effects of technology misuse.

Information sessions to review specific aspects of technology that seem to be causing problems for your customers or to preview new technology. Vendors will be willing to help you with technology previews.

As your customers become more comfortable with Internet technology, you might want to conduct on-line forums on specific topics from your Help Desk Web site.

Hold an open house event to demonstrate standard hardware and software and to show how different areas within the company are using technology. You can invite some of your expert customers to

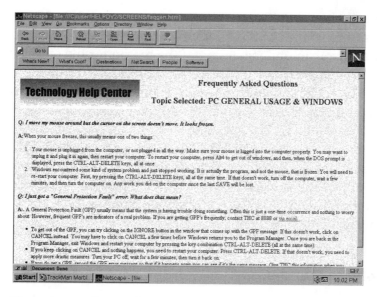

Figure 10.5   Example of a Help Desk intranet web site FAQ.

give demonstrations. Offer short seminars on topics customers have expressed an interest in.

Work with a third-party training provider, if your Help Desk doesn't offer training, to provide training options for your customers. Trainers can rotate through customer areas providing just-in-time training as customers are working. Trainers can also provide "getting started" training to people who have just received technology.

Communication

It's late in the evening and you're in the process of bringing the network down to do an upgrade. You're very excited about it. Response should improve considerably. Your customers will be a lot happier. Suddenly, the phone rings. Oops. You forgot to let everyone know about the service interruption. Someone who stayed late to work on a critical project is not very excited about your upgrade and not very excited about your Help Desk as a whole. A little communication on your part would have given that person an understanding of the reason for the service interruption and a chance to plan around it.

Marketing involves two-way communication with your customers: keeping customers informed about what is going on in the technological environment and giving them a chance to give feedback. Informed customers call the Help Desk less often, are more understanding and pleasant to deal with, and can make more effective use of their time. Encouraging feedback from customers results in good information for improving the Help Desk and enhances your relationship with your customers.

Communicating to Customers

What do you need to communicate to customers? Anything that affects their technological environment. For example:

- Planned service interruptions
- Emergencies or bad news (e.g., mainframe down)
- Good news, such as "faster lines are now available"
- Changes in the environment (e.g., software upgrade)

Service Interruptions

Post planned service interruptions to your Help Desk Web site as soon as you know about them, then issue frequent reminders via E-mail and/or logon messages. Customers should also receive reminders the day before and the day of the interruption.

Emergencies and Bad News

When something goes wrong, how you handle the communication is just as important as how you fix the problem. Here are a few tips for communicating bad news:

Describe the problem and its impact—don't try to justify it or lay blame. Customers are more interested in getting the problem fixed than in whose fault it is.

Let people know what you're going to do about the problem. This might be as general as "We do not yet know what the problem is, but we have notified the vendor and are expecting technicians on site any minute." People want to know that you are doing something about the problem.

Communicate often. No news is worse than bad news. To a customer, no news means that you are doing nothing. Tell customers how often you will communicate, and then stick to that schedule. For example, you may tell customers "Call in to the Help Desk Emergency Information Line for updates on the problem. Updates will be posted every thirty minutes on the half hour starting at 1 P.M." Make sure that you do change the information message every half hour. Even if nothing new has happened, time-stamp the message and say as much as you know.

Let customers know when there is a resolution. Notify customers as soon as the system is up so they are not sitting there waiting to start work.

Emergencies and bad news situations need to be communicated quickly. Good communication vehicles include the following:

Use voice mail messages to let people know there is a problem. Set up a phone group that allows you to send a phone message automatically to designated people in each customer area. The designated people can then notify everyone in their departments. Use these same groups to let people know when the problem has been resolved.

Set up an option on your Help Desk phone menu to point people to a system status information line that people can access when there is a major problem. They can get the most current update on the problem without talking to a Help Desk analyst.

Other vehicles that might be useful in your company: overhead electronic displays to let people know when a problem occurs, what is going on to fix it, and when it is resolved; a public address system; a fax system to fax messages to designated customers letting them know the status of problems.

Changes and Good News

Changes that need to be communicated include software upgrades, upcoming technology changes, and new Help Desk services such as expanded hours or interactive voice response (IVR)—anything that will affect the technological environment of the customers. Customers need to know about changes well ahead of time so they can get any required training, and they need frequent reminders right up to the time of the change. For example, if word processing software is being upgraded to a new version, let customers know about two months ahead of time. Then remind them on a weekly basis. During the last week, daily reminders might be a good idea. Communicate after the fact also. Let people know that the upgrade was put into place and that everything is as it should be.

Good news to be communicated includes improvements that customers have been waiting for, such as "more lines available for dial-in" or "company templates have now been added to our word processing software."

Vehicles for communicating changes or good news include the following:

E-mail, especially if the information is something that needs to be communicated immediately

Messages that appear at logon time

Articles in company newsletters

Posters

Your Help Desk Web site

Getting Feedback from Customers

Make giving feedback easy for customers. Vehicles you might use include the following:

E-mail to a special feedback ID.

Response lines. Customers can call in, anonymously if they wish, and leave a message.

Callbacks. Call customers after their problems have been closed to ask if they have any suggestions for improvements, as well as to ensure that the problem was really fixed. If you are already doing callbacks, add a question asking the customer for suggestions for improvement.

Surveys. Keep surveys short and fun. You might want to survey customers on a rotating basis so your survey information is always current. For example, you may survey a different department every month or two, and then follow the surveys up by attending departmental meetings to communicate survey results and any planned improvements. Surveys can be sent out via E-mail on postcards that customers fill in and return, in company newsletters, or at the Help Desk Web site. Figure 10.6 shows an example of collecting feedback using an intranet web site survey.

Meetings. Attend customer meetings and ask for feedback. Let people know ahead of time that you'll be there so they can prepare their comments.

Focus groups. You may already be holding regular focus groups for users of specific software such as spreadsheets. You can collect feedback on software performance and the quality of Help Desk support at these groups.

Gather feedback at any open house events that you host. Have a feedback box prominently displayed and have a designated Help Desk analyst available so that feedback can be given anonymously or in person. If feedback is given in person, have the analyst record it so that the customer feels that the feedback is being taken seriously and won't be forgotten.

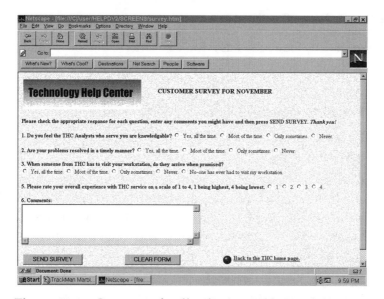

Figure 10.6   Customer feedback via a Help Desk intranet web site.

Acknowledging Feedback

Feedback will stop coming in if you don't acknowledge it. You can acknowledge feedback by summarizing it in vehicles such as newsletters, report cards sent to customers, or an option in your Help Desk Web site. Figure 10.2 illustrates acknowledging feedback using a survey response card. You can also attend customer meetings to talk about the feedback you have received. Besides simply summarizing feedback you must tell customers how you plan to act on it. If the feedback comes from an upset customer who includes a name, then you should get back directly to that customer. Similarly, if a customer gives you an idea that you use, thank the customer personally before you publish feedback results.

Make sure you let customers know how to give feedback and that you welcome it. Mention this at the end of any newsletter articles you submit, in your Help Desk Web site, and in any general communication you send out.

Marketing Vehicles

In deciding how you are going to get information to your customers, you can choose from a wide variety of communication vehicles—everything from a memo to an open house. Regardless of the vehicle you choose, you will have the challenge of communicating to people who are deluged with information and who are very busy. In order to help ensure that your communication gets through to them, whatever vehicle you choose, you need to do the following:

1. Cater to Your Audience

   Know who your audience is, and design the communication specifically for them. If your audience is your customers, go back to the customer profile you created when you were getting your Help Desk focused, back in Chapter 1. This will tell you who you need to market to, where they are, how technology-literate and technology-friendly they are, what technology they use, and what they use it for. You need to make sure you send information to your customers in a way that will ensure they receive it. If they have access to and use E-mail, then E-mail is available to you as a marketing medium. If they use voice mail, then voice mail is also available to you. If you have pockets of customers who are not (yet) technology-literate, use other media, such as posters or newsletters, to get your information to them.

   Be aware of any companywide initiatives that will affect your communication, such as paper conservation. If you are putting out reams of paper when the rest of the company is trying to conserve, you will annoy a lot of people, and they probably won't get the information you're sending.

2. Be Concise

   Your customers are being inundated with information from a variety of sources. They do not have time to read long missives or listen to long, repetitive messages. Make your communications short and to the point. Tighten up meetings and seminars so you use only the time you need to get what you want accomplished.

3. Think Image

The more consistent you are about having each Help Desk communication reflect the image you want to portray, the greater the likelihood that your customers will connect that image to your Help Desk.

Making Use of Existing Vehicles

Your company already has several communication vehicles in place. Make use of them in your marketing wherever possible. For example:

Company newsletters. Contribute regularly, or have your own section. Editors who are trying to fill space will welcome your contributions.

Company intranet. Set up your own home page.

Customer departmental meetings. Customers often have regular departmental meetings. Make use of these meetings for selling performance, teaching, communicating changes, and gathering feedback.

Performance review meetings. Your own department most likely has meetings set up to communicate performance to upper management. Make sure Help Desk performance is included, and try to be there to communicate it. If you can't be there, take a look at what is being communicated and make sure it is accurate and communicates what you want.

Being Creative

If you are sending paper, make it paper that people will look at. People like to look at pictures, and they like to laugh. Use graphics and humor wherever possible, and don't be afraid to laugh at yourself. Humor can lighten up even a poor "Help Desk Report Card" that you are sending to customers. If you're afraid that your communication vehicle is too creative, try it out on a few customers first to get their feedback.

Fourteen Vehicles to Consider

1. **Help Desk newsletters.** The newsletter can contain technology hints and tips, answers to customer questions, news about product upgrades, and performance information. Depending on your environment, you may wish to publish your newsletter on paper (some customers like to read on the bus or at home) or electronically. You could include a copy in your intranet web site.

2. **Faxes.** You could fax news of coming events, changes, and various updates to predesignated departmental servers. Or, if you have the technology, you could set up a fax-back system that customers could use to request specific documents such as "how-to" information.

3. **Laminated priority lists or service-level agreement terms.** Have these printed on fluorescent paper and laminated so that customers can pin them on the wall next to their phones.

4. **Postcards.** These can be used for surveys, invitations to seminars or presentations, or announcements of upgrades.

5. **Reports** (paper or on-line). Good for formally communicating performance to management and customers.

6. **E-mail.** For emergencies, notes to individual customers, and any kind of information that customers need to receive immediately.

7. **Help Desk intranet or Internet sites.** The site could contain all Help Desk–related information such as policies, procedures, hints and tips, priorities, service-level agreements, training information, upgrade announcements, performance information, and so on. There could also be a facility at the site to allow customers to give feedback on Help Desk service (see Chapters 8 and 15).

8. **Voice messaging.** A phone option could be set up to run off of the main Help Desk phone menu to be used as an emergency information line that customers could call for updates when a major service interruption occurs. Options could also be set up to

allow customers to leave feedback or to provide customers with general Help Desk information.

9. **Scheduled technology demonstrations.** Set up demonstrations to showcase new technology or new uses of existing technology.

10. **Seminars.** If your Help Desk call statistics indicate a need for customer training in specific software or procedures, a seminar might be just the thing. A seminar could also be used to address recurring questions. If your Help Desk does not provide training, outsource it. Bring in a third party to do it.

11. **Meetings.** Set up information meetings or attend customer meetings to gather feedback and/or communicate changes and performance. Attending customer meetings is an excellent way to prepare departments for the arrival of technology.

12. **Focus groups.** Focus groups are especially good for introducing new products or upgrades. Customers in the groups will do a lot of free advertising for the Help Desk. If the product is not appropriate and is discarded, it is good to find that out as early as possible. Customers will feel that you have really listened to their feedback. If the product is appropriate and is purchased, you will have a group of customers already familiar with it and telling others about it. They will also have positive things to say about a Help Desk that listens to their input.

13. **Open houses.** Holding an open house increases the visibility of the Help Desk, allows you to meet your customers face to face, and gives you a chance to do a wide range of marketing. Ask some of your expert customers to demonstrate how they use specific software. Give demonstrations of standard desktop software, with lots of time for questions and answers. You can give miniseminars on high-interest topics, offer tours of your computer or server room, show customers what a PC or server looks like inside, and even demonstrate the life cycle of a problem that is called into the Help Desk. Refreshments and door prizes will add a sense of fun to your open house.

14. **Specialty marketing vehicles.** Mouse pads and inventory stickers make great marketing vehicles when imprinted with your Help Desk phone number, E-mail ID, and Web site address. They're hard to lose so customers will always have Help Desk contact information at hand.

A Marketing Plan

Why do you need a marketing plan? A marketing plan will help you accomplish the following things:

Maintain a consistent Help Desk image.

Measure the success of your Marketing initiatives and ensure that they really get carried out.

Be prepared for emergencies. If you plan how you will communicate bad news, such as unplanned service interruptions, then chances are you will do a good job communicating when a service interruption does happen. If you aren't prepared, you may go into panic mode, and communication will suffer. Customers will perceive you as not being able to handle big problems.

Prepare customers for future changes in the environment. Customers hate surprises. What may seem like a great surprise to you— "Hooray! The new upgrade to Windows is here!"—might be perceived as a disaster to your customer: "What the #$@! is this? What's happened to my Windows software? How do I do my work?" Putting together a marketing plan will help ensure that customers get adequate notification of any changes and are prepared for them.

What's in a Marketing Plan?

A marketing plan typically consists of the following items for each marketing initiative:

- Your objectives—what you want to accomplish through marketing
- The information you need to communicate to achieve your objectives
- The marketing vehicles you plan to use
- The audience you are trying to reach
- The frequency of the marketing initiative

Each of your major Help Desk activities (e.g., hardware and software upgrades, automation, installation of new tools) should be accompanied by a marketing initiative. Other activities and events you need to plan marketing for include:

- Significant, unplanned service interruptions
- Planned service interruptions
- Help Desk performance
- Customer surveys
- Changes in standards, policies
- Creating and maintaining hints and tips
- Creating and maintaining answers to frequently asked questions
- Technology upgrades
- Features of specific software
- Changes in Help Desk services

Your marketing plan should also show how you plan to maintain (or improve) your Help Desk image.

Keep It Current!

As with any plan, your marketing plan is only useful if it's current. Update it quarterly, along with your Help Desk objectives.

Sample Marketing Plan

Table 10.1 is a sample of a Help Desk marketing plan. Note that the plan addresses all four components of marketing.

Table 10.1   Example of a Marketing Plan

Initiative	Objective	Vehicles	Audience	Frequency/Date	Responsibility
IMAGE					
Training	Upgrade communication skills.	HD102 seminar	John, Martin	May/97	John, Martin
Image Consistency	Set up standard communication template.	E-mail, Word document	N/A	June/97	John
Image Review	Review all marketing materials. Check quality.	N/A	N/A	Quarterly: February, May, Aug, Nov.	Jim
Image Survey	Check customers' perception of all.	E-mail (mail-in response)	Rotating 10 percent of customers	Quarterly: February, May, Aug., Nov.	Paul
SELLING VALUE					
Quarterly Performance Report	Inform management of Help Desk Value.	Performance Report	Management	Quarterly: January April, July, Oct.	Peter
Performance Updates	Inform management and customers of Help Desk value.	Newsletter	All customers	Monthly	Jim
		Web site	All customers	Monthly	Jim
COMMUNICATION					
Planned Service Interruptions	Make customers aware of downtimes.	Web site	All customers	Post schedule monthly.	Paul
		E-mail	All customers	Day before and day of interruption	Paul

(continues)

Table 10.1   Example of a Marketing Plan *(continued)*

Initiative	Objective	Vehicles	Audience	Frequency/ Date	Responsibility
Emergencies, Bad News	Make customers aware that emergency exists and inform them of impact.	Phone group	Key customers	Twice. Immediately and when emergency is over.	Monica
		Information Message	All customers	Update every thirty minutes.	Monica
Changes in Technological Environment	Prepare customers for changes in environment.	Web site	All customers	One month before change.	Tina
		E-mail	All customers	Two days before change.	Tina
Feedback	Get suggestions from customers.	E-mail ID, running off of intranet web site	All customers	Set up by July. Monitor daily.	Jim
EDUCATION Updates to Standards, Procedures, Policies,	Keep customers aware of changes to technology standards.	Web site	All customers	Ongoing.	Tina
		E-mail	All customers	Once, at time of change.	Tina
Frequently Asked Questions (FAQs)	Give custom-ers answers to FAQs so that they don't have to call.	Web site	All customers	Update monthly from Help Desk database.	Jean
Technology Misuse.	To minimize theft of laptops.	Web site	All customers	May	Kelly
		Article in Newsletter	All customers	June	Kelly

Ideas for New Help Desks

If You Haven't Started Your Help Desk up Yet

If you haven't started your Help Desk up yet—get focused. Getting focused isn't only a marketing issue (see Chapter 1), but it's so important that I've included it here. Get feedback from customers, management, and other IT groups on what your Help Desk should be.

Are you delivering a Help Desk facility that will meet your customer's needs? You will start off on the wrong foot if what you deliver falls far short of customer expectations. If you can't deliver what they expect, perhaps you can deliver a first step. Discuss this with customer groups before you set your Help Desk up. Go to customer departmental meetings or arrange focus groups.

What does senior management expect from you? If management expects you to answer every how-to question that customers send your way but you know you won't have enough staff to do this, you are set up for failure. Create a budget-versus-services estimate that lists the services you think you can provide for the budget (including staff) you have. It won't be completely accurate, but it will help keep senior management, and your own, expectations realistic. Once you've been in business for a few months you will have a better handle on what services you can provide for how much, substantiated with call statistics, and can communicate this to senior management in your performance reporting.

Talk to IT groups to make sure that nothing "falls through the cracks." There are few things worse for a customer than being bounced back and forth between support areas.

Very Busy Help Desk Analyst: *"We don't support this . . . you'll have to call Application Support."*

Very Unhappy Customer: *"But Application Support passed me here!"*

Start marketing what's coming about a month before you open for business. The information you need to communicate includes:

When you will be open for business. Make sure your marketing is very specific about when your services will be available, otherwise people will be frustrated trying to get hold of you. Be very sure that you can meet the date you advertise. If you give out a phone number in your marketing, put a message on that number letting people know when your service will be available.

What services you will be providing. You want to include Help Desk hours, systems supported, and any other services such as training, technology purchase, and the installation of software that you will be providing.

How people can access your services. Let customers know what number they will have to call or what E-mail ID they will have to use to get help.

Suggested marketing vehicles:

Articles and teasers in company newsletters. The articles should describe the services you plan to provide and, if you've gone to your customers for input, can include customer comments. Your teasers can appear as ads letting people know that "help is coming soon."

E-mail messages. Send out an initial message describing what Help Desk services will be available and when. After the initial message, send out shorter messages weekly reminding customers when your Help Desk will be available and how to access it. If you have already set up a Help Desk Web site or some kind of on-line information application, let customers know how they can access it.

Pamphlets describing your services. Paper-based information gets out of date quickly so try to build some kind of central on-line Help Desk information application or Web site as soon as you can.

Posters. Use posters as teasers. For example, "All the help you need . . . coming on August 15th." (But remember, don't market a date unless you're sure you can meet it!)

Don't be afraid to get creative in your marketing. If you have doubts about a specific marketing technique, go to your customers for feedback.

Once You're Open for Business

Put out an E-mail message and/or logon message the day you start business. The message should state that you're open for business and should include the Help Desk phone number and E-mail ID. Give out mouse pads sporting the new Help Desk phone number, E-mail ID, and Web site address. You can also include this information on the inventory stickers that you put on each piece of hardware.

Survey your customers often. These surveys should be informal and conducted either over the phone or in person. You will be going through a period of adjustment. Let customers know that you are willing to listen to them and adjust your services accordingly. Don't forget about your remote customers. Call them for feedback and visit them when you can.

When you distribute PCs or install new technology, give customers some kind of introduction to Help Desk services. This might be in the form of a postcard left with the PC telling customers how to access Help Desk services and where to go for more information. You might prefer to make this introduction in person and give each customer a one-hour "getting started" session. This may be something that you can outsource.

As You Continue to Expand and Update Your Services

Communicate updates to Help Desk services in the company newsletter. Use posters for those updates you really want to emphasize. Keep your Help Desk Web site current and have a "What's New" option so customers will quickly be able to see what has changed.

Once you've collected a few months' worth of call statistics, market them from your Web site and in newsletters. For example, you may want to show growth in number of calls (broken down by type) and in number of customers supported, so people are aware of the growth you are supporting. Don't forget to market good news such as reduced resolution times and problem prevention or elimination.

Stay close to your customers. Send your Help Desk analysts to customer meetings regularly. If your customers are remote, don't forget about them. Set up a schedule to visit them if you can, or call them often. Get everyone on the Help Desk involved in attending customer meetings. Knowing what is important to customers—what they actually do—is invaluable to someone trying to solve a customer's problem.

Ideas for Established Help Desks

Use the information you are collecting about the kinds of calls you're getting to create a regular *hints and tips column* in your company newsletter and/or on your Help Desk Web site. If you provide this information on a regular basis, people will start to look for it. If you notice recurring questions or problems in specific areas, offer *one-hour seminars* for customers. Pass the idea by a few customers first to see what kind of response you get and to pick a time that would be best for them.

Contract a trainer to come into specific departments on specific days to provide *just-in-time training* to customers as they work. Use your Help Desk call statistics to justify the cost of this training to your management and/or customer management.

Create customer focus groups for each major software package. You probably know which of your customers are expert in each of the major packages you support. Work with these customers to set up user groups. The groups should meet regularly (e.g., monthly) to share knowledge about the software, how it is being used in different areas, and how it can be used. Encourage customers to invite vendors. Help the groups get started, but let the customers run them. Make sure someone from the Help Desk attends each meeting to answer questions; provide news of updates, fixes, and future plans; and gather customer feedback. If your customers are very comfortable with intranet/Internet technology, you might want to set up an on-line forum for your customers, to discuss use of specific software packages. Responsibility for moderating the forum could be rotated among customers.

Hold an open house to give customers a behind-the-scenes look at the Help Desk and increase awareness of the Help Desk and its services. Ask expert users from among your customers to demonstrate how they are using software. Demonstrate standard hardware and software; show people your plans for the future; provide tours of, or talks describing, the server room (or mainframe room); and have a mini-Help Desk set up at which people can ask questions and report problems. Offer refreshments and door prizes.

If you have customers at remote locations, offer *one-day on-site help sessions* at regularly scheduled intervals. Use these visits to answer questions, resolve current problems, and update remote customers on Help Desk plans, services, and any upcoming technology changes. If you don't have enough staff to provide this on-site service, you may be able to outsource it.

Keep close to your customers. Offer customers various feedback options: E-mail, an anonymous response line, surveys. Call customers back after closing calls to ask about your level of service and gather suggestions for improvements. Make sure everyone on the Help Desk team has a chance to attend customer meetings so they can get feedback first hand and can get to know their customers face to face. Use these meetings to keep customers informed. Make your presence at these meetings the rule rather than the exception. The more you know about the business, the more you can help the business.

If you still don't have an on-line Help Desk information system or *Help Desk Internet or intranet Web site,* set one up. If you do have one, expand it to include references to various sources of self-help, such as seminars, books, magazines, or CDs (yes, some customers actually do read reference material). If your customers have access to the Internet, include references to sites that would be of interest to them.

Create a rolling twelve-month picture of Help Desk activity. Do this in graphical format showing call load, systems supported, call breakdowns, and response times. You can include this in your Web site (update it monthly) or in company or Help Desk newsletters and/or you can present it at customer departmental meetings.

Increase the visibility and understanding of your Help Desk by getting it profiled in the company's annual report. How do you do this? Write (or present) a proposal to senior management describing and justifying your request. You can include reasons such as the following: The Help Desk helps the business realize return on expensive technology investment, helps the business take advantage of new developments in technology, helps employees make more effective use of technology, and so on. Use Help Desk statistics to back your assertions up.

Key Points Covered in This Chapter

Marketing has four components:

Image. Image stems from the quality of your services, from you, and from your communications. Image is how you're perceived—all the things your words and actions are saying without you necessarily verbalizing them. You need to cultivate a customer-friendly, customer-focused, and image-aware Help Desk environment.

Selling value. The products of a Help Desk are not always tangible, its value not always obvious, its successes often very quiet. In order for you to keep customers and management aware of the value the

Help Desk is offering the business, you need to demonstrate this value on a regular basis via quarterly performance reports and more frequent, informal reports.

Education. Ignorance, not intent, is the cause of many technology-based disasters and inefficiencies. The more you can teach your customers about using their technology, the more effective use they can make of it. They will make fewer calls to the Help Desk, cause fewer mistakes and disasters, and make better use of their own time.

Two-way communication. If you keep customers informed about what is going on in the technological environment, you will be rewarded with customers that call the Help Desk less often, are more understanding and pleasant to deal with, and can make more effective use of their time. If you encourage feedback from customers, you will get good information for improving the Help Desk and a more productive customer relationship. Good two-way communication heads calls off at the pass. Customers will have fewer reasons to call the Help Desk.

A note of caution. Marketing is not a substitute for poor performance. You cannot market what you don't have. If you are performing poorly, no amount of marketing will hide this from your customers, at least not for long.

Marketing vehicles need to do the following:

Cater to your audience.

Be concise.

Project your Help Desk's image.

A marketing plan should take all of your major Help Desk activities into account. You should plan a marketing initiative for all planned events, such as technology upgrades, and for unplanned events, such as emergency service interruptions. Your marketing plan should include the following, for each initiative:

Your objectives; what you want your marketing to accomplish.

The information you need to communicate to achieve your objectives.

The marketing vehicles you plan to use.

The audience you are trying to reach.

The frequency of each marketing initiative.

Cost-Benefit Analysis

"Common sense is genius dressed up in its working clothes."
—Ralph Waldo Emerson

Whether you're just starting a Help Desk or have an established Help Desk and are trying to make improvements, you're going to have to go through the process of justifying the cost of what you are proposing. You might see the value in what you're trying to do very clearly and wonder how anyone could doubt the worth of a Help Desk or improvement, but management might not see it quite like that. They have to make sure you're spending the company's money on something that will bring value to the business. They need to understand the business value of what you're trying to do. The purpose of the cost-benefit analysis you prepare will be to demonstrate that value.

In This Chapter

The first section in this chapter will discuss how to show business value—the measures to use, and the steps involved in putting a cost-benefit analysis together. The next three sections will give examples of cost-benefit analyses, showing all of the data behind the calculations and the rationale for the justification of the costs. The scenarios used in the examples are as follows:

- Cost justification of a Help Desk
- Cost justification of an Interactive Voice Response (IVR) system
- Cost justification of the outsourcing of the training function

Business Value

Demonstrating business value might not be as much of a challenge if you were in the business of producing widgets. You could calculate the cost of producing, marketing, and selling each widget versus the price you got for it. On the Help Desk, you aren't producing anything. Instead, you are enabling other people to produce, sell, and distribute things, be they widgets or information. This makes it difficult to put a value on the Help Desk function.

In order to show the business value of a Help Desk, it is necessary to look at the situation from a different perspective: What would the environment be like without a Help Desk? What would it be costing the business, in terms of extra time users would have to spend solving problems, figuring out where to go to get problems resolved or performing any activity associated with support? What would it be costing the business not to have a technology environment that was stable enough to support critical production applications? The difference between this environment and the same environment with a Help Desk added is the business value of your Help Desk. This is what you have to try to estimate when you're putting your cost-benefit analysis together.

The same applies to doing a justification for an improvement, such as installing interactive voice response (IVR). Consider what it is costing the business not to have an IVR in terms of customer time, support staff time, and strategic direction. Then consider the same environment with an IVR: The costs may have disappeared, and extra benefits been realized. This is the business value. In the case of an IVR, you will have data from your call-tracking statistics to help you estimate business value. When you're setting up a Help Desk for the first time, you don't have those statistics.

Creating Measures

In order to put a value on the difference between the existing situation (that is, no Help Desk) and the one you are proposing (Help Desk), you need to create some kind of measure. You may not have any real data for the current situation, but you do have information that you can gather from users and support staff. For example, users might be taking much longer than required to accomplish their work because they are doing things inefficiently. They don't know how to pass data along the network, so they are putting their work on diskettes and sending them to people via internal mail; they don't know how to download from the mainframe and so are rekeying data; or their PCs are incorrectly configured, which is slowing them down. You estimate that half of all users (there are 1,000 in total) experience situations like these and that this is costing each user on average six hours each month. This means that in any given month, 500 users are spending six hours that they shouldn't have to. Over a year, this is 36,000 hours or 4,500 eight-hour days. Broken down by user, this means that on average, users are spending 4.5 days per year, or 2.4 percent of their time (assuming 188 available days per year), on unproductive tasks that would not be necessary were they in a supported environment. You could break this number into minutes or hours per day or week if it were more relevant. You now have a business cost associated with the unsupported environment. You also have a business benefit for the supported environment: You are freeing up 2.4 percent of user time. Add any other benefits that your supported environment brings, and you have your measure.

You need to be careful when dealing with these kinds of measures. They are very rough estimates meant to show trends and magnitudes, not exact figures. It would be almost impossible to get this kind of information accurately. When you talk in terms of user time spent or saved over a period of time, you have to remember that you can't simply add it up and present it as a cost or savings in terms of people. First of all, it is a very rough estimate. Second, what you are adding is bits of time from many users. You can't take all of this time, put it together, and talk about staff savings—you are putting bits of people together, not whole people. For example, say you have 500 users and you claim that you are saving them each three days per year. This is 1,500 user days. You cannot say that this is equivalent to eight people (at 188 days per year). This would imply that you could get rid of eight people, and this isn't true—you are giving 500 people three days each a year to spend on something of greater business value, which is quite a different story. Management will be very quick to pick up on any hint of staff savings, so be careful about making inadvertent promises in this direction. Keep any time measures to per-user units—such as three days per user per year or 1.5 percent of users' time.

Depending on the situation, you can also convert hours into dollar values using a fixed hourly rate that includes benefits and other employee overhead. Your human resources or finance department should be able to give you this figure for your organization.

Preparing Data for the Analysis

In order to put your cost-benefit analysis together, you are going to have to do the following:

Describe the current situation in terms of cost to the business.

Describe the proposed situation or improvement in terms of eliminating some or all of that cost and adding more value.

Describe the Current Situation

You need to determine what the problems are with the current situation and what each is costing the business in terms of person time, money, or strategic growth. If you are trying to cost-justify a Help Desk and you don't have any historical data to work with, you will have to interview customers and support staff to get an idea of the problems they face and the time it costs them. Don't worry too much about being 100 percent accurate. You're trying to get indications, magnitudes, and trends, not 100 percent accuracy. Give consideration also to other, tangible costs: equipment that has to be maintained or any extra help that has to be hired.

If you are trying to cost-justify improvements to the Help Desk and you have historical data, you can use this along with user and support staff interviews (if they are necessary) to get the data you need. For example, support traffic might be so high that a customer spends ten minutes trying to get through to the Help Desk to get a terminal reset. That ten minutes could be a combination of trying, hanging up, and trying again, or it could be just staying on the line for ten minutes waiting for a free support person. If it were the former, you'd have to actually talk to that customer to find out that the total time wasted was ten minutes.

Besides costs for individual problems, you need to consider costs to the business as a whole, now and in the future. For example, if a company has no PC Help Desk, the development of critical business functions using client/server might be impaired because there would be no support for them.

Describe the Proposed Situation or Improvement

Here you need to describe your proposal and what it would mean to the business. Would all of the problems disappear? Would the business realize other value? What would this mean in terms of the company's future? The improvement could be stated in terms of time saved, money or staff saved, and opportunities for the business. For example, your proposal to put in a Help Desk might mean that each technology user can free up 3 percent of the time spent struggling with technology to focus on the business. It could also mean the very real savings associated with centralized software purchase. The LAN environment would be more stable so the business could use client/server for critical production applications.

Building a Proposal

Besides doing the cost-benefit analysis for what you are proposing, it would be wise to have the support of your customers or potential customers. Talk to the customer managers, show them drafts of your proposal, and ask for their feedback. The more support you have, the easier it will be to get what you are asking for. If possible, go to senior managers who are willing to advise you about how to put the proposal together—try to get their support. It would be frustrating and embarrassing, to say the least, to put the whole proposal together just to have the customers tell senior management, "We're okay as we are. We don't need a Help Desk." Going through this whole justification exercise and talking to various managers should indicate, very early on, whether you have a case for putting a Help Desk together.

The level of detail required in a cost-benefit analysis will vary depending on your own environment, the dollar amount you're trying to justify spending, and whether you need expense or capital. Some organizations have standard forms for cost-benefit analyses. If your management believes in what you're trying to justify, or you have a champion somewhere higher up, you may require a much less detailed document. Expensive initiatives need more detailed analyses than less expensive ones, and something that can be written off as an expense usually requires less detail (if any at all) than a capital outlay.

A cost-benefit analysis can be divided up into five sections:

1. A brief description of the current situation (you may also give a brief overview of what you are proposing)

2. The problems with the current situation and their impact on the business

3. A description of what you are proposing and the benefits it will bring to the business

4. The implementation options and cost

5. The recommendation

If your proposal is longer than a few pages, you will want to preface it with a management summary containing all of this information in a very summarized form. Your proposal may require a discussion of the risks involved in the proposed undertaking, such as when outsourcing is being considered. This can be added to the section containing what is being proposed and the benefits to the business.

When discussing implementations and cost (the fourth item in the preceding list) you should always include the cost of doing nothing. This figure is a very powerful indication of what the current situation is costing. The focus should always be on business value. As much as you can, describe problems in terms of how they affect the business.

Presenting Your Case

Once you have put your proposal together, you need to present it to some level of senior management. Hopefully, you have shown enough evidence and offered enough solutions that management will realize the value of your proposal and accept it. The way you present your case is important. Sending off a report in the mail isn't usually the best way. You want to make sure your report is looked at by the right people and given enough attention. If possible, present your case in person and hand the reports out at the presentation. You will be able to handle comments and concerns as they come up. Ideally, one or more of the managers at the presentation will have helped you put the proposal together.

In the sections that follow, three examples of cost-benefit analyses are presented. The first is a justification of a Help Desk. Although the example is set up for a Help Desk, much of the material in the section can be used to justify other business initiatives, including improvements to the Help Desk. The second example deals with justifying an interactive voice response (IVR) system. The third example deals with outsourcing. It is a cost-benefit analysis to justify outsourcing the training function of the Help Desk. A management summary is presented at the end of each of the three analyses. Normally, and especially for proposals presented to management, the management summary is included at the very front of the document. For the purposes of this book, however, it is placed at the end to show the natural progression of data collection, analysis, and summary.

Example No. 1: Justifying a Help Desk

The following example is a cost-benefit analysis for a Help Desk. The environment currently has no Help Desk. Its 2,000 users generate approximately 1,000 support requests each month. The actual number is probably much larger—1,500 or 2,000. The 1,000 estimate was made by the staff from network support, software support, and hardware maintenance, who provide some PC support as a sideline to their real jobs. Users get a lot of help on their own, either by going to vendors directly or by asking their colleagues for help. No one is responsible for customer support, and no calls are logged. When users need help, they phone around until they get a network support person, a hardware maintenance person, a software maintenance person, a vendor, or a colleague who knows something about computers. There is no coordination between support staff. They often work on the same problem without knowing it. People in management who introduced PCs (and who are no longer there) felt that the technology wouldn't require any support and that users could be self-sufficient. Training was left up to individual users and generally wasn't taken. A lot of time is being wasted by people who don't really understand how to use the technology and who are constantly running into trouble. A lot of the equipment that was purchased initially is now slow and has incompatibility problems with some of the newer equipment. PCs are purchased centrally, but no standards exist—all users just purchase what they want.

The Help Desk being proposed draws all support areas together and adds three front-line staff, an automatic call distributor (ACD), and Help Desk software. I present a management summary at the end of the example.

1. Summary of Current Situation

Currently, there is much confusion among technology users about whom to call when they experience a problem with any of their PC technology or want to ask a question about using it. Users are getting support for their PCs, monitors, and printers by going to the technical staff who install and maintain the PCs, going to a colleague who can help, or calling a vendor directly. There are 2,000 PC users who generate an estimated 1,000 support requests per month. The number is probably actually much larger, but support requests are not logged and users often get their own support. These users are spending a significant amount of their time trying to get the support they need for their technology, which is time they could be spending contributing to the business. They are also not making as effective use of the technology as they could—the return on the company's PC investment is not nearly at the level it could be. No one is fully dedicated to providing support for PC users, and many aspects of the purchase, installation, and use of PC technology remain nonstandardized, uncoordinated, and unplanned. Support staff who install and maintain PC technology are the main source of support. This support load is such that in addition to their other responsibilities they are unable to perform functions that would make the technology environment more stable and lessen the number of problems that users are experiencing.

A Help Desk would offer a central point of contact for problems, questions, and requests for users of PC technology. It would bring all PC support staff and functions under one roof and give them tools to do their jobs more effectively. Users would know where to call when they had problems, would have their technology set up for maximum effectiveness, and could take advantage of organized training to learn how to use it to its full capabilities. Technology standardization efforts could be started, equipment could be kept up to date, and problems could be logged and tracked to identify negative trends for resolution and to help manage the support load. Users could get their focus back on the business and off the tools that support it.

2. Problems with Current Situation and Impact on Business

Five support staff and 40 (out of 2,000) users were interviewed to get the data in the following tables. Working days are assumed to be eight hours. The problems can be summarized as follows:

- Lack of centralized and coordinated support for PCs
- Untrained technology users
- Lack of upgrade strategy for equipment
- Lack of standards and strategies
- Lack of planning

These problems are shown in Tables 11.1 and 11.2.

Impact on the Business

Lack of centralized support is causing technology users to spend significant time trying to get help on their own. This is time away from the core business, away from their jobs. This time is also causing projects to take longer and making employees less productive. Employees cannot use the technology as effectively as they might because they do not receive the training they need, and the nonstandard environment often makes information sharing difficult. Support staff do not have the organization or the tools required to identify and solve recurring problems, to handle problems efficiently, or to put standards into place.

Using the examples from Tables 11.1 and 11.2, which are representa-

Table 11.1 Problems from Users

Problem	Effect	Est. Yearly cost (in eight-hour days)
Don't know whom to call when they have a problem.	Time away from business trying to call various people to find some support. **Estimate:** 50% of callers don't know whom to call; take approximately ten minutes to find out. (Yearly Cost: $500 \times 10 \times 12 \div 60 \div 8$ days)	125 days
Don't know when support will come or how long fix will take.	Time not fully productive while waiting for support; difficult to plan alternatives because don't know how long fix will take. **Estimate:** Time waiting is, on average, only 70% productive; 10% of calls have average wait time six or more hours. (Yearly Cost: $100 \times 6 \times 30\% \times 12 \div 8$ days)	270 days
Often go to colleagues for help.	Users who can help others have to take time away from their jobs to do so. **Estimate:** Approximately 5% of all 2,000 users help others; average help time is ten hours per month. (Yearly Cost: $100 \times 10 \times 12 \div 8$ days)	1,500 days
Individual users sometimes hire consultants off the street to help.	Consultants don't know environment; some of their work has to be redone. **Estimate:** Two incidents per month; one day each to recover. (Yearly Cost: 2×12 days)	24 days plus any data loss

Table 11.1 *(continued)*

Problem	Effect	Est. Yearly cost (in eight-hour days)
Often have to redo work because of incorrect use of technology.	Time and work lost through errors that could have been avoided by getting help or training. **Estimate:** For three examples: a) Files not saved often enough; data lost; rekeying necessary. b) Bought wrong software; wasted time trying to get it to fit the application. c) Incorrect use of formulas in spreadsheet. (Could cause misinformed business decisions.) For these three examples: Approximately 10% of all 2,000 users; Average of two hours lost per month. (Yearly Cost: 200 × 2 × 12 ÷ 8 days)	600 days plus cost of any data lost or misinformed business decisions
Subtotal for problems from users		2,519 days plus cost of any data loss and misinformed business decisions

tive but by no means comprehensive, employees using technology are spending slightly more than 3 percent of their time, or fifteen minutes each day, struggling with some aspect of technology while returning nothing to the business. If we put a dollar figure to this, using the standard hourly wage of $60 for the organization, we get a total of $5,531,520 of wasted user time per year. That's 11,524 days times eight hours per day times $60 per hour. Lost support time comes to $108,000 per year (225 days times eight hours per day times $60 per hour). The cost of total time lost is $5,639,520 per year. On top of this is the cost to the business of any data that has been lost and of not being able to provide a stable production environment for future business applications. The

Table 11.2   Problems from Staff Doing Support

Problem	Effect	Est. Yearly cost (in eight-hour days)
Users are doing things inefficiently, due to lack of knowledge and availability of standard setup.	Tasks take longer to accomplish. **Estimate:** For three examples: a) Users don't know how to pass data along network; instead, they copy to diskettes and deliver or mail. b) Users are rekeying rather than downloading data from mainframe. c) Incorrectly configured files are slowing individual workstations down. Approximately 35% of all 2,000 users are doing at least one of these; Taking approximately six hours each month. (Yearly Cost: $700 \times 6 \times 12 \div 8$ days)	6,300 days
There is a lack of coordination. Users are down longer than necessary because a support person working on a problem would not know if another person had already worked on it and resolved it.	Time wasted in duplication of effort; customers are down longer than necessary. **Estimate:** Happens almost daily; Approximately 20 hours per month; (Yearly Cost: $20 \times 12 \div 8$ days)	30 days for users 30 days for support staff
There are no firm hardware or software standards, so compatibility and communication between users can be difficult and time consuming.	Customers waste time reformatting data in efforts to interface with each other. **Estimate:** For this example: Have three different word processors (Word Perfect, Word for Windows, and Ami Pro) and the mainframe text editor;	800 days

Table 11.2   *(continued)*

Problem	Effect	Est. Yearly cost (in eight-hour days)
	Documents need to be imported and reformatted when being shared; True of approximately 10% of all 2,000 users; Takes approximately twenty minutes per document; Happens eight times per month per user. (Yearly Cost: 200 × 20 × 8 ×12 ÷ 60 ÷ 8 days)	
Old, obsolete equipment is still in use and making the users very inefficient. No standards or upgrade strategies are in place.	Time is lost through inefficient and slower processing. Also, the cost of maintaining old equipment is high, and time to get new software working on it is high. **Estimate:** For users: Users on 200 old PCs are approximately 10% less productive in a given day than users with newer models, due to a much slower processing speed and higher maintenance time; Average user time spent on a PC is three hours per day; Loss of productivity is approximately six hours per month. (Yearly Cost: 200 × 6 × 12 ÷ 8 days for users) For support staff: 10% of the 200 machines require approximately four hours of extra support in a month, just to keep them running. (Yearly Cost: 20 × 4 × 12 ÷ 8 days)	1,800 days of user time 120 days of support time

(continues)

Table 11.2   Problems from Staff Doing Support *(continued)*

Problem	Effect	Est. Yearly cost (in eight-hour days)
Planning for any aspect of PC technology is very difficult. Support staff work in reactive mode to solve continuous crises (e.g., viruses, lack of backups, software upgrade requirements).	Time is spent cleaning up and fixing problems rather than preventing them. There is also a very real cost associated with virus damage, loss of backups, etc. **Estimate**: For these examples: Virus damage: two-hour re-create time per ten users per month; Lost data (no backups): three-hour re-create time per ten users per month. (Yearly Cost: $5 \times 10 \times 12 \div 8$ days)	75 days of user time, 75 days of support time (at least) Cost of data lost or destroyed Cost of inability to provide secure environment for mission-critical applications
Subtotal for problems from support staff		9,005 user days 225 days for support staff plus cost of any data loss and business cost of inability to provide secure environment for mission-critical appplications
TOTAL		**11,524** user days *(6 days per user per year = 15 minutes per day = 3.2% of user time)* **225** support staff days *plus* cost of data loss, misinformed business decisions, and inability to provide secure environment for mission-critical applications

technology environment cannot safely support any client/server applications until some kind of centralized support is in place.

3. Proposed Solution and Benefits

A solution to the current situation needs to address the following issues:

- Lack of training of technology users
- Lack of upgrade strategy for equipment
- Lack of standards and strategies
- Lack of planning
- Lack of centralized and coordinated support for PCs

A Help Desk Solution

A Help Desk would provide a single number to call for all PC problems, questions, and requests. Services offered would be as follows:

One number to call for support, 6 A.M. TO 6 P.M.; pager support after hours

Hardware maintenance

LAN maintenance

Customer support for PC hardware and software

Management of hardware and software inventory, including upgrades

Testing and installation of software upgrades

Source and purchase of hardware and software

Organization of training

Coordination of planning for the PC environment

Coordination of PC standards and security

Benefits

There are four major benefits of creating a Help Desk. First, technology users could spend more time on the business. They would not need to waste time looking for help or dealing with external resources whenever they had a problem. The Help Desk would take care of all aspects of support. Informal support networks would no longer be necessary, and those employees who had been providing informal support could once again focus on their own jobs. Problems would be responded to more quickly. Users would know the status of their problems and could plan around any anticipated downtimes.

Second, users could make more effective use of the technology to support the business. Training needs would be tracked and organized training made available so users could learn to use technology correctly and avoid costly errors.

Third, technology use would be more cost-effective. Standards would be in place so that economies of scale could be realized in hardware and software purchasing and licensing. Obsolete equipment could be either upgraded or replaced so that users could make use of more current software and spend less time waiting for a response. Maintenance and support costs for the equipment would be lessened.

Finally, the technological environment would be more stable. Problems would be tracked so that recurring errors and duplication of effort could be eliminated. The creation of standards would be coordinated and promoted so the technology between departments was compatible. Sharing documents and data would be easier. Support staff would be able to do preventive maintenance and planning to decrease instances of downtime and last-minute emergencies. They could install virus and security software, monitor hardware and software use so that licensing and upgrades could be accomplished before any limits were reached, and set up proper backups. Client/server development initiatives would have a much greater chance of success.

These four benefits translate into a significant savings of customer and support staff time, specifically $5,639,520 per year.

Impact on the Business

Technology users would no longer have to be in the business of support. They could make more productive use of the technology because it would be more stable and because they would have a better understanding of how to use it. Technology downtime would be diminished because support would be faster and more effective: Calls would be logged, tracked, and handled on a priority basis. The more stable technology environment could handle mission-critical applications.

As technology is added, these benefits would be compounded—greater gain could be realized through the greater stability and more effective use of the technology. Current spending on PC technology is approximately $4 million annually. The business cannot hope to see a return on this investment without a support organization to ensure that it is working properly and being used effectively.

4. Implementation Options and Cost

The Help Desk would incorporate and enhance several areas that are currently in existence and would require three additional staff members to provide a first line of support for logging and resolving problems. Existing areas that would be incorporated into the Help Desk are as follows:

Hardware maintenance

LAN support

Management of hardware and software inventory

Testing and installation of software upgrades

Source and purchase of hardware and software

Functions that would be added include the following:

Management of hardware upgrades

Organization of training

Coordination of planning for the PC environment

Coordination of PC standards and security

Setting up the Help Desk would take one internal support staff member approximately eight weeks. Table 11.3 shows option 1, an internally staffed Help Desk. Table 11.4 shows option 2, which is to outsource the three new positions as part of an existing maintenance contract.

Option 3 is do nothing. The cost of option 3, over one year, is $5,531,520 of customer time plus $108,000 of support staff time, which

Table 11.3   Option 1: Internally Staffed Help Desk

Component	One-Time Cost	Yearly Cost	Other Consideration
Three new internal staff (could be new hires)	Possible finder's fee if hiring from outside	$150,000 (including benefits)	Need increase of three head count
Training cost Replacement staff for training, vacation, illness (six weeks each)		$6,000 $36,000 (18 weeks @ $2,000)	
Help Desk software	$20,000	$1,000	
ACD	$50,000	$5,000	
Help Desk setup	Eight weeks, one staff member: $8,000		
Total	$78,000 plus any finder's fee	$198,000	

Table 11.4   Option 2: Outsource the Three New Positions as Part of an Existing Maintenance Contract

Component	One-Time Cost	Yearly Cost	Other Consideration
Three contract staff; added to hardware maintenance contract. Located on site.		$180,000	No head count increase; no vacation/ sickness/etc. issues. Two staff will always be there. Save by using same contract as hard- ware maintenance.
Help Desk software	$20,000	$1,000	
ACD	$50,000	$5,000	
Help Desk setup	Eight weeks, one staff member: $8,000		
Total	$78,000	$186,000	

totals $5,639,520. On top of this is the cost to the business of any data that has been lost and of not being able to provide a stable production environment for future business applications.

5. Recommendation

The recommendation is option 2. Information services is very satisfied with the service being provided as part of the hardware maintenance contract. The firm providing the service is also in the business of providing Help Desk staff and is willing to expand the existing contract to include three such people at an advantageous price. The Help Desk would be relieved of the responsibility of training the three staff, staffing during sickness and vacation, and adding head count. This option has a one-time cost of $78,000 and an annual cost of $186,000. Option 3, because of its cost, was not really an option.

6. Management Summary

Background

The PC environment has grown to its present count of 2,000 over the course of only a few years. Hardware and software are sourced and purchased centrally, but no one is concerned with standards, so there is a mix of technology. There are several different groups involved in working with some aspect of support for PCs. Hardware maintenance has been outsourced and is looked after by three on-site third-party staff members. LANs are looked after by an internal group, as are testing and the installation of upgrades. There is no group for customer support. Every time customers run into a problem, they have to figure out who to call and then try to chase that person down. Support staff are very busy trying to maintain a growing environment and don't have time to support customers. There is no coordination between them, so they are often working on the same problem without knowing it.

Customers often spend time struggling with problems on their own or going to colleagues for help—a very expensive network of informal support has been created. There is no organized education. Older equipment is now out of date and slow and is not always compatible with other technology. The company has started work on client/server, but the current environment does not provide the stability that such an environment would require.

Proposal

A PC Help Desk is a central support group to provide front line support for PCs and LANs and to coordinate the efforts of all support groups. The group would take on the additional functions of coordinating planning and policies, organizing training, and upgrading hardware.

Cost of Not Having a Help Desk

The 2,000 employees are spending, on average, fifteen minutes each day (just over 3 percent of their work time) struggling with some aspect of technology. Employees are not trained, so they often misuse the technology; this results in lost data and misinformed business decisions. Cost of employee time lost is estimated at $5,531,520 per year and cost of support time lost at $108,000.

Support staff have no coordination and often find themselves spending time working on the same problems as other support staff. The company does not have the stable microcomputer environment required to support future business applications.

Benefits of a Help Desk

- Employees would have at least 3 percent more time to spend on their own part of the business. Supporting the technology they use would become someone else's (the Help Desk's) business.

- Employees would make more effective use of technology to support the business. There is a $4 million annual investment in technology for which return cannot begin to be realized until the technology is performing at some level of stability and people understand how to use it.

- A more stable technology environment. The business could implement fully supported client/server.

- More cost-effective use of technology through standardization.

- The business would no longer be wasting $5,639,520 yearly in lost employee productivity.

Implementation Cost

Many components of the Help Desk exist currently as separate entities but must be organized and consolidated into one group. Three additional (outsourced) staff and Help Desk software are required.

Initial setup cost would be $78,000. Cost required annually, over and above the cost of the existing Help Desk components, would be $186,000.

Example No. 2: Justifying an Interactive Voice Response System

When you are justifying a Help Desk tool, or some other form of improvement, you can use statistics from your call-tracking data to strengthen your case. In the case of automation—for example, an interactive voice response (IVR) system—these statistics are often how opportunities for improvement and solutions to problems are identified.

In this example, we will be putting together a cost-benefit analysis for an IVR. The situation is as follows:

The Help Desk requesting the IVR supports both PC and mainframe users. The front line is staffed by four people, and an automatic call distributor (ACD) is used to distribute calls and gather statistics. Help Desk software also gathers statistics. The current volume of calls is 3,600 per month: 60 percent for PC issues and 40 percent for mainframe issues. There are currently about 1,000 PCs and 2,000 terminals being supported. Terminals are decreasing in number, while PCs are exploding.

The support load has increased by about 50 percent in the past nine months, and support staff are having a hard time keeping up. Customers are having a hard time getting through to the Help Desk—it is taking them longer. Some 38 percent of calls are for functions that could easily be automated. The Help Desk wants to use an IVR to automate all of these functions. The IVR could also be used by the automation project currently taking place in the data center. The following is the cost-benefit analysis for the proposal to introduce the IVR. A management summary is given at the end.

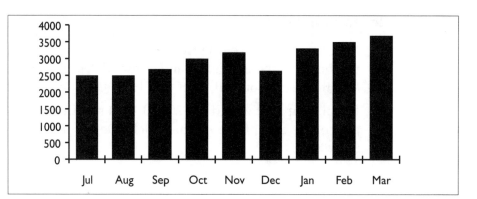

Figure 11.1   Growth in number of calls per month has been 50 percent over the past nine months.

1. Summary of Current Situation

Support calls to our Help Desk have increased by 50 percent in the past nine months (see Figure 11.1) due to the ongoing introduction of newer and more complex technology, specifically in the PC area. PCs have been increasing at a very strong rate, as shown in Figure 11.2. The Help Desk now supports 1,000 PCs as well as 2,000 terminals. The trends of increasing calls and PC growth show no sign of slowing down. The support staff cannot handle the current support load effectively; customers are forced to spend a longer time getting through to the Help Desk and then they have to wait for service.

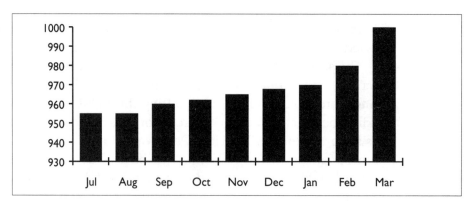

Figure 11.2   Growth in number of PCs.

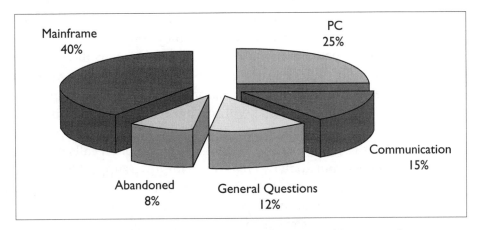

Figure 11.3   Distribution of the 3,600 calls received in a month.

The mainframe environment has been fairly stable and accounts for 40 percent of all calls to the Help Desk (see Figure 11.3). Of mainframe-based calls, 65 percent are repetitive requests for routine tasks such as printer resets, terminal resets, and password resets (see Figure 11.4). These requests, which make up 26 percent of total calls to the Help Desk, place a significant demand on support time. A further 12 percent of total calls are general questions. These questions are also repetitive, have routine answers, and are a drain on support time.

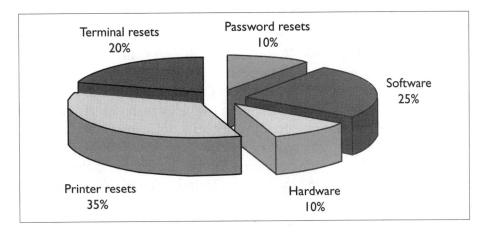

Figure 11.4   Distribution of mainframe calls.

The Help Desk needs to find some way to contain the increases in calls. If these increases continue, they could degrade service to the point where customers would be forced to develop their own informal networks of support—a very expensive proposition. At the same time, it needs to channel support efforts away from mundane, repetitive tasks and toward work that will add more value to the business, such as preparation for client/server. IVR would allow the Help Desk to automate handling of repetitive tasks—38 percent of all calls could be automated almost immediately. This would improve support levels and free staff to investigate further automation; call levels could be kept down to allow the Help Desk to support the coming client/server environment. The voice response system would also be a valuable addition to the data center automation initiative that is taking place. It could be used for various functions, such as remote support.

2. Problems with Current Situation and Impact on Business

Routine, repetitive tasks are draining time away from the Help Desk and preventing it from providing the levels of service required by the rapidly expanding technological environment. Table 11.5 provides details of the time being spent by the Help Desk on repetitive, administrative tasks and the detrimental effect this is having on service. The table also shows how workload could be alleviated and service improved through automation.

Impact on Business

Help Desk customers are facing increasing wait times for service from the Help Desk. Routine, repetitive tasks are taking up significant Help Desk resources, in effect doubling the time a customer must spend getting through to the Help Desk and then waiting for service. PC technology is experiencing explosive growth, which has been accompanied by a corresponding increase in support requirements. PC-based client/server applications, which will further increase support requirements, are being planned for the near future. Unless something is done to alleviate the load on the Help Desk and allow it to focus on what is most important to the business, it will not be able to adequately support the growing PC environment. This lack of support will endanger the integrity of any PC-based applications that are developed.

Table 11.5 Details of Help Desk Time Allocation and Effect on Service

Tasks or Problems	Effect on the Help Desk and on Service	Estimated Monthly Cost without IRV	Estimated Monthly Cost with IRV
Terminal resets, password resets, printer resets	Mainframe calls = 40% of 3600 = 1440 Terminal, password, printer resets = 65% of 1440 = 936 Average customer time to get through to Help Desk and get terminal reset is ten minutes. Average support time is five minutes. **Estimate**: 936 calls 10 minutes per user per call = 20 days 5 minutes support per call = 10 days	20 days customer 10 days support	2 days customer (with 1 minute per call) 0 days support
General questions	General questions make up 12% of calls. 12% of 3,600 = 432 Average customer time to get through to Help Desk and get information is 6 minutes. Average support time is 2.5 minutes. **Estimate**: 432 calls 6 minutes per user per call = 5 days 2.5 minutes support per call = 2 days	5 days customer 2 days support	1 day customer (1 minute per call) 0 days support
Increased wait time	3,600 calls Average customer wait time to get through now has increased by three minutes. $3600 \times 3 \div 60 \div 8 = 23$ days 30% of Help Desk calls (1,080) cannot be resolved at point of call. Average resolution time for these calls is eight hours (up from an average of four hours over the past nine months).	23 days customers 324 days customer	0 days Resolution time would go back at least to previous levels: 162 days

(continues)

Table 11.5 Details of Help Desk Time Allocation and Effect on Service *(continued)*

Tasks or Problems	Effect on the Help Desk and on Service	Estimated Monthly Cost without IRV	Estimated Monthly Cost with IRV
	Estimated average productivity loss during wait time is 30%. 30% of 8 hours is 2.4 hours $1080 \times 2.4 \div 8 = 324$		
Totals		372 customer	165 customer
		12 support	0 support
Notes on totals	Calls that can be automated include the 936 mainframe resets and 432 general questions. This is 1,368, which is 38% of the total calls. $(1368 \times 100 \div 3600 = 38\%)$		With automation, save 207 customer days. This is a decrease of 56%. With automation, save 12 days of support per month = over half of a support person's time.

As Table 11.5 shows, monthly costs without an IVR are 56% more than they would be with an IVR. We can use our organizational standard of $60 per hour to put a dollar figure to this percentage. An IVR would save 207 customer days, which translates into 207 days times 8 hours per day times $60 per hour, or $99,360 per month. Value of support time saved would be 12 days times 8 hours per day times $60 per hour, or $5,760. Not having an IVR is costing us $105,120 per month in time lost.

3. Proposed Solution and Benefits

An IVR would automate the handling of approximately 38 percent of Help Desk calls—those dealing with terminal, printer, and password resets and general questions. All manual handling of these would be eliminated, improving service to customers and freeing Help Desk staff for more important work. The IVR would also provide a basis for future growth. As repetitive, recurring processes were identified, they could be automated.

Benefits

Each user would typically see a 56 percent decrease in time spent dealing with and waiting for the Help Desk. As shown in the previous section, this comes to a total of $105,120 in time savings per month.

Help Desk staff could focus on work more important to the business, such as automation and problem elimination to make sure that the Help Desk could handle the support requirements of the growing PC environment. This is especially important since critical applications are being developed for client/server.

The data center automation project could make use of the IVR in areas such as remote problem handling. The IVR could handle most of the mainframe calls so that Help Desk staff could focus on the PC environment.

4. Implementation Options and Cost

Three options are presented. The first involves internal staff doing the work while outsourced staff temporarily look after calls. It is shown in Table 11.6. The second option, shown in Table 11.7, involves outsourced staff doing the work. The third is doing nothing. The cost of the third option is $105,120 dollars per month in wasted employee time. Over one year, this can become $1,261,440.

5. Recommendation

The recommendation is option 1. Having some in-house expertise in IVR will allow the Help Desk to plan and use the IVR in other ways. These could include improving the effectiveness of the Help Desk and the uptime of customers and consulting with other areas of the company that might be contemplating IVRs.

Table 11.6   Option 1

Component	Description	Cost (One-Time)	Other Consideration
Staffing	One internal staff to work on IVR project	Would be performed by current Help Desk staff; would require $2,000 in training	IVR expertise would stay in-house
	Two temporary staff to work on Help Desk to field calls at acceptable service levels	$80,000 for six-month time period	
IVR		$100,000	$15,000 yearly maintenance
Total		$182,000	$15,000 yearly

Table 11.7   Option 2

Component	Description	Cost (One-Time)	Other Consideration
Staffing	IVR outsourced	$60,000 for six months	IVR expertise would be outside; would lose knowledge that could help us find other uses
	One temporary staff to help work on Help Desk to field calls at acceptable service levels	$40,000 for six months	
IVR		$100,000	$15,000 yearly maintenance
Total		$200,000	$15,000 yearly

6. Management Summary

Background

Support calls to our Help Desk have increased by 50 percent in the past nine months due to the ongoing introduction of newer and more complex PC technology. The number of PCs has grown to 1,000 and continues to grow. Neither trend shows signs of slowing down. The business will soon be implementing client/server applications, which will further increase the support requirements. The mainframe environment is fairly stable, and 38 percent of calls to the Help Desk are requests for administrative functions that could easily be automated.

Proposal

IVR would allow the immediate automation of 38 percent of the calls coming into the Help Desk, improving support to customers and lessening the load on staff.

Cost of Not Having an IVR

PCs are experiencing explosive growth, and client/server applications will soon be rolling out. Given the current growth of technology and support, the Help Desk will be unable to support these applications with current staffing levels.

Approximately 56 percent of the time that customers spend each month getting through to the Help Desk and waiting for support is taken up by routine tasks and delays that could be eliminated through automation. This translates into $105,120 dollars per month in wasted employee time. Over one year, this becomes approximately $1.25 million.

Of all calls, 38 percent require that a support person perform repetitive, administrative functions that could be automated. More than half of a support person's time is spent providing these functions. As the environment that is being supported grows, this situation will only worsen.

Benefits of an IVR

There are three major benefits of an IVR. First, each user would see, on average, a 56 percent decrease in the time spent dealing with and waiting for the Help Desk. Second, Help Desk staff could focus on work more important to the business: eliminating problems and automating resolutions to ensure that the Help Desk can handle the support requirements of the growing PC environment. Finally, the data center automation project could make use of the IVR in areas such as remote problem handling.

Realizing these benefits would mean that the yearly loss of $1.25 million in employee productivity would cease.

Implementation Cost

There would be a total initial cost of $182,000: $100,000 for the hardware and $82,000 to set the project up. Yearly maintenance costs would be $15,000.

Example No. 3: Justifying Outsourcing of the Training Function

In this example, we will be putting together a cost-benefit analysis for outsourcing the training function. The situation is described in the following paragraphs.

Providing training in PC software is currently a Help Desk responsibility. All aspects of training are provided by three trainers. The Help Desk currently supports 1,000 PCs and 1,000 terminals, but terminals are rapidly being replaced by PCs, and additional PCs are being added almost daily. Most customers are still fairly new to PCs, but a growing number are becoming more experienced and require more advanced training.

New versions of software come out so quickly that trainers are having trouble learning them and modifying courses before the new versions are introduced. They can't provide courses that customers are requesting for new software because they have no time. Learning, course administration, and preparation are taking up all their time outside of actual training. The whole training function has become very expensive for what it provides.

The solution being suggested is to outsource the training function and to bill customers directly for the training they take. Currently, the cost of training (as part of the whole cost of the Help Desk) is charged back to departments at a very high level in background transactions.

The cost-benefit for outsourcing follows. A management summary is included at the end of this example.

1. Summary of Current Situation

The Help Desk currently offers PC training to all the customers it supports. Three trainers handle all aspects of training, from sign-up, scheduling, and administration through course design and course delivery. The supported environment consists of 1,000 PCs and 1,000 terminals, but this is changing rapidly as terminals are being replaced by PCs and additional PCs are added. A large proportion (approximately 65 percent) of customers are new to PCs and require extensive but very basic training, while a smaller percentage are quite experienced and are looking for more advanced training.

The trainers cannot keep up with the rate at which new versions of PC software are introduced and implemented. They seem to be consistently one version behind: by the time they modify their courses for a new version, the next is already waiting to be installed. The trainers also can't keep up with requests for new courses. As new software is purchased, customers request training, but the trainers cannot learn software and develop courses quickly enough to give customers what they need. As it is, they are learning software just steps ahead of their students. Customer feedback indicates that this is affecting the quality of training. Customers do not have confidence in the trainers' knowledge of the software being taught.

As a result of all of this, customers are not getting the training they need when they need it. They are wasting, on average, from ten to fifteen hours each month struggling to learn and use the software they need to use. Some customers are going out to external vendors to get training at their own cost, but this often is not an ideal solution. Customers don't always know exactly what they need, and the whole training experience can be frustrating and a waste of time if they choose a course that is either too basic or too advanced.

The training function has become very expensive for what it provides. Maintaining three trainers on staff to handle only a small number of PC courses does not make financial sense. Trainers are spending 30 percent of their time on all the administration that goes along with teaching—registration, changes, and schedules—which is an expensive use of their time. On top of this, the rate of no-shows and last-minute cancellations is 15 percent. Customers don't always take their training commitments seriously. They don't see the cost involved in their actions.

The existing training function is one that worked well in the mainframe world, where things did not change as quickly or as often, but in the PC world it just does not suffice. It is creating a bottleneck for people who need training and forcing a certain level of inefficiency and productivity loss upon them.

Outsourcing the training function would give customers better access to a wider variety of training at a lower cost. Courses would be offered more frequently, at a greater variety of levels, and trainers would be more experienced. Training administration would no longer be a Help Desk responsibility but would be looked after by the company providing the training. The training company would take responsibility for interaction with customers, scheduling, sign-ups, and billing. Customers could call the company directly (via an internal phone number) to arrange for training and would be billed directly. Charging the customers directly for each course (currently, a high-level charge-back process goes on in the background) would give them a vested interest in showing up. No-shows would decrease. Training could be offered on site in the existing training facility or off site in the third-party facilities.

Outsourcing the training function would mean redeploying or laying off the three training staff.

2. Problems with Current Situation and Impact on Business

Quality and Timeliness of Training

PC training is not current. Trainers cannot keep up with the pace at which PC software changes.

PC training is limited to a few (five) standard software packages. Customers are forced to go elsewhere for training for other packages and often find that training inappropriate because they did not understand what they were signing up for.

Trainers are learning software just a few steps ahead of the classes they are teaching, and their lack of experience with the software shows in their training. Customers do not have confidence in the trainers' knowledge of what they are teaching.

Impact on the Business

Customers are hampered in their efforts to make effective use of technology in their jobs. Customers who can't get the training they are looking for from the Help Desk (approximately fifty per month) estimate that they lose between ten and fifteen hours each month because they don't know or use the software properly. That's fifty customers each losing approximately 12.5 hours per month.

These same customers need to spend time looking for alternate training. If the training turns out to be inappropriate, then further time is wasted. Averaged out, this cost is estimated to be approximately thirty minutes for each of the fifty customers per month.

Adding the two quantities of time lost, we get fifty customers each losing thirteen hours per month. At $60 per hour, this becomes $60 × 13 hours × 50 customers = $39,000 per month = $468,000 per year. This does not include the cost of errors in data, or the poor business decisions made on the basis of the erroneous data, which could be caused by incorrect use of the technology.

Lack of training has become a bottleneck to the effective use of technology that will inhibit business improvements and advancements. This situation will only worsen as the PC environment expands.

Cost of the Training Function

The cost of the training function (shown in Table 11.8) is very high for the value it provides.

3. Proposed Solution, Benefits, and Risks

The proposed solution to the problems just described is to outsource the entire training function to a third-party training provider. The third party would take over all aspects of training, including the following:

- Registration
- Scheduling

Table 11.8   Cost of the Help Desk Training Function

Item	Annual Cost	Notes
Salaries	$140,000	For three trainers.
Training materials	$40,000	Manuals, notes, etc.
Cost of training room	$12,000	Part of office rental.
Miscellaneous office costs and supplies for trainers	$10,000	
Training equipment and maintenance	$20,000	
Training for trainers	$6,000	
Variety of training offered		Five different courses are taught: three at an introductory level, two at both introductory and advanced.
TOTAL:	**$228,000**	
Cost per training day:	**$1,583**	Using current average of twelve training days per month (=144 per year).
Cost per student per training day:	**$264**	Assuming a full class of six students.
Cost per student per training day taking no-shows into account:	**$310**	No-show rate is 15%. This means an actual rate of 5.1 students per class.

- Advertising scheduled courses
- Training
- Measuring training effectiveness
- Tracking training statistics
- Billing

Business Benefits

There are four major business benefits of outsourcing training. First, customers would have access to training for a wider variety of courses at all levels, and courses would be offered more frequently. Trainers would be more experienced. Customers would receive the training they needed when they needed it, effectively reducing or eliminating the thirteen hours currently being wasted each month by approximately fifty customers. This is a savings of $39,000 per month or $468,000 per year in customer time.

Second, the training bottleneck inhibiting business improvements and advancements would be removed, and the occurrences of errors due to the improper use of technology would be reduced. Third, customers would be billed directly for training and charged for no-shows and last-minute cancellations, which would almost eliminate the occurrences of these. Finally, the cost of training would be reduced from $310 to $196 per student per training day.

Cost of Outsourced Training

The cost of outsourced, on-site training is shown in Table 11.9.

Table 11.9   Cost of Outsourced Training

Item	Annual Cost	Notes
On-site training, at $1,000 per day	$180,000	Average of fifteen days of training per month.
Cost of training room	$12,000	Part of office rental.
Training equipment and maintenance	$20,000	
Variety of training offered		Fifteen different courses are taught, each having from one to three levels. A much wider variety of courses are available at the third-party site.
TOTAL:	**$212,000**	
Cost per training day:	**$1,178**	Will be training fifteen days per month (=180 per year).
Cost per student per training day:	**$196**	Assuming a full class of six students.

Risks

Outsourcing the training function entails two major risks. First, outsourced training must still be managed and measured to ensure that it is meeting the requirements of the business. If this is not done and training fails to meet the needs of the business, the anticipated benefits will not be realized and the current problems will continue to grow.

Second, if training is outsourced, three current training staff will need to be laid off or redeployed elsewhere. Every effort needs to be made to redeploy these staff within the company. This process needs to be handled very carefully and fairly, with honest communication to all Help Desk staff at timely and frequent intervals. Failure to do this could impact morale and the performance of Help Desk staff.

4. Implementation Recommendations and Cost

The implementation recommendations are as follows:

All training functions, from registration to billing, to be performed by a third-party training provider (yet to be selected).

Third party to report to the Help Desk regularly.

Customers will be billed directly for training.

Courses to be offered on site, except for more specialized courses, which are typically attended by fewer customers. These will be taken at the third-party site at discounted rates.

Implementation, initial advertising, and so on to be performed by the selected third party at no cost.

Every effort must be made to redeploy the three training staff within the company. If redeployment is not possible, staff layoffs will be necessary.

Cost of On-site Training

Estimated at $1,178 per training day, or $196 per student per training day (assuming a full class of six students).

Cost of Off-site Training

Will range from $300 to $400 per student per day, depending on specific course.

5. Management Summary

Background

The PC environment is changing and growing so rapidly that the Help Desk training function is unable to keep up. Training is not current enough, is offered for a limited selection of software, and is provided by trainers who have little experience in the software itself. As a result, PC users are wasting time trying to learn software themselves or find someone who teaches it, and they are not using it as effectively as they could. The training function has become very expensive for what it delivers.

Proposal

Outsource the training function to a third-party training provider. Continue to offer on-site training through the third party.

Problems with the Current Situation

There are a number of problems with the current situation. First, customers who can't get the training they are looking for from the Help Desk estimate that they lose an average of thirteen hours each month because they don't know how to use the software properly and have to spend time looking for alternative training. That's fifty customers each losing approximately thirteen hours per month. At $60 per hour, this becomes $39,000 per month or $468,000 per year.

Second, the inability to use technology properly can cause errors in data, which can lead to bad business decisions. Third, the lack of training has become a bottleneck to effective technology use that will inhibit business improvements and advancements. This situation will only worsen as the PC environment expands. Finally, the cost of the training function is very high for the value it provides, on top of which there is a 15 percent no-show rate. The cost per student per training day is $310.

Benefits of Outsourcing

Outsourcing training offers four major benefits. First, customers would have access to training for a wider variety of courses at all levels, and courses would be offered more frequently. Trainers would be more experienced. Customers would receive the training they needed when they needed it, effectively reducing or eliminating the thirteen hours currently being wasted each month by approximately fifty customers. That's $468,000 over one year.

Second, the training bottleneck inhibiting business improvements and advancements would be removed, and occurrences of errors due to the improper use of technology would be reduced. Third, customers would be billed directly for training and charged for no-shows and last-minute cancellations, which would almost eliminate the occurrences of these. Finally, the cost of training would be reduced from $310 to $196 per student per training day.

Implementation and Cost

The cost of on-site training would be $1,178 per training day, or $196 per student per training day. The cost of off-site training would be between $300 and $400 per student per training day. Implementation costs will be absorbed by a third-party training provider. Management of the outsourced function would remain the responsibility of the Help Desk.

Risks

One of the risks is that outsourced training must still be managed and measured to ensure that it is meeting the requirements of the business. If this is not done and training fails to meet the needs of the business, the anticipated benefits will not be realized and the current problems will continue to grow.

A second risk is that if training is outsourced, three current training staff will need to be laid off or redeployed elsewhere. Every effort needs to be made to redeploy these staff within the company. This process needs to be handled very carefully and fairly, with honest communication to all Help Desk staff at timely and frequent intervals. Failure to do this could impact morale and the performance of Help Desk staff.

Key Points Covered in This Chapter

A cost-benefit analysis illustrates the business value of what you are proposing. This is a challenge when you're dealing with all the intangibles involved in the Help Desk function. A Help Desk doesn't produce anything; it enables other people to do so. This makes it difficult to put a value on it.

The way to evaluate the Help Desk function is to consider what it would cost the business to not have a Help Desk. This would include the extra user time required to get problems resolved, the money being spent on maintaining out-of-date equipment, and strategic considerations such as not having an environment stable enough to handle production applications. Then consider the difference between this environment and the same environment with a Help Desk. This is the business value. In order to put a measurable value on this, you need to estimate the costs based on data gathered from users and support staff.

In order to put your cost-benefit analysis together, you are going to have to describe the current situation in terms of the cost to the business—what the problems are and what they cost—and describe the proposed situation or improvement in terms of eliminating some or all of that cost and adding more value. It's a good idea to get support from user management as you do this to help ensure that your proposal gets accepted.

A cost-benefit analysis can be divided up into five sections:

A brief description of the current situation

Problems with the current situation and their impact on the business

A description of what you are proposing and the benefits it will bring to the business (may include a discussion of the risks involved)

Implementation options and cost—including the option of doing nothing, which can be very powerful in making your case.

Recommendation

A management summary should be included at the front if the analysis is longer than a few pages. Once you have put your proposal together, you need to present it to management. Try to present your case in person so that you can answer concerns directly and provide more detail as required.

CHAPTER TWELVE

Outsourcing

There are two extremes of thought about outsourcing:

It's a dirty word.

It's a panacea for all your ills.

The truth for you will depend on where you're sitting. If you're caught in the middle of a consolidation or takeover or the outsourcing of the complete IT (Information Technology) function, you'll probably lean toward the first point of view. If you have a problem area that you've just outsourced with a big sigh of relief, the ink on the contract is still wet, and you think that's the end of that, you'll probably be leaning toward the second point of view. If you're an executive who wants to impress the board with dramatic cost-cutting and outsourcing, you'll probably also be leaning toward the second perspective.

If you don't fall into any of these categories, then the truth for you is probably somewhere in between. Outsourcing doesn't have to be a dirty word. You can use it as a tool to add value to your Help Desk. Outsourcing certainly isn't any kind of panacea. You may have outsourced a part or all of your Help Desk, but someone, most likely you, will still be responsible for its successful performance. Things will not necessarily go smoothly simply because they have been outsourced. Outsourced work needs to be managed and measured. You still have customers and a business to keep satisfied. Something as simple as outsourcing a PC hardware and software inventory can become a nightmare if it is not managed. Data that is incorrect, incomplete, inconsistent, or in the wrong format can make what was supposed to be a no-brainer into an administrative headache. This kind of situation can and has happened, as many of us can attest from painful personal experience.

In This Chapter

In this chapter we'll cover the following topics:

- Business value
- Outsourcing benefits
- When to outsource
- When not to outsource
- Outsourcing options
- The outsourcing process
- The human factor (people issues)

Also included, at the end of the chapter, are two examples. The first is a hardware maintenance agreement; the second is a request for proposal.

Business Value

When you think of outsourcing, you should be thinking in terms of value to the business. Sometimes it just does not make business sense to do something in house that could be done more cost-effectively by a third party. Unfortunately, you don't always have a say in what is considered good business value. A decision might have been made higher up in the organization, without your input or knowledge, to outsource the Help Desk—either on its own or with the rest of IT. On the other hand, sometimes you do have a choice. You can choose to make sure your Help Desk is effective and adds value to the business, or you can choose to leave things as they are and run the risk of not being able to meet the company's strategic needs. Choosing the former may involve using outsourcing to allow your Help Desk to focus on the work that is most important to the business. Tasks such as telling customers how to put a border around a WordPerfect document can be given away. Outsourcing can free staff to work on projects such as automation, fixing the causes of recurring problems, and eliminating the reasons for customer calls to the Help Desk—all activities that add business value.

When your Help Desk is engaging in these kinds of activities and marketing them so that management realizes what is being accomplished, it is in little danger of being outsourced because it does not offer business value. If a third party can do a job better and more cost-effectively than your Help Desk without taking anything important away from the business, then you need to either give up and be gone or change the way you're doing things, and that might include using outsourcing.

Outsourcing Benefits

If outsourcing is used as a tool that is applied only where it is needed and is managed and measured, it can bring tangible benefits:

A reduction in costs

An improvement in productivity and performance

Increased flexibility, so business requirements can be responded to more quickly

A wider range of services

Increased skill level

Most importantly, outsourcing provides the following benefits:

More control over the Help Desk function

The increased ability to focus on what really matters to the business

Reduction in Costs

Third parties, who are focusing on servicing several customers, can realize economies of scale that your Help Desk could not possibly achieve. They can spread the cost of research, purchases, training, marketing, and consulting over many customers. They are motivated to stay on top of emerging technologies so they can benefit their customers and nurture their businesses.

Third parties can afford to give their staff the ongoing training required to keep staff current and ensure their expertise in various products. You might not be able to. Staff who have been trained and are current on new technologies are less likely to make costly on-the-job decisions than those who do not completely understand the technology and alternatives.

Training isn't the only cost associated with keeping current. The shelf life of packaged software is estimated to be approximately nine months. This means that to keep up with current versions, you need to not only train staff but purchase, test, and install each new piece of software approximately once a year. That is an expensive proposition in terms of staff time. A third party may be able to do this more cost-effectively.

Some support skills, such as those required for networks, are particularly expensive to keep and maintain. Staff require significant (and expensive) training and are in great demand by the industry, and turnover is high. If you feel you need to keep these skills in house, you can choose to outsource some network support positions and keep the rest in house. This will allow you to stretch the staff you do have without completely handing the skills away.

Third parties can also afford a higher quality and wider assortment of tools than you might be able to. For example, one outsourcing company specializing in banking applications has a state-of-the-art call center that offers specialized call management software, knowledge of all the standard banking software, automated call distribution, remote LAN management, established processes, and a guaranteed response time. Setting that kind of structure up from scratch would be an expensive and time-consuming proposition, involving significant management time, learning, and pain. To buy into one that you know is working, especially when you don't want to be in the business of Help Desks, means that you can become operational quickly and have plenty of experience at your disposal without a large capital outlay or a big learning curve.

For small businesses, outsourcing means being able to provide support services they could not have otherwise. For example, they can outsource the whole creation and maintenance of a support Web site or offload support calls to a third party for times during the day when no one is in the office.

Improvement in Productivity and Performance

Staff who are completely focused on their jobs naturally produce more and perform better than staff who are constantly being interrupted and pulled off current work to do other things. Outsourced staff are allowed to be focused, while full-time staff are not always allowed or encouraged to be. Not only are they being pulled in several ways, they have to worry about company politics, about what the company is or is not planning, about their future. Outsourced staff worry about their performance. If they work for themselves, their whole reputation and future employment is based on it. It is relatively easy for a company to get rid of contract staff who are not performing well. If they work for a third party, the third party will make sure that they are performing; again, their future business depends on it. Outsourced staff have a vested interest in performing well. Full-time staff can be more complacent about their stability. They don't necessarily have to worry quite as much about where their next paycheck is coming from or about their reputation. If they miss a deadline by a day—what's a day? To outsourced staff, a deadline is part of the contract. Miss it and you're out.

One outsourcing company reports that it constantly gets the same feedback from its customers: After four to six weeks on the job, outsourced Help Desk staff are more productive than equivalent internal staff. Even Help Desk customers comment on how focused the staff are. A Help Desk manager reports similar findings. One person on the Help Desk was responsible for the mass production of cartridge tapes containing new releases of internally developed application software. The person was not doing a good job and was constantly complaining about the monotony of the task. The Help Desk was forced to cut costs, and the Help Desk manager decided to outsource that position. At the suggestion of management, and against the Help Desk manager's better judgment, the function was outsourced to the person who had been doing it. The result was amazing: a 100 percent improvement in performance and innovation. Soon after the function was outsourced, the person was developing various efficiencies, including bar coding the cartridges. The Help Desk manager is now extremely pleased with that person's performance.

There are, of course, exceptions. Almost everyone has outsourcing disaster stories: maintenance staff who came in to fix a server and destroyed it in the process; network maintenance people who accidentally took a LAN down and then couldn't get it back up; network designers who designed and implemented a state-of-the-art network with several points of failure that quickly made their presence known; a consultant who came in to reconfigure some PCs, which then actually had to have their hard drives replaced. The fact that you've outsourced a function is no guarantee that it's going to be performed well. It might take you several tries to find an outsourcing company and staff that work well in your environment.

If your Help Desk has well-defined tasks that you can outsource, you might find them being done faster and more effectively by outsourced staff. At the same time, internal staff could do the work that was more important to the business. They could be more focused because someone else would be there to handle the routine work and at least some of the interruptions.

Outsourcing could also help eliminate the problem of absences on the Help Desk, where a person taking a vacation or calling in sick leaves a big hole. If you've outsourced the position, the third party will have the responsibility of making sure a qualified person is there every day—and with good motivation: Your business and your reference are at stake.

Increased Flexibility so Business Requirements Can Be Responded to More Quickly

On a Help Desk, especially on the front line, staffing requirements vary from one time period to the next. During the day, there are peaks and slow times for call traffic; over weeks, months, and the whole year there might be peaks and slow times for all the various tasks that your Help Desk performs. Outsourcing can help you meet the peaks without being overstaffed during the slower times. Outsourced staff can be used to handle daily traffic peaks, perhaps even from a remote location. They can be used to provide extra staffing to handle the increased call volume that results from the installation of a new software package or some other form of new technology. They need only be on the Help Desk for a period that covers the customers' learning curve. Some outsourcing contracts allow staff to be increased or decreased as required. Unusually large Help Desk requests, such as a big PC order that needs to be tested, configured, and installed, can be completely outsourced so the workload of the internal staff won't be disrupted. Outsourcing allows you to keep your Help Desk staffed for the straight line and let someone else worry about the blips.

A Wider Range of Services

If the business you support is demanding services that you don't have enough staff, budget, or skills to provide, you can use outsourcing to fill the gap. If your customers are using too many different software packages for you to support effectively with the resources you have, you could outsource support for those packages. You could even outsource some or all of the installation, testing, management, and training. A third party who is serving several other customers and has the skills required can probably do these more cost-effectively than your Help Desk.

Increased Skill Level

Outsourcing can provide the Help Desk with skills and experience in areas in which it is weak or in which it simply has no skills. Third-party staff can often provide knowledge and experience in the various options that technology allows and in the identification and resolution of problems that may crop up with the technology. They may be familiar with problems and methods that the Help Desk has not seen before. Using third-party staff may be a more cost-effective and quicker way to increase skill level than hiring new staff.

More Control over the Help Desk Function

Outsourcing can actually provide you with the tools or people you need to manage the Help Desk more effectively. If you don't have the staff or tools to do network monitoring, you might be able to outsource that function. A third party could dial into your network and monitor it remotely, providing you with accurate and timely reporting for traffic patterns, network performance, and situations that need immediate attention. This information would help you prevent, eliminate, or quickly resolve problems, making your environment more stable. A third party could also perform (or even set up) some or all of your Help Desk management functions in this way, providing you with problem management reporting and information on Help Desk performance. Having a third party do this, even for a limited time, would give you valuable feedback from which you could plan improvements.

If your Help Desk is in an out-of-control problem cycle, outsourcing extra help can give you some breathing room to determine and implement a strategy for getting out of the cycle.

Increased Ability to Focus on What Really Matters to the Business

When you're trying to focus your Help Desk on delivering business value and you don't have an unlimited head count, it doesn't make much sense to be spending time and resources on nonstrategic activities that take away from your ability to do this. Ordering PCs, matching purchase orders to invoices, or explaining to someone how to use Word for Windows to rotate an address on an envelope don't add a lot to your business value, and you would not lose anything of value by outsourcing them. Help Desk staff would be able to focus on work that is more important to the business: automation, planning for upgrades to ensure the environment can handle new mission-critical software, giving customers tools to make them more self-sufficient, finding and eliminating the causes of recurring problems, and making the environment better able to support the business.

A Caution

Figure 12.1 summarizes what outsourcing can do for you. What out-sourcing will *not* do for you is free you from having to manage what you've outsourced or from being accountable to your customers. Functions are not guaranteed to run smoothly just because you've out-sourced them. Regardless of whether you are performing the function or

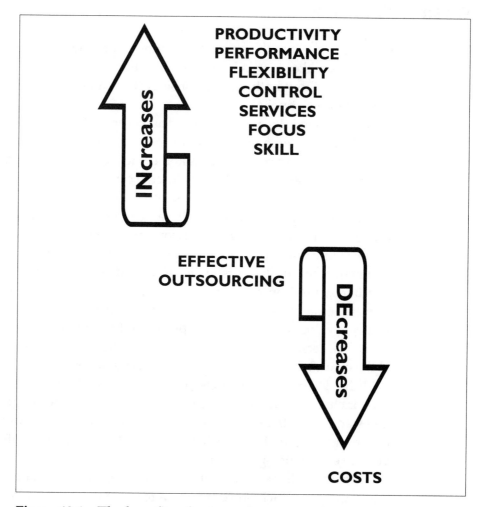

Figure 12.1   The benefits of outsourcing.

are paying someone else to do it, you need to make sure that objectives are met, customers are satisfied, and the business is being served effectively. You will need to set objectives and performance measurements with the outsourcing party and communicate often to review these. Failure to do this can result in work that does not meet expectations and in customers and a business that are not happy with your performance.

When to Outsource

Outsourcing as much as possible without stopping to consider the consequences makes just as little sense as stubbornly refusing to outsource anything without bothering to consider the potential benefits. It is a tool to be used selectively.

Outsourcing does not have to be an all-or-nothing proposition. It can involve a complementary blend of in-house and outsourced functions. There are as many combinations and choices in outsourcing as there are companies to provide them. Outsourcing can fill in gaps; it can stretch or build onto existing staff, skills, or services. It can be as simple as providing one person to handle peak call traffic remotely or something as complex as taking over the whole network management function.

Deciding what to outsource is more complex than using the formula. A function should be outsourced if a third party can do it more cost-effectively. Environments are too complex for the decision to be that simple. Sometimes the loss in cost-effectiveness is worth something in strategic value, in having the expertise in house to help make strategic decisions. Technology is no longer isolated from the business. It is often at the heart, with the success of the business depending on it.

What Help Desk functions you outsource will depend on many factors, including your technological environment (how large, complex, and stable it is), the variety of services you provide, the growth you are experiencing, the staff you have (skills, ability, number), the demand you are experiencing, and the focus of your business.

The possibilities for outsourcing are almost endless. Some of the circumstances in which outsourcing might help you are as follows:

Your customer base is experiencing rapid growth.

Routine work seems to be taking over your resources.

The Help Desk is drowning in support.

You simply need more people.

You really don't know how the Help Desk is performing.

You're going through a transition.

You're finding it difficult to support remote locations.

You require expensive tools that you can't afford.

You have a requirement for a skill that you use infrequently.

You need one or more people with very expensive skills.

You require skills that are specialized but not strategic.

You're in a business you want to get out of.

You need to support a wide variety of packaged software.

The Help Desk is getting a lot of how-to questions for packaged software.

Each of these is discussed separately in the following sections.

Customer Base Is Experiencing Rapid Growth

PCs are being rolled out at a rate that is making the environment unstable and causing your support calls to skyrocket. You can either outsource some of the support to help your staff handle the load, or you can outsource the whole support load for a specific time so your staff have time to investigate why the environment is unstable and what the Help Desk could do to eliminate the problems being experienced. It would give you time to see just how much support the Help Desk will need to provide. Once the time was up, you could either staff permanently or leave some or all of the outsourced staff there so your other staff could focus on more strategic activities.

Routine Work Seems to Be Taking over Your Resources

If routine, repetitive work is consuming more and more Help Desk time and keeping you from doing other more important work, such as making improvements or becoming more proactive in managing the environment, you should consider either outsourcing or automation. If you can't automate, outsource—or outsource some of your support so you have time to automate.

The Help Desk Is Drowning in Support

There are so many problems that you just can't get ahead. You can barely keep up with the calls, and that's all you do. You don't have time to identify and solve recurring problems or to look into what is required to reduce the number of calls. A solution would be to outsource part or all of the support while your staff researches and implements ways to reduce calls.

You Simply Need More People

You just don't have enough staff to provide your customers with what they need. You can't get an increase in head count, but you might be able to get money for outsourcing.

You Really Don't Know How the Help Desk Is Performing

You're too busy to do the work necessary to measure your performance, but you might be able to outsource that function. A third party could come in, put in place the reporting that you would like to see, and leave the rest for you. Alternatively, that same person (or persons) could do your performance measurements on a regular basis, even designing and distributing customer surveys. Having an outside person do this would serve as a good audit.

You're Going through a Transition

Perhaps you are moving all your customers to a new hardware or software platform and you need someone to support the old environment while you prepare for the new one. Several software companies have this same problem. They solve it by outsourcing customer support for their older products while in-house staff focus on learning and supporting the new products.

You're Finding It Difficult to Support Remote Locations

Supporting remote locations can be expensive, especially if you constantly have to send staff there. Outsourcers might be able to manage it remotely or may be in a location where they can support it more cost-effectively than you can.

You Require Expensive Tools That You Can't Afford

If you need to perform functions that would require a large investment in tools and skills, such as wide area network (WAN) management, it might be wiser to outsource this function to a third party who has the tools, skills, and experience necessary to do the job. You would be saved the capital outlay.

You Have a Requirement for a Skill That You Use Infrequently

If you require a skill to perform a function that you need only occasionally, it doesn't make a lot of sense to support the cost of that skill. Outsourcing would probably be more cost-effective. An example is hardware installation in an environment that is experiencing almost no growth.

You Need One or More People with Very Expensive Skills

Some skills, such as LAN support (e.g., network engineers), are very expensive to maintain. The people with these skills require a lot of training, and if you don't pay them enough they will leave because they are in great demand. Turnover, which is very expensive, could be high. It might be more cost-effective for you to keep some of these skills in house and outsource the rest. The knowledge would still be in house to some extent but could be stretched and made more efficient through the use of the outsourced staff.

You Require Skills That Are Specialized but Not Strategic

An example of this is hardware maintenance. The skill is expensive to maintain because technology is changing so quickly. Maintenance technicians are portable from environment to environment—their skills are based on the tools, not on the company. It is not necessary for them to know anything about your business. Just as the photocopier repair person can go into any company, so can the PC maintenance person. Having your own maintenance staff would mean having not only staff costs but the costs of stocking and replenishing parts. A third party could do this more cost-effectively because of economies of scale.

You're in a Business You Don't Want to Be In

If you're a Help Desk with internal training staff, you might be spending too much time and effort in a business that could be done more cost-effectively by someone whose business is training. To support your training business, you need to support the trainers while they learn software packages and put together and prepare for courses. You also need to support all the administration that goes along with training: scheduling, course signups and cancellations—and perhaps even internal records and billing. A training company would have all of this set up and would have enough trainers to cover all the software packages you need training for. It could spread the expense of keeping all of this running over several customers, which could include you.

You Need to Support a Wide Variety of Packaged Software

One person can learn only so many software packages in the detail required to support them. Supporting a wide variety of packages means increased staffing requirements and increased training requirements. As mentioned, the shelf life of a software version is roughly nine months, so training requirements will be high. A third party will have staff that knows the software and can learn the details of the customer's configuration and environment so time is not wasted finding all this out when a call comes in.

The Help Desk Is Getting a Lot of How-to Questions for Packaged Software

If your customers are demanding more software support than you have the staff to provide or want to provide, you can outsource support for standard packaged software. If funding or misuse was an issue, you could distribute the cost among the customers using the service.

Figures 12.2 through 12.5 show examples of situations in which you might want to outsource.

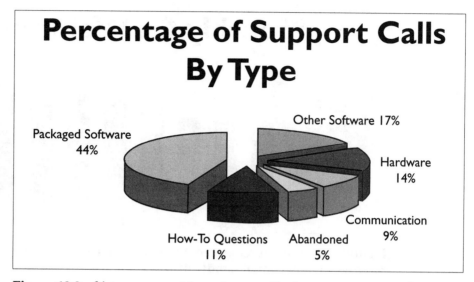

Figure 12.2   You may want to outsource if a large percentage of support is for packaged software.

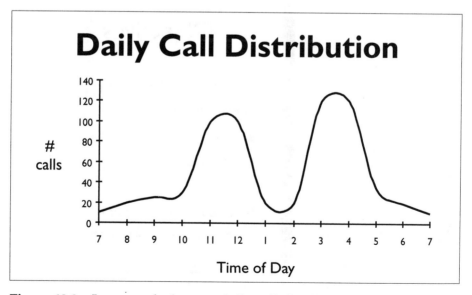

Figure 12.3   Large peaks in your daily call distribution might indicate a good time to outsource.

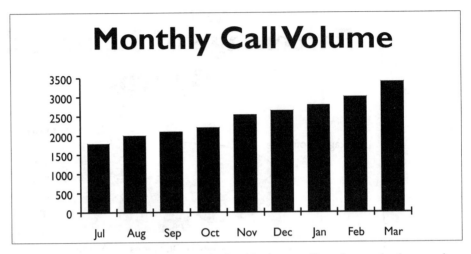

Figure 12.4   Outsourcing can help if your call volume is increasing rapidly and you cannot handle the load.

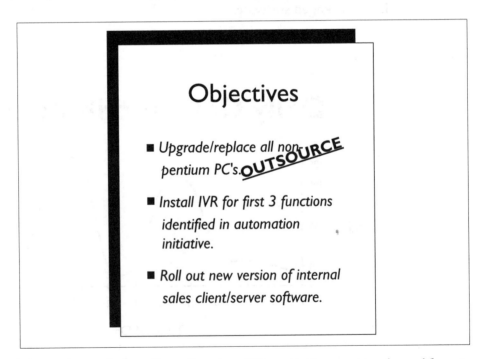

Figure 12.5   Going through a transition can become easier with out-sourced help.

When Not to Outsource

This is a well-debated topic. Some companies don't want to outsource any functions that involve strategic decision making or planning; some refuse to outsource anything that is part of the core business; others won't outsource understanding and mastery of advanced technology; still others will outsource anything that is cost-effective; and some will outsource anything.

If you are unsure whether or not to outsource, and money is not the issue, you will have to decide the costs, in terms of business value, of not having that function in house. Then you'll have to decide how important that value is to the business and make your decision from there. Your outsourcing decision will be easier if you understand which Help Desk services are critical to the business and/or give it a strategic advantage in some way and which services are simply a commodity. These will vary from business to business; what is strategic for one company could be a commodity for another. For example, a hardware retailer would probably not hesitate to outsource the maintenance of telephone systems and voice networks, but a telephone company, or any other company dealing in voice communications, might not be as eager to do so.

One function that companies often hesitate to outsource is network management. Some won't outsource anything that has to do with the network: support, design, and management. The reasons for this include the following:

"We need to know everything about networks and how they work so we understand the different ways we can use them to benefit the business."

"Networks can get very complicated. If an outsourcing company makes a mistake in your network, it's a big deal. You might be stuck with a network that you don't know anything about and a very expensive price tag to try to get it fixed. You won't understand your network, so how will you know if the company you hire to fix it will do any better?"

"Networking requires knowledge and understanding of the business. Outsourced network engineers don't have this and will find it hard to get it in the short time they have to design or reconfigure a network. They might overlook alternatives or make critical mistakes that might limit the company's ability to compete in some way later on down the road."

You may require skills specific to your business in order to provide support to your customers. You might not want or be able to outsource these. One Help Desk supporting a real-time retail environment found that in order for Help Desk staff to support the customers effectively, they needed to have store experience. That became one of the prerequisites for working on the Help Desk. A support person with store experience would understand what the customer was experiencing and would know the environment. That kind of knowledge and experience would be almost impossible to get from an outsourcer.

You also probably wouldn't want to outsource the support of applications that are unique to your business. The more people you have who understand these applications, the better for the business. Outsourcing companies might not be able to support these applications any more cost-effectively than you since they could not share the cost across any customers other than your company. They would also have the overhead of learning the application and your environment.

Another environment that would not be cost-effective to outsource would be a nonstandardized environment that included a wide variety of technology. A newspaper company with just such an environment was investigating the possibility of outsourcing the LAN support area, and the potential outsourcer reached the following conclusion: "LAN support consists of seven staff. The workload analysis shows that their responsibilities are diverse and varied over many different platforms and require very unique skill sets. Each individual has a specialized area of expertise and must be capable of supporting other platforms as well. Also, the selection of the router environment is a software solution as opposed to a hardware choice, making it impossible to monitor the environment remotely. Because of the diversity and requirement for on-site support, the only option in this scenario would be to hire the seven support staff to maintain this environment. However, this option makes the business case prohibitive in terms of cost savings."

Outsourcing Options

When you are outsourcing, you can mix and match between what you need and what third parties can offer. They want your business, so they are usually more than willing to accommodate any special requirements you might have.

The following are some of the most commonly outsourced Help Desk functions. Each can be partially outsourced and combined with other functions, giving you several options for the kinds of outsourced services that are available to your Help Desk:

- Hardware maintenance
- Software management
- Customer support
- Training
- Transitional work

Hardware Maintenance

Outsourcing maintenance for mainframe equipment has long been a given. The costs and skills involved in doing this in house are prohibitive. Maintenance is typically outsourced either to the vendor or to one or more third-party service providers. Some service providers specialize in specific products, such as mainframe printers.

The maintenance of PC/LAN technology is also something that many companies are deciding to outsource. Service providers abound for PC/LAN hardware maintenance. Some provide maintenance for both types of environments—mainframe and PC. This discussion will focus on PC/LAN hardware maintenance.

Description

Outsourcing hardware maintenance for PC/LANs involves having a third party look after the maintenance and repair of all your PCs, printers, servers, monitors, and all associated hardware (network cards, modems, CD-ROM, etc.). How this is actually implemented will vary widely from company to company. Some options are the following:

Third-party staff on site full-time. One or more technicians from the third-party service provider are actually on site full-time. They do preventive maintenance on all equipment and service or replace equipment that needs repair. They become part of the Help Desk team and are dispatched to customers to investigate potential hardware problems. They use the Help Desk call-tracking system to track problems. The technicians maintain a spare parts inventory and often take on the responsibility of maintaining hardware inventory. In fact, they often perform tasks other than maintenance, such as setting up and configuring new PCs for Help Desk customers. Because these staff are on site, they become very familiar with the environment and the Help Desk customers.

Third-party staff on site half days. This option is identical to the preceding one, except that the technician is only at the customer's site for half of each day.

Third-party staff on an on-call basis. Another option for hardware maintenance is to have the third-party staff visit your site only for specific problem instances. If a problem occurs, you call the service provider and a service technician is dispatched within an agreed-upon response time.

Carry-in service. This option involves taking the equipment directly to the service provider for repair.

Which of these options you choose depends on how large your customer base is. If you have enough PCs to justify a full-time service technician, then that option is preferable. The response time is best, and you have control over that person's time.

Some companies choose a mix of options: a full-time technician at their main site and on-call service for remote sites. If you choose the option of having a technician on site, you will most likely be getting services other than simply hardware support and proactive maintenance. Other services often incorporated into maintenance contracts are as follows:

- Maintenance of hardware inventory
- Asset tagging

- Setup, testing, and installation of hardware
- Hardware relocation
- Hardware upgrade

The customer organization can specify how technicians are to report on services performed and parts used.

Other service maintenance options involve the response time to calls. (If you have an on-site technician, this is taken care of.) You can pretty much set up whatever kind of response you want, if you are willing to pay for it. Some standard offerings are as follows:

Four-hour, eight-hour, same-day, or next-day response. A technician will be on site looking at the problem within the time specified. Or—and this is usually reserved for critical hardware—replacement equipment will have been put into place within that time.

Once-a-week visit. Another option is to have one or more service technicians visit your site at a specific interval—say, weekly—to perform all required maintenance.

Choosing among these options will depend on how important your hardware is to your business (how much downtime you can afford) and how much redundancy you have. If you are supporting a mission-critical application on your PC technology, then service once a week is not going to suffice. You need not limit your response time specifications to one option. You can have several alternatives for hardware at different levels of criticality. For example, you might have four-hour service for your production and testing applications and next-day service for any other applications.

Another option to consider is business hours. You can specify that hardware support is to be provided during regular business hours or up to twenty-four-hour support if you need it. The cost of support will increase as response time decreases and as after-hours coverage increases.

The hardware maintenance contract is usually set out for a year and is typically a flat rate; services performed above and beyond those specified in the contract are charged back on an hourly basis. See example no. 1, at the end of this chapter, for a sample of a hardware maintenance agreement.

Software Management

Keeping up to date with releases of packaged software is expensive and time consuming. Software must be purchased, installed, and tested, Help Desk staff and customers trained, and the product rolled out. The more standard packaged software packages you have to maintain, the more time consuming this is. Outsourcing the whole or part of this process is an option.

Description

Software management involves the responsibility of keeping software up to date and working smoothly. Tasks that you can outsource include the following:

Maintenance of licensing. Keeping software licensing up to date is an arduous task, especially when you have a mix of standalone and networked PCs. Third-party service providers are willing to do this for you. They will make sure that you have adequate licensing at all times, that licenses are reused when someone no longer needs one, and that software upgrades are properly licensed.

Testing and installation of software. Service providers can test and install packaged software or software upgrades across the network or on individual PCs.

Training. Service providers can train Help Desk staff and customers in upgrades.

Complete management. The third-party service provider can take over all of the software functions. Even customer support can be outsourced.

Customer Support

Many organizations are outsourcing their customer support for packaged applications. They cannot afford to expend the money for the necessary people and time to train for and support the calls.

Description

A third party provides support for Help Desk customers. Service can vary from answering software questions remotely to fixing all problems on site. Some of the options include the following:

Third-party staff on site, as part of Help Desk team. The third party provides staff to either take over support on your Help Desk or add to the staff you have. Staff would become part of the Help Desk team. This is a good way to expand the skills you offer customers, staffing for peaks and transitions and lessening the support load so that in-house Help Desk staff can focus on improvement projects.

Use of third-party call center. Customers call the third party directly when they have a problem. You could set up your phones so this happens automatically when customers call a Help Desk number and select the support option.

Outsource only support for packaged software. Support that is most easily outsourced is for standard packaged software. Some third parties specialize in certain applications, such as banking, so companies using those applications could also outsource fairly easily. For a third party to take on the support of your in-house applications, the cost to you would have to be very high. The expense of learning and supporting your application could not be shared over any other of the third party's customers.

First-line support provided by third party, second-line by customer. For this option, the third party would take all of the calls and try to resolve them. Any calls that could not be resolved over the phone would be passed to the customer's second-level support area. Third parties report being able to handle approximately 80 percent of the calls without having to go to second-level support. (This depends very much on the environment, of course.)

Support for off hours or peak times during the day. One way of extending your service to seven days a week, twenty-four hours a day, is to outsource any after-hours service. You can have the phones automatically switch over to the third-party phone center as soon as your business hours are over. If the problem can't be handled over the phone, your staff can be paged to take care of it. This may also be a good way to handle your peak times; you can switch one or more lines to the third party for specific times during the day.

When you choose to outsource to a remote call center, you need to do some work up front to make sure that the staff at the call center are familiar with your environment so customers don't have to spend time explaining the environment to them. Third-party staff can serve your internal customers more effectively if they have an understanding of the environment and standard configurations.

Outsourcing partial customer support to third parties is a popular solution for reducing support load on staff. Software development companies use it extensively.

Training

Training is outsourced by companies that don't want to be in the business of providing training. They don't want to take on the cost or management burden associated with keeping training staff up to date on all packages for which training is required, supporting the trainers while they develop courses, and supporting administrative functions such as registration. Third parties make much more cost-effective use of their trainers and are able to offer courses more frequently and with greater course variety. Each trainer can provide training for several clients. Their economies of scale are passed on to customers to make this an attractive outsourcing option.

Description

The third party is responsible for providing training to customer employees. Some of the options are as follows:

Training at customer site in facilities provided and maintained by customer. The customer maintains a training facility that the third party uses to provide on-site training. This option is attractive to those customers who already have some kind of training facility.

Customer employees attend training at third-party site. Customer employees attend either the third party's regular course offerings or course offerings that have been set up specifically for the customer.

Outsource training only for standard packaged applications. Training for company-specific applications is not as cost-effective as training for the software that the third party already provides training for. Training for the customer-specific applications can be kept in house.

Have the third party handle all aspects from registration to billing. Third parties providing training have all of these functions set up already and can provide them to customers at an attractive rate.

Customize training to customers' environment. Training, even at the third-party site, can be customized so it reflects the environment of your internal customers. How to access software or information about common libraries, how to use the network, even how to call the Help Desk or access security and standards documents can be included— everything that is particular to your organization.

Just-in-time training. Third-party staff come into the company and coach company employees in the use of technology while the employees are performing their daily tasks. This kind of training could be scheduled at regular intervals on a rotating basis throughout the company.

You may want to offer your customers a few options: attending training on site or—if the times are more suitable—attending a regular course offering at the third-party site. If your Help Desk supports some packages that have fewer users, training for those packages can be left at the third-party site. If you are charging your clients directly for the training, the training company can also take care of that for you. They can provide promotional material, such as training schedules, and take care of registration, scheduling, and billing.

A side benefit to outsourcing training is that sometimes internal staff don't take in-house trainers as seriously as external trainers, even though the skills may be equal. They might have more respect for, and tend to be more satisfied with, third-party trainers who have more experience. Also, having the third party charge customers directly may cut down on no-shows and last-minute cancellations.

Transitional Work

Outsourcing can help during times of transition. If you need to focus your resources on new products, outsourcing support for the old ones can make sense. Software development companies often do this. You can also outsource part of the work for the new product, especially if it is something you will probably only be doing once or very infrequently.

Some examples of outsourcing transitional work include the following:

Outsource support so that staff can focus on upgrading the environment for client/server.

Outsource the installation and initial setup of interactive voice response (IVR).

Outsource the extra support that is required in the early stages of the introduction of a new product or environment.

The Outsourcing Process

When you're considering outsourcing, you need to know who might be able to provide the services you need. Chances are that as a Help Desk manager you're already getting endless calls from vendors about every service imaginable. It is sometimes difficult to make time for vendors, but by not listening you can miss some valuable ideas. If you don't have time to talk to all of the vendors when they knock on your door, at least keep a file of cards and services so you can go back to them when you need something.

Request for Proposal (RFP)

Unless what you're doing is very small, you'll want to put together a request for proposal (RFP) to distribute to prospective service providers to explain what you need. The RFP should set out the details of the service(s) you are looking for. See example no. 2 at the end of this chapter for a sample RFP.

Know the Third Party

Once you have a short list of potential service providers, you should do some serious investigation into the service organizations themselves, if you have not done so already.

Check into the financial stability of the organization. Annual reports can provide valuable information on a company's financial health, as can any industry news source or even gossip. Taking a contract with someone who goes into receivership soon thereafter is something you want to avoid.

Visit the head office. Make sure there is something solid behind the salesperson.

Meet the staff who will be working at your organization. If you are not confident that they can do the job, then maybe you should go elsewhere.

Check into their quality control. What measures does the service provider take to ensure that you are getting the service you require?

Find out how they plan to communicate progress and performance to you. They should have reporting and procedures already in place for this.

Check all references. This is an absolute imperative. Don't make any final decisions without talking to other customers of the company.

Take your time. Don't rush into a decision if you're not sure about the outsourcing firm. You're going to have to live with the decision for a while, so take your time. You want to do everything possible to avoid making an expensive and time-consuming mistake.

A Clear Agreement

When you are ready to create an agreement with the third party of your choice, you need to make sure that each of you understands exactly what is expected of the other:

Make sure the vendor understands what your objectives are and is ready to meet them. You have objectives to meet, and by outsourcing you are attempting to meet them through the third party. If the third party does not meet them, you will be held accountable.

Define responsibilities for each party clearly, with nothing left to chance. Regardless of any "that-goes-without-saying" promises, make sure that everything you expect from the third party is clearly documented. In the same way, what is expected of you must also be clearly stated.

Build performance measures. You're going to have to have some way of measuring whether the outsourcing is working. Building these measures up front will not only make it easier to understand whether the contract is successful but will also help clarify performance expectations, ensuring that they get met.

Put it all in writing. If it isn't in writing, it isn't in the contract, and the vendor cannot be held to it.

Monitor

Once the agreement is signed and the work has started, your responsibility is still not over. You have to monitor the contract, make sure that it is working. You will have to set up some form of communication with the company—face-to-face meetings are probably best—at which you review performance from both sides to see how successful the contract is. Start off by meeting frequently to make any adjustments required and then settle into a schedule of perhaps a meeting every month or so.

An Example

One third-party service provider meets with each of its customers monthly to review performance. Customers rate each of its services on a scale of 0 to 7. Customers also evaluate the following:

- Performance against the service-level agreement—for example, speed of resolution
- Quality of the front-line staff—skill level and call handling
- Call statistics—wait time, response time, resolution time, abandoned calls

Evaluation can sometimes be fairly subjective, and often the service provider finds that success depends largely on how customer employees get along with third-party support staff. Individual personalities make a difference.

The Human Factor

Don't expect your outsourcing suggestion to be greeted with open arms by your staff. Even if they are stressed and overworked and you are providing relief in some form of outsourcing, they may not see it as help but rather as a threat.

There is no such thing as overcommunication when it comes to letting staff know that you're considering, or have decided on, outsourcing. Staff will start to worry as soon as you mention the word. They'll be concerned about the following issues:

Losing their jobs

A change in working conditions—"What will be expected of me? Will I be able to do it? Will they train me?"

Their careers—"Will I lose my seniority? If they keep outsourcing, there won't be anywhere left for me to go."

They may feel as if they've been betrayed. A way to help combat all of these worries and feelings of betrayal is to make your staff aware of what is going on as early in the process as possible:

Get them involved in making the outsourcing decision. Explain what you're trying to achieve and how outsourcing will help you achieve it within the constraints of your budget, or any cost-cutting measures the company has put into place.

Provide opportunities for them to ask questions and express their concerns. Be honest.

Let them help form the agreement, getting them involved in setting up performance measurements.

Make them part of the third-party review and selection process.

Include staff in regular performance meetings with the third-party service provider.

By making your staff aware of the outsourcing process early on you will make them feel like a part of the process, and they will be much more likely to give the outsourcing their support. Trying to make the outsourcing work without the support of your staff will be very difficult, especially in cases where an outsourced employee has to work with your staff.

When People Lose Their Jobs

Sometimes an outsourcing decision involves laying people off. You should be honest with staff from the beginning if there is a possibility of this. How you handle the situation will be very closely watched by other staff. If they feel you are hiding things or not telling the whole truth, you are less likely to get their buy-in. They might worry that you are planning to outsource everything.

Don't write off the staff you are laying off. Make every effort to find different positions for them. Sometimes the outsourcing firm will hire the people whose positions you are outsourcing. They will train them and often place them back with you. The advantage to the outsourcers is that they have someone who is familiar with your environment.

This seems like an ideal solution, but what can and does happen is that the outsourcing firm lays those same people off a while later. The people have no seniority and get very limited severance. This solution is very cost-effective for the company that handed them over to the outsourcing firm but very severe and financially damaging for the employees, who would have been much better off had the original company simply laid them off.

It is the original employer's responsibility to make sure that staff who are laid off get help finding employment and receive the severance that is due them. If staff do go to the outsourcing firm, the original company can specify a guaranteed length of employment for them as part of the outsourcing contract, but the company should not force the outsourcing firm to take on employees that they don't need. That is not fair to either the outsourcing firm or the employees. If a company cannot find a place for its employees internally and if the outsourcing firm has no place for them, the fairest thing to do is to lay them off with proper severance.

This is more than just a matter of moral responsibility. Staff who think they have been treated unfairly can do more than moan and groan. They can sue. Never underestimate the importance of the support of your in-house staff in any kind of outsourcing endeavor. Treat your staff fairly, especially when you have to let them go.

Example No. 1: Hardware Maintenance Agreement

The Support Program

The third party proposes that it will provide three on-site engineers to the customer. At the direction and discretion of the customer, the engineers will perform tasks as defined in Schedule A (see Schedule A later in this section). The hours of the engineers will be staggered at the discretion of the customer to include coverage from 7:00 A.M. to 7:00 P.M.

The third party promises to provide and maintain spare parts inventories at designated customer locations. The third party proposes to provide hardware maintenance on all customer equipment outlined in Schedule B (see Schedule B later in this section) according to the following annual investment:

Three field engineers:	$195,000
Refundable parts retainers:	$ 48,240
Total:	**$243,240**

Please note: The parts retainer is capped so the customer will not be charged for any parts in excess of the $48,240 figure; so the maximum charge for this program is $243,240. Any unused balance of the retainer is 100 percent refundable to the customer, so the actual amount paid may very well be less than the maximum price indicated, as illustrated in Table 12.1.

The Hiring of Existing Staff

The third party agrees to make every fair and reasonable effort to hire the existing support engineer at the customer site and agrees that an offer of employment will be extended to this individual (signed by third-party company president).

Table 12.1 Program Cost

Failure Rate	Failures	Average Parts Cost	Total Parts Cost	Annual Total
10%	134	$120	$16,080	$211,080
20%	268	$120	$32,160	$227,160
30%	402	$120	$48,240	$243,240

Schedule A: On-Site Engineer, Duties and Capabilities

Software Support. Third-party on-site field engineers will perform software support and installations as directed by the customer. Based on our understanding of the customer's environment, the third party will provide field engineers trained in the Microsoft suite of products and other software packages deemed appropriate by the customer.

Service Call Tracking. Service call tracking will be performed by the third party as specified by the customer. For example:

Department, location, and contact name

Make and model of equipment requiring repair

Date and time the service call was requested

Date and time the service call was completed

The repair description

Asset Tagging. Asset tagging procedures will be performed by the third party as specified by the customer.

Hardware Maintenance and Support. Items covered include:

All personal computers and printers in standalone and LAN environments

Advanced diagnostics

Installation of parts

End-user support

Hardware Installations. Areas covered include:

Setup

Testing

Relocating equipment

Equipment upgrades

Disk drives (transfer data, partitioning)

Video cards

LAN cards

RAM

Monitors

Batteries

Proactive Support. Proactive support helps eliminate equipment failure and leads to increased performance and longevity. At the discretion of the customers, each personal computer and printer will be supported proactively.

Proactive support for personal computers involves the following procedures:

Virus scanning

Disk defragmentation

An external cleaning

An internal vacuuming and lubrication

Proactive support for laser printers involves the following procedures:

An external cleaning

An internal vacuuming and lubrication

Corona wires cleaned

Fuser assembly inspected for wear

Photo drum inspected for scarring

Physical Inventory and Audit. The third party will maintain a complete microcomputer inventory and generate inventory documents on request. This valuable physical asset listing will contain standalone and network-specified information for all physical components and resources. At the discretion of the customer, the types of information collected may include the following:

Model of computer

CPU type and speed

Floppy drive size and capacity

Hard drive capacity and type

Disk controller type

RAM, conventional and extended

Serial and parallel port number and configurations

Network interface card

Node address

Disk coprocessor board model

Video board type

ROM BIOS version

Other internal hardware (modem, mouse, etc.)

Software in use

Warranty tracking, with the objective of eliminating any cost incurred for parts of equipment under warranty

The serial numbers of the major hardware and software components are included as part of the physical inventory and audit.

Schedule B: Equipment List (Summary Only)

Personal computers:	938
Printers:	
Laser printers:	123
Dot matrix printers:	261
Other printers:	14
Total units:	1,336

Note: In this contract, nothing is said about growth of the environment. Because growth is low and coverage was considered more than sufficient, management did not consider this an issue. Other environments might want to specify how much growth was allowed before the contract had to be renegotiated or a premium charged.

Example No. 2: Request for Proposal

Request for Proposal for Help Desk Support

For:	Good Hotels Corporate Help Desk 125 Good St., 1st floor Ottawa, Ontario, Canada
Contact:	Jane Do Tel: 613-111-2222 Fax: 614-111-3333
Deadline:	Proposals must be received on or by January 31, 1997.
Contract:	Contract is expected to start on June 1, 1997.
Contents of This RFP:	1. The Company 2. Summary of Requirements 3. Our Current Help Desk Environment Customers Help Desk Function Standard Desktop Packages Being Supported Call Volume Hours of Operation 4. What We Are Looking For Responsibilities of Third-Party Service Provider Service Levels Required from Third-Party Service Provider 5. Details of RFP Response Format 6. Selection Process and Schedule (1998) 7. Attachments A. Chart showing details of call distribution over a week B. Inventory summary for technology to be supported

1. The Company

Good Hotels is an international company with 200 luxury hotels, resorts, and conference centers all over the world. The head office is in Ottawa, Canada.

2. Summary of Requirements

The Corporate Help Desk of Good Hotels is looking to outsource support of packaged desktop software so it can focus on supporting business systems.

3. Our Current Help Desk Environment

Customers. The Corporate Help Desk supports approximately 3,500 users of standard desktop software. Eight hundred of these are employees at the home office, the rest work in the hotels, resorts, and conference centers.

Help Desk Function. Support requests come in by phone and by E-mail.

An IVR handles some basic functions such as terminal resets.

All calls are logged.

Call tracking and logging is done via tracking software.

Calls that cannot be handled by the first line (approximately 15 percent) are passed on to the second or third levels of support.

Standard Desktop Packages Being Supported

- Desktop operating system
- Word processor
- Spreadsheet
- Presentation software
- Database software

For details, please see the Summary of Technology Being Supported, attached to this RFP.

Platform. Networked PCs, ranging from 486 to Pentium. Standard network operating system. *For details, see the Summary of Technology Being Supported, attached to this RFP.*

Call Volumes. Calls for standard desktop software are about 1,000 per week. For details of call distribution, see attached chart showing average call distribution over a week.

Hours of Operation. Twenty-four hours per day (to handle all time zones).

4. What We Are Looking For

We are looking for a third-party service provider to take over our Help Desk support function for packaged desktop software. Support calls would go directly to the third party.

Responsibilities of Third-Party Service Provider:

Support the standard desktop software as it runs in our current environment. See previous section for details.

Become and remain familiar with the environment our customers function in and have the technical knowledge and skills to support it effectively.

Log every call from our customers using the tracking software.

Resolve problems via phone and E-mail. Follow the Help Desk procedures that we have established for call tracking and closure.

Dispatch on-site technician or call second-level support as required. Maintain control of problems until closed.

Provide twenty-four-hour service. Calling patterns and volumes are as per attached graph.

Do random customer call backs daily on 10 percent of calls.

Generate weekly call statistics (e.g., number of calls, resolution time, call wait time, abandon rate, etc.), details to be worked out as part of a service-level agreement.

Keep third-party staff trained in advance of new software releases.

Service Levels Required from Third-Party Service Provider:

A 90 percent first-level call resolution rate.

Call waiting of less than thirty seconds.

Abandonment rate of less than 3 percent.

Customer surveys must generate a 90 percent positive response: i.e., staff are polite, service-oriented, knowledgeable.

Contract will be set up so that it can be canceled at any time if service levels are not met.

Monthly meetings will be held between the third-party service provider and the manager of the Good Hotel Help Desk.

5. Details of RFP Response Format

Responses should be directed to:

Jane Do
Good Hotels, Corporate Help Desk
125 Good St., 1st floor
Ottawa, Ontario, Canada
613-111-2222
On or by
January 31, 1997

The response to this RFP should contain the following information:

1. Company Information

   Name and address of company.
   Contact name, phone and fax number.

2. Proposed Staffing

   Table or graph showing number of staff to be allocated to Good Hotels support for the same time frames as in the attached call volume/distribution graph.

   Profiles (short resumes) of the suggested staff.

3. Services

   A list of services that the third-party service provider will provide to Good Hotels for the price shown in the following section.

4. Pricing

   To be shown in chart format: Person-hours per week, range of number of calls per week, price per year. For example:

No. Person-Hours	Range of No. Calls/week	Cost per Year
200	1,000-1,500	$n

Include as many ranges as you wish and as many variations as you wish.

We welcome suggestions and alternatives.

Include information on any cost penalties (i.e., if range increases, etc.).

5. References

Include three customer references: company name, contact name, and phone number.

6. Other Information

Feel free to include any other information that you feel would be useful.

6. Selection Process and Schedule (1998)

To Be Completed	Activity
January 31	All RFPs collected.
February 21	RFPs reviewed by Good Hotels.
February 28	Candidates considered will be notified by telephone for interviews. Unsuccessful candidates will be notified via mail.
March 3 to April 4	Candidates under consideration will be interviewed during this time. Also during this time we may request interviews with candidate staff who may be working on our Help Desk.
April 25	Final selection. Unsuccessful candidates and successful candidate will be notified by telephone.
May 16	Contract negotiated and service-level agreement drawn up.
May 23	Contract and service-level agreement signed by all parties.
June 1	Contract starts.

7. Attachments

A. Chart showing details of call distribution over a week goes here.
B. Summary of Technology Being Supported goes here.

Key Points Covered in This Chapter

Outsourcing is a tool that can add value to your Help Desk. Using outsourcing as a tool, applied where necessary, will bring tangible benefits:

Reduction in costs

Improvement in productivity and performance

Increased flexibility so business requirements can be responded to more quickly

A wider range of services

Increased skill level

More control over the Help Desk function

Increased ability to focus on what really matters to the business

Some of the circumstances that might indicate outsourcing are as follows:

Your customer base is experiencing rapid growth, and you need support relief while you try to deal with it and bring the environment up to pace with it.

Routine work seems to be taking over your resources, and you are unable to get to the work that adds business value.

The Help Desk is drowning in support, and you could use someone to handle the support while your staff implements improvements to reduce the volume of calls.

You simply need more people to handle everything that needs to be done.

You really don't know how the Help Desk is performing, and no one has the time to measure performance.

You're going through a transition.

You're finding it difficult to support remote locations.

You require expensive tools that you can't afford.

You have a requirement for a skill that you use infrequently.

You need people who have very expensive skills.

You require skills that are specialized but not strategic.

You're in a business (e.g., training) you want to get out of.

You need to support a wide variety of packaged software.

The Help Desk is getting a lot of how-to questions for packaged software.

Functions that you may not want to outsource are as follows:

Complete network management and control

Skills specific to the business

Support of in-house applications that are unique to the business

Support of an environment with few standards and a wide variety of technology

Some of the most common functions that Help Desks outsource are as follows:

Hardware maintenance

Software management

Customer support

Training

Transitional work

When it's time to select a third party to provide the functions you want to outsource, you need to take the time to make sure that the party you select is the best choice. You need to do the following:

Check into the financial stability of the organization.

Visit the head office to make sure there is something solid behind the salesperson.

Meet the staff who will be working at your organization.

Check into their quality control.

Find out how they plan to communicate progress and performance to you.

Check all references.

Once you have selected a vendor, you need to put together a clear agreement, making sure that the responsibilities and expectations of each party are written down. Performance measurements should be agreed upon and documented, and a schedule of meetings should be set up between both parties for monitoring performance.

Never underestimate the importance of having the support of your internal staff for any outsourcing you are planning. You need it for your outsourcing efforts to succeed. In order to help ensure that your internal staff are supportive, you should get them involved in making the outsourcing decision. Provide opportunities for them to ask questions and express their concerns, and be honest in your responses. Involve them in all aspects of third-party selection and management.

PART SIX

Case Studies and Example

CHAPTER THIRTEEN

Help Desk Case No. 1: Setup

In this example, a PC support group is set up amid incredible growth and support requirements.

Current Technology Environment

- Some 1,000 PC and LAN users are spread over several remote locations. Users access the mainframe via the LAN and wide area network (WAN).

- Hardware and software standards exist, and most users access a standard set of desktop applications from the LAN.

- Client/server applications are just starting to be developed, but no critical applications run on the LAN yet. Several performance and stability issues must be addressed before this happens.

Current Help Desk

- Staff consists of three front line staff, one of whom is a student. Hardware maintenance is outsourced and performed by two on-site third-party staff. Two people look after PC ordering and invoicing. Five staff look after the LANs.

- Most (but not all) calls are logged via a Help Desk package called Quetzal.

- The call volume is 80 to 100 calls per day.

- There is no call distribution system. Calls into the Help Desk are fronted by a phone menu.

- Training is administered by an outsourcing firm, which takes care of everything from signup to billing.

- Support is from 7 A.M. to 6 P.M., and the hours are covered by staggered shifts.

History

This company went into PCs in 1990, very late in the game. Prior to this, PCs had not been allowed into the company for a number of reasons, one of which was that they were considered a security risk. Along with a change in management came a change in policy. PCs were allowed in, and in they came—in droves. Everyone wanted one. Unfortunately, because none had been allowed in up to that point, there was no expertise in the area. Very few people in the company knew anything about PCs. The mainframe technical support group was given responsibility for them. A standard configuration was hastily put together, and an ordering process set up. The technical support group could not handle the volumes of requests that came in. The PCs were set up with terminal emulation cards to enable communication to the mainframe. The first attempts at networking were fairly disastrous, as was the first network operating system that was selected. Neither the LAN operating software nor the PC operating system (OS/2) was very stable in the new environment, and neither was accepted by the users. People begged to be taken off the network and went out and bought themselves Windows software. PC support was hit and miss. There just weren't enough technical support staff, and those who were there were just learning PCs.

In 1991, the first of many corporate reorganizations happened, and a proposal was put forward for a PC support group. Interestingly enough, management had a hard time accepting it, even with all the problems, because PCs were being touted as tools that made users completely self-sufficient. Eventually, the proposal was accepted, and a PC group was put together. The team was designed, and job descriptions were created for the participants.

Unfortunately, when it came time to staff the group up, the makeup of the group was largely determined by the reorganization and consolidation that had just taken place. Some functions didn't seem to have a home in the organization, so they were put into the PC group—for example, administration of E-mail and an entire training function. The group was staffed from inside the company with people transferring or people who had lost their jobs through consolidation. Only two people on the team had PC experience: one of the technical support staff and a person from another division who had very extensive experience and knowledge.

The team that was formed consisted of a manager, five staff to support PCs and LANs, two staff to administer the mainframe E-mail system, three trainers, a training administrator, and a technical writer.

What Was Done

1. A plan was developed and objectives set to try to stabilize the current PC environment. It included setting up processes, support procedures, and training. The first thing on the list was switching all existing PCs and LANs to Windows and Novell Netware.

2. A standard desktop was developed and tested, and a rollout schedule was put together. The rollout started, and all existing LANs and PCs were converted over the course of four months. At the same time, the trainers developed courses for the standard desktop and how to use the LAN. They were just learning PCs

themselves. After the first LAN rollout (to an IT area), a survey was sent out to determine the quality of the work (not great). Procedures were updated for next time based on survey results.

As all of this was going on, a new mainframe E-mail package, which the team had inherited by reorganization, was being rolled out. One trainer and two administrators were kept busy training, providing support, and answering questions. The package was not popular, and users complained bitterly about its lack of functionality.

There were many struggles with PC/LAN technology, the volume of support, and the volume of requests for PC purchases and installation. The feeling at the time was that manufacturers and developers purposely designed their products in such a way as to prevent them from interfacing cleanly with any other product. As some LANs were being converted, new ones were being installed. Customers were still not happy. PC staff were picking up calls for PC support, but no logging or tracking was taking place.

3. A Help Desk phone number and user ID were selected and publicized. The Help Desk number was prefaced with a phone menu so users could select hardware, software, mainframe, or E-mail support. Some options contained commonly asked questions about E-mail so people could get their own answers.

   A list of services was developed.

   Pamphlets were sent out explaining the services of the group and how to use the phone menu. Inventory stickers were printed up with the support number.

   Trainers took the PC software calls, and PC support staff took the hardware calls. Customers still weren't happy with support. Problem resolution took too long.

4. Standards and ordering procedures were put together and published for hardware and software. Convincing customers that standards were vital to a supportable environment was not easy. Everyone had a favorite spreadsheet or word processor and just couldn't live without it. Fortunately, within six months, standards were adhered to almost 100 percent. They were sold on the basis

that not having standards cost too much in support and incompatibility. Many users using nonstandard software had experienced that incompatibility, and everyone could relate to the cost issue.

5. A Help Desk package was purchased (Quetzal). The PC staff reorganized so that someone was almost always available for PC help, and began to log calls.

6. A hardware maintenance agreement was set up with a hardware supplier. One very welcome on-site technician provided hardware maintenance support and helped with the setup of new PCs, which were still coming in at an unmanageable rate. Relationships were formed with various suppliers to make ordering processes easier. The administrative work involved in ordering PCs and maintaining software licensing was horrendous.

7. An Open House was held (about five months after the Help Desk was formed) to market the standard software, the services of the group, and the capability of the technology and to explain the concept of PCs and LANs. The event had demonstrations, seminars, an open server on display, and tours through the computer room. It was extremely successful.

8. Standard software was upgraded to new versions. Trainers gave upgrade seminars. Customers and trainers had a hard time accepting the rate at which PC software changed.

9. A year after the original team was formed, the PC support staff were split off into a separate team. The support function required a full-time person to look after it, and one of the staff was promoted to manager. Two staff were added. A separate support desk area was set up, and staff took turns on the Help Desk—one person full-time, a second when things got busy. Most requests were logged. LAN monitoring software was purchased and installed.

The Result

- After one year, PC support had its own dedicated team and manager. Processes and procedures, standards, and a standardized environment were all in place. Customers knew what the PC Help Desk did and how to get service.

- The PC environment had grown in one year from 200 PCs to almost 600, with eight LANs (three remote), all able to communicate with the mainframe.

Challenges

The Help Desk's challenges centered on growth, staff, lack of knowledge and experience, and administrative tasks:

- **Growth.** In the first year, the Help Desk never really got control of the support load or the growth. The business was very demanding, and there were a lot of emergencies.
- **Staff.** Some staff found it difficult to accept the fast pace of change in the PC environment. These people sometimes hindered progress.
- **Lack of knowledge and experience.** So many people were learning at the same time that it was very difficult to do things right. It took a while before the quality of work was reliable.
- **Administrative tasks,** such as PC ordering and invoicing and software licensing. They just took too much time.

Observations

- Make every effort to get the staff you need, not the staff you're given.
- Planning is all important, even when there is no time.
- Market—make time to go out and talk to your customers.
- Outsource whatever business you don't want to be in.

PC Support Proposal

The following is the original proposal for PC support.

Proposal for Support of Personal Computers

Two plans for support are required: short term (six to twelve months), to deal with immediate issues and concerns, and long term, to deal with ultimate direction and strategy. The long-term PC support plan should be integrated with business plans and with plans for other technologies. It must address questions such as: What will the technology requirements for our strategic applications be in the future? How will we be building future applications?

Short-Term Plan for PC Support

Objectives:

1. Stabilize our current PC environment: Get the PCs and LANs working.
2. Increase PC expertise in both IT and the client areas.
3. Get control of the processes involved in PC support, including the following:

    Request, approval, ordering, delivery, and installation of PCs

    Maintenance of an inventory of PC technology

    Support/problem logging

    Training

    Maintenance/upgrading

    Security
4. Provide PC support and consulting to IT and the client areas.

What we have to do:

1. Develop, with the clients, an interim PC policy that covers the following:

    Suggested standard hardware and software configurations

    Nonstandard configurations—if IT cannot provide support, we must find out who can; we must make sure that all configurations are supportable

Number and location of LANs to be installed over the short term (six to twelve months)

Printing

Software upgrades

Host access

Remote access

Hardware maintenance

Security

2. Solve the outstanding major problems (e.g., LAN system hang-up, LAN printing).

3. Off-load work from technical support as much as possible. Appoint and train LAN administrators and persons who can perform LAN maintenance. If possible, hire a consultant for approximately 6 months for skills exchange.

4. Put processes or people in place for:

Request for PC hardware/software

Approval—for example, ensure client sign-off at appropriate level

Ordering

Receiving

Inventory control

Delivery and installation

Billing and payment

A coordinator should be appointed to monitor PC orders, from request to installation. This person (with the help of a PC inventory package) would schedule installations with the clients and the installers to ensure that all necessary equipment was received and would be installed at a mutually convenient time. This person would also ensure that the client received a quick PC lesson immediately after the installation so the client could make immediate use of the system.

5. Develop an education/publicity strategy to propagate PC knowledge as quickly as possible throughout IT and the client areas. Be-

sides formal courses, this might include lunchtime demonstrations by clients or IT. We would be emphasizing self-learning.

6. Assign IT staff to visit client PC users regularly to see if there are any problems and to make sure clients have everything they need from us.

7. Set up a PC phone hotline. Staff a support desk. Log problems. There are PC packages available to keep track of problems and to display possible problems and their solutions.

8. Appoint IT staff to handle PC consulting.

9. Leverage client PC expertise wherever possible—can clients take their turn on the hotline? in consulting? in R&D?

Note: *Regarding PC application development, we need to learn more about this and to stabilize our PC base before we embark on major work in this area. PC application development should be treated as any other project—it must be part of our strategy and must be prioritized accordingly.*

Proposal/Action Plan

1. Work with the clients to determine the real PC requirements for the next year. Based on these, work out an interim (six- to twelve-month) PC strategy. We need to understand the problems and priorities.

2. Put together a dedicated (i.e., not matrix) PC support team. In order to ensure proper support for this very specialized technology, all PC functions should be covered by this group—everything from LAN setup and maintenance to administration of the request, purchase, and delivery cycle for PCs. The team could be composed of the following staff:

   A coordinator for PC processes (as described in the previous section)

   Two PC LAN/operating system/communications experts

   Three or four PC support persons. These people would do client support, consulting, and some training. IT staff could rotate in and out of some of these positions to ensure cross training.

The team should be headed by a manager, who would work with the clients to develop the interim strategies and who would be involved in setting longer-term direction.

3. Stabilize our current environment—define, prioritize and address the problems, and ensure that all required tools (e.g., for LAN management) are in place.

4. Define and set up a management system for the PC processes (as in step 4 above). Communicate these processes to all IT and client areas.

5. Design and start a hotline Help Desk function.

6. Plan, communicate, and implement informal education sessions, self-help sessions, visits by support staff to clients, and so on.

Time Frame

From startup through team selection and education, environment stabilization, process setup, and Help Desk education, implementation would be roughly four months.

CHAPTER FOURTEEN

Help Desk Case No. 2: Working Well

In this example, we examine an established Help Desk that is functioning very successfully.

Technological Environment

- Approximately 500 retail outlets, most run by their own AS/400 hooked to a front-end cash register system and back-end data storage system. Stores are hooked to a satellite network for access to the head office mainframe for E-mail and various other retail applications.

- The Help DeskSupports a live retail environment and works out of the head office location.

- Consists of ten people. Two are outsourced staff who support older systems that are gradually being phased out.

- The staff work in shifts to keep the Help Desk staffed from 7 A.M. to midnight (to handle the different time zones), seven days a week. The call load is approximately 2,400 calls per month.

Background

This group is part of a larger IT department that supports the retail locations directly. The whole department is partially funded by store owners, so costs are watched very carefully. The Help Desk has been in existence for many years and has matured into a very effective and successful function. Its customers, a tough group at best, are very pleased with Help Desk service.

Call Handling

All calls go directly into an integrated voice response (IVR) system. The caller is asked to enter the store number, a system code, a priority code, and a voice message describing the problem. By the time the caller hangs up, the IVR has sent all the information to the AS/400, which has logged the call. Help Desk staff pick the call up from the AS/400 and look after it in order of priority. All calls are resolved in less than five hours. There is no such thing as an outstanding call.

Reasons for Success

There are several reasons for the success of this Help Desk. It is very focused, with clear priorities. Staff understand the business, the Help Desk is accountable to its customers and staffing is flexible. Each of these reasons is looked at in more detail in the following sections.

Very Focused

There are no questions about whom the Help Desk serves or what services it provides. Everything is written down and understood by both sides. A service-level agreement was recently put into place. Some services other than those specified in the agreement are provided, but at extra cost.

Priorities Are Clear

Priorities are well established:

1—System failure

2—Critical programs

3—Noncritical programs

4—Hardware

5—General questions

They are printed on fluorescent paper, laminated, and sent to each customer. Two sets of priorities are printed for two different systems. Customers keep these lists by the phone for easy access and abide by them. They have to give a priority when calling into the Help Desk. The priority list also contains symptoms to look for, so identification is easier. For example, "You cannot create or process customer work orders" or "Isolated hardware such as the printer or screen is not working."

Staff Understand the Business

All staff on the Help Desk have spent time as employees in the retail outlets. They understand the business and understand customer concerns and problems. When there is a problem, they know which other store functions or systems might be affected and can get all aspects of the problem resolved quickly. Customers really appreciate the knowledge that the Help Desk staff have.

Help Desk Is Accountable to Its Customers

Help Desk customers pay for Help Desk service, and they are very demanding about getting value for their money. This forces the Help Desk to maintain a high level of efficiency. This isn't always a positive. Getting funding for improvements is sometimes difficult.

Flexible Staffing

The Help Desk has ten staff, two of whom are contract staff working on older systems that are being phased out. Each of the remaining eight staff take turns working off hours from home. When it is a person's week to work at home, that person works from 8:30 A.M. to midnight, with two hours off in the middle of the day. One disadvantage of having staff work at home for a week is that they are out of the communication loop. A lot happens on a Help Desk in a week.

Measures of Success

There are two major measures of success for this Help Desk: whether the customers want to pay the Help Desk and whether it meets the service-level agreement.

The agreement contains the following elements:

- The method of operation, describing the responsibilities of each party, the hours of service, after-hours service, priorities, and response times.

- Support and services, describing what systems are supported, what third parties are involved, who supports what, and what the procedures are for interacting with each of the parties involved in support.

- Fees, detailing out regular support fees and additional services and their related charges.

Challenges

Stores are growing and expanding and will require extra support. Unfortunately, there is to be no increase in head count. Outsourcing is being investigated, but there is a major drawback: The Help Desk requires very specialized knowledge (as well as two languages) not generally available. Help Desk contract positions have been advertised at stores, but store staff generally like where they live and don't want to move close to the head office. An option being investigated is to set up contract staff with remote support capabilities so they can work for the Help Desk from home without moving.

CHAPTER FIFTEEN

Example: A Help Desk Intranet Web Site

This chapter walks through a sample of a Help Desk intranet site that could be handling a significant part of the Help Desk's business. Figure 15.1 shows the home page of the site. It has a very simple layout. All options are grouped under six categories. The Help Desk mission appears at the top of the page, and its meaning is reflected in the menu of functions.

Clicking on the happy face brings up the cartoon shown in Figure 15.2. Customers aren't forced to load up the cartoon, but they can look at it if they choose to. Clicking on the letter icon labeled "Feedback" will bring up an E-mail screen. Any messages entered will be sent to a feedback ID, not to the regular Help Desk help ID. This will keep them out of the problem queue and help ensure that they are addressed.

The hot news of the moment is indicated by the "Virus Alert" message. Customers will notice this immediately upon bringing up the home page, so they are made aware of the problem situation. They can click on "check your PC for viruses" to get information on how to check for viruses.

In the "Hardware/Software" category customers can select to view current policies, as shown in Figure 15.3. On the policies screen the new policy is clearly marked, and dates most recently updated are given for

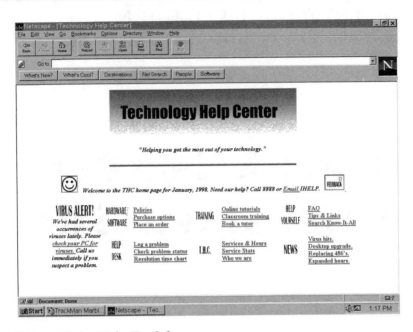

Figure 15.1   Help Desk home page.

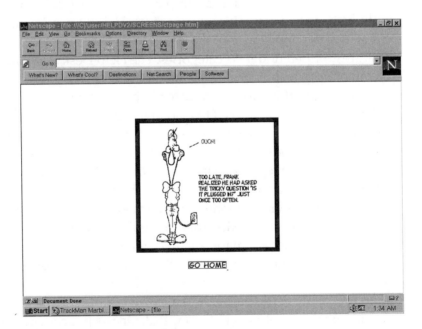

Figure 15.2   Help Desk humor.

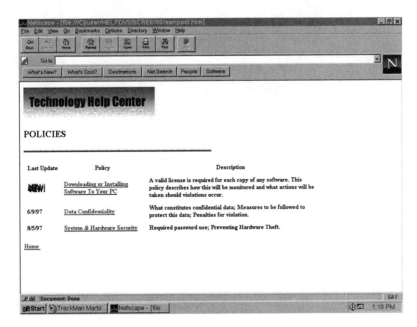

Figure 15.3   Policies page.

the other policies. Contents are described so customers don't end up where they don't want to be.

Customers can also view purchase options in the Hardware/Software category. This is a list of technology packages the customer can order. Information for each package includes what functions the package is meant to be used for (e.g., heavy graphics and mathematical applications versus word processing), sign-offs required, and cost.

· The final option in the Hardware/Software category is "Place an order." Customers can fill out an on-line form to initiate a technology purchase.

The "Training" category on the home page shown in Figure 15.1 offers customers access to on-line tutorials, schedules, and information on classroom training as well as the ability to book a personal tutor.

Clicking on the "Tutorials" option will take customers to a list of available on-line tutorials, shown in Figure 15.4. Tutorials are listed and described, with a new one clearly indicated. Customers click on the one they want to view. A message at the top of the screen asks them to fill out a short survey that is embedded at the end of each tutorial. This will give

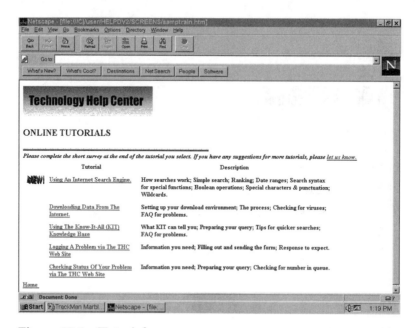

Figure 15.4   Tutorials page.

the Help Desk valuable feedback on the quality of the material. The message also gives customers an opportunity to suggest topics for tutorials.

The "Classroom Training" option offers a list of all classroom training available, descriptions of all courses, and a schedule showing locations and times. An on-line registration option is also available. The customer would fill out the form, and one copy would be sent to the customer's manager for authorization and another to the training department.

The "Personal Tutor" option allows a customer to book one hour of time with a trainer. A schedule showing tutor availability for the next three months is posted, and the customer fills out a form, selecting a slot. A response is sent back to the customer indicating that the booking was (or was not) successful.

The "Help Yourself" option gives customers an opportunity to try to resolve their own problems. The FAQ page, shown in Figure 15.5, lists a set of carefully categorized FAQs the customer can access and a description of each. The FAQs were built based on the most frequently occurring questions coming into the Help Desk.

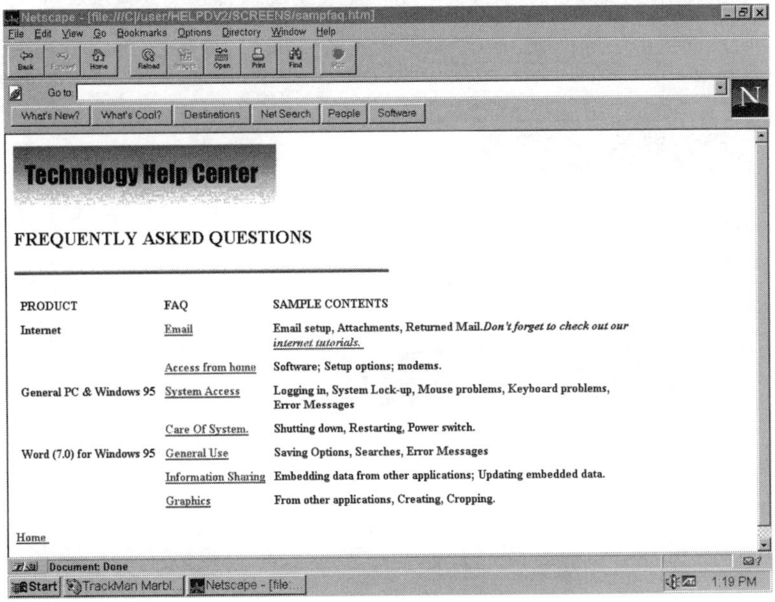

Figure 15.5 FAQ page.

The "Tips & Links" option gives customers access to a variety of technical tips, categorized and built on the basis of data collected from Help Desk calls. Links to useful sites on the Internet are included for each category.

The third "Help Yourself" option ("Search Know-It-All") gives customers access to the Help Desk knowledge bases. Customers can query three different knowledge bases (two prepackaged ones) to try to find an answer to their problems. An on-line tutorial (see Figure 15.4) is available to help customers make more effective use of the knowledge bases. The Help Desk option on the main page (Figure 15.1) allows customers to log problems and requests, check on problem status, and check out resolution times for the past week. The graph, shown in Figure 15.6, is a good marketing tool for the Help Desk. It gives customers a chance to see one aspect of actual performance.

If customers chose to log a problem or check on problem status, they would be given direct access to the Help Desk management system.

The "THC" option on the main screen tells customers about THC's (Technology Help Center's) services, hours of operation, performance,

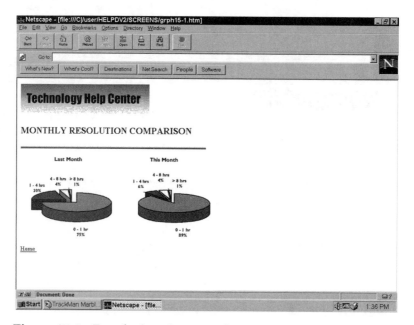

Figure 15.6   Resolution time graph.

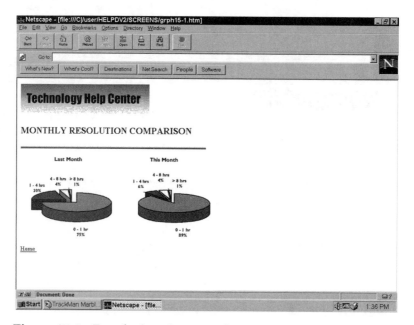

Figure 15.7   Services and hours of operation.

and employees. Selecting services and hours will bring up the screen shown in Figure 15.7. The customer is able to access some of the services listed (e.g., tutor's service) directly from this screen.

The "Service Stats" option lists all available service-level agreements, which the customer can choose to view, and performance graphs such as calls per workstation, calls categorized by type, and percentage of calls resolved at point of call. Graphs are presented for the previous month's worth of data.

"Who We Are" is a list of all Help Desk employees. Clicking on an employee's name will bring up the photo of that person.

The "News" option on the main page lists recent events or developments of importance. Clicking on any of the listed headings (for example, "Desktop Upgrade") will bring up an article describing the event or development in detail. All of the articles are contained on one screen, but selecting a specific article will take the customer to the location of that article on the screen.

A Further Resource

Visit the companion Web site, which was made available to provide readers and Internet surfers with ideas, guides, and information to complement this book. You can reach the Web site at www.wiley.com/compbooks/czegel.

The site includes the following information and templates:

- Examples of
    Mission statements
    Customer surveys
- Templates for
    Skills requirement grid
    Help Desk operating cost
    Service-level agreement
    Cost-benefit analysis
    Marketing plan
    RFP
- Checklists for
    Help Desk consolidation
    Service-level agreement
- A Sample Help Desk Web site
- Useful Help Desk links
- Updates and new thoughts on the material in this book

References and Further Reading

Bexar, D. 1996. "Long Road to CTI," *LAN Times Online*, July 22, www.wcmh.com./96jul.

Chamberlin, B. 1993. "Knowing When It's Time to Outsource," *LAN Times*, vol. 10, no. 24 (December 6), page 80.

Computer Conference Analysis Newsletter. 1993. "Outsourcing," *Computer Conference Analysis Newsletter*, no. 320 (May 25), page 12.

Condon, Ron. 1997. "Intranet Benefits, Dangers Outlined by Report," *Client/Server World*, March 1997, page 22.

Crevier, D. 1993. *AI: The Tumultuous History of the Search for Artificial Intelligence*, New York, NY: Basic Books.

Daly, Cinda. 1997. "Help Desk Software Vendors: Understanding the Product Features Can Aid in Tool Selection," *Service News*, vol. 17, no. 4 (March), page 46.

Danielle, D. 1997. "Equipping Your Help Desk: 4 Products to the Rescue," *Network Computing*, vol. 8, no. 2 (February 1), page 44.

Dolan, T., and S. Smith. 1993. "Getting Support," *LAN Magazine*, vol. 8, no. 11 (October), page 77.

EDGE: Work-Group Computing Report. 1993. "Software Support: Software Publishing Outsources Support for Selected Products," *EDGE: Work-Group Computing Report*, vol. 4, no. 177 (October 11), page 3.

Ellison, C. 1993. "Tech-Support Hold Blues," *Computer Shopper*, vol. 13, no. 2 (February), page 836.

Falcone, P. 1997. "96 Great Interview Questions to Ask before You Hire," AMACOM, American Management Association.

Gibbs, M. 1997. "Push and Pull for Suckers," *Intranet Journal*, September, page 5.

Goldmann, N. 1997. "Extranet: The Third Wave in Electronic Commerce," *Journal of Internet Banking and Commerce*, January, www.arraydev.com.

Hamilton, K. 1996. "Web Page Reduces Help Desk Calls," *Service News*, vol. 16, no. 12, November.

Hamilton, K. 1997. "Help Desks Turn to Self-help Support," *Service News*, vol. 17, no. 1, January.

Harding, E. U. 1993. "Help Desk Practices Change; Firms Must Automate, Add Technical Expertise," *Software Magazine*, vol. 13, no. 1 (January), page 25.

Harding, E. U. 1993. "IS Explores Multisourcing: Trend toward Selective Use of Third Parties," *Software Magazine*, vol. 13, no. 9 (June), page 28.

Hare, C. C. 1992. "Downsizing Changes Role of Help Desk; Network Managers Face New Expectations of Quality Support, Service," *LAN Times*, vol. 9, no. 16 (August 24), page 55.

Help Desk Institute. 1997. *Help Desk and Customer Support Practices Report*, Colorado Springs, CO: Help Desk Institute.

Hibbard, J. 1997. "Banking on Intranets," *Intranet Journal*, September, page 9.

Hibbard, J. 1997. "Companies Putting Intranet Policies in Place," *Client/Server World*, March 1997, page 14.

Kohlhepp, R., and A. Frey. 1997. "Intranets: How to Cut through the Cobwebs of Internal Information," *Network Computing Online*, www.networkcomputing.com, Interactive Network Design Manual.

LaPlante, A. 1992. "Help Desk Consolidation Simplifies User Access, Reduces Costs," *InfoWorld*, vol. 14, no. 37 (September 14), page 66.

Leland, Karen, and Keith Bailey. 1995. *Customer Service for Dummies*, Foster City, CA: IDG Books.

Microsoft Corporation. 1995. *Microsoft Sourcebook for the Help Desk*, Redmond, WA: Microsoft Press.

Newton, H. 1994. "Headsets All Around: Computer Telephony Moves onto LANs," *PC Magazine*, vol. 13, no. 3 (February 8), page NE1.

Palleschi, A. 1997. "Document Management Hooks onto 'Net," *Network World*, vol. 7, no. 3, page 21.

Patch, K., and M. J. Turner. 1993. "A Fresh Outlook on Outsourcing: Users Find Farming out of the Network Operations Pie Has Its Benefits," *Network World*, vol. 10, no. 8 (February 22), page 34.

Rigney, S. 1996. "NetWatch. CTI Brings Call-Processing to Your LAN," *Computer Shopper*, July, www.zdnet.com.

Sterne, J. 1996. *Customer Service on the Internet*, New York, NY: John Wiley & Sons Inc., 1996.

Stevens, L. 1993. "Choosing Hardware Support Means Weighing Trade-offs," *MacWEEK*, vol. 7, no. 13 (March 29), page 12.

Straguzzi, Nick. 1997. "Models, Cases, and Trees, Oh My . . . Which One to Use?" white paper, Advantage kbs, ww.akbs.com.

Wallace, P. 1994. "Help Desk Consolidation Speeds Tech Support," *InfoWorld*, vol. 16, no. 4 (January 24), page 55.

Withington, F. G. 1993. "Outsourcing: Flower or Weed?" *Datamation*, vol. 39, no. 21 (November 1), page 124.

Index

ACD, *see* Automatic call distributor
Analyst, Help Desk, *see* Help Desk analyst
Analyst roles, *see* Roles
ASP, *see* Association of Support Professionals
Asset management,
    benefits of, 137
    in managing Internet access, 199, 201
    in measuring performance, 261
    tools for, 12, 24, 36, 148, 159, 165, 175–176,
        181, 183, 243, 273
    see also Hardware and software inventory
Association of Support Professionals (ASP), 161,
    182
Automated attendant, 165, 167, 169, 170, 183
Automatic call distributor (ACD), 165, 167, 169,
    183, 269 322, 335
    on a front line, 47
Automation,
    candidates for, 144–145, 153, 259
    cost justification for, 335, 338, 341, 343–344
    in procedures, 117–118, 124, 132
    in senior management expectations, 7, 18,
    of Help Desk processes, 240, 244, 306, 357,
        362, 366
    on a front line, 45–46
    to improve Help Desk environment, 89

B

Budget,
    as part of Help Desk manager's responsibili-
        ties, 92
    considerations in Help Desk focus, 3, 4,
        309
    for a small business, 193

for Help Desk tools, 157,174
improving through asset management, 139
in determining number of staff, 50, 52, 54
    67
in services, 24–25, 27, 28
in training, 86
negotiating with customers, 15, 21
stretching through outsourcing, 361, 383
see also Performance
Business value
    communicating, 276, 282–284, 287, 288–291,
        307, 313–314
    in a cost-benefit analysis, 315–317, 320,
        352–353
    in determining priorities, 107, 113
    in outsourcing, 356–357, 371–372
    increasing through outsourcing, 356–357,
        362, 371, 394
    of tasks, 4
    marketing, 283, 285
    measuring, 227, 234, 242, 244, 258
    see also Performance

C

Call distribution
    determining, 16
    in calculating number of staff, 49, 57
    in determining when to outsource, 358, 369,
        389, 390, 393
    in measuring performance, 261, 265–267,
        278
    marketing, 215
    tools for, 165, 359, 400
    see also Automatic call distributor